Praise for
TEACHING THE CAT TO SIT

"Theall's tightly wrought account serves as a powerful testimony to the healing power of language."

—*Publishers Weekly*

"In a narrative that deftly moves between past and present, Theall tells the moving story of how she found self-acceptance as a lesbian mother of faith. . . . A searingly honest memoir of faith, sexuality, and motherhood."

—*Kirkus Reviews*

"An unusually moving memoir of alienation and discrimination. . . . Theall's heartbreaking and heart-affirming coming-of-age, respect-seeking, and truth-telling tale ultimately demonstrates that openness is all."

—*Booklist*

"Through unflinching prose, Theall returns to her youth and untangles the complexities of her life. She walks readers through her feelings of insecurity and loss with such sincerity that, were it not for the elegant writing, you might mistake the memoir for a diary."

—*5280, The Denver Magazine*

"Painfully honest. . . . Theall records her story with skill and humor."

—*Windy City Times*

"Despite its inherent sadness, *Teaching* is hard to put down because author Michelle Theall is a first-rate storyteller. . . . The book works because of its deliberateness and its ultimately empowering message of truth to self. For that, and for the great biography it is, *Teaching the Cat to Sit* is a must-read, especially for those who can relate."

—*Washington Blade*

"At once powerful and touching, Michelle Theall's moving memoir captures the meaning of family—the families we inherit and the ones we make."

—Piper Kerman, *New York Times* bestselling author of
Orange Is the New Black

"A clear-eyed, brave-hearted, and utterly unforgettable memoir about life's big things—love, faith, identity, and justice—and the sometimes ferocious effort it takes to balance them. At this book's center is a beautifully rendered relationship between a mother and daughter that's as complicated and memorable as any I've ever read. Here is a story told with grace, honesty, and remarkable spirit."

—Sara Corbett, *New York Times* bestselling coauthor of
A House in the Sky

"Michelle Theall can really write. This is a little story packed with big issues and told with real mastery."

—Kelly Corrigan, *New York Times* bestselling author of
The Middle Place

"Powerful down to the last page. This book shows the resilience of its author and the universal quest to belong at all costs."

—Julia Scheeres, *New York Times* bestselling author of *Jesus Land*

"Theall's written a memoir that is genuinely moving, compelling, and, at times, hilarious. As she grapples with the basic questions of family, faith, love, and identity, she expresses with great poignancy the transformative power of love in all its forms."

—Wendy Lawless, *New York Times* bestselling author of
Chanel Bonfire

"Michelle Theall tells the story of learning to fight for her truth and the journey is engaging and evocative. *Teaching the Cat to Sit* is life under the microscope—a struggling family, the rigid Church, the mean kids at school, and the coaches who took the time to care. It's an emotional ride as this mama bear finds home."

—Jennifer Wilson, award-winning author of
Running Away to Home

"*Teaching the Cat to Sit* is a powerful reminder of the ways that discrimination and cruelty still flourish, even as laws shift to recognize more of the LGBT population. Michelle Theall beautifully captures the effects of bigotry on a community, a family, and on an individual psyche both afraid and determined to change."

—Cris Beam, author of the *New York Times*
Notable book *To the End of June*

"*Teaching the Cat to Sit* is about the most important thing of all: unconditional love. Michelle Theall's beautiful, compassionate book touches on many of today's thorniest subjects, from marriage equality to adoption to the politics of the Catholic Church, but ultimately hers is a simple tale of parents, children, and the courage that loving one another—and ourselves—truly requires."

—Buzzy Jackson, award-winning author of
Shaking the Family Tree

"Michelle Theall is a fighter, and in her warm, courageous, deeply honest, heartbreaking, heart-mending memoir we bear witness to the staggering number of times she gets knocked to her knees, and cheer at increasing volume every time she comes up swinging. This timely reckoning with Catholicism, homosexuality, abuse, adoption, and illness ultimately gives rise to a celebration of tenacity, forgiveness, and love. *Teaching the Cat to Sit* could convince the most committed outsider to come inside, and teach the rest of us how best to invite her."

—Pam Houston, critically acclaimed author of
Contents May Have Shifted

"Michelle Theall's memoir is all heart—painfully and beautifully so—with a moving message about how powerful a mother and church can be—for better or for worse."

—Lori Duron, critically acclaimed author of *Raising My Rainbow*

TEACHING

THE CAT

TO SIT

A Memoir

MICHELLE
THEALL

G

GALLERY BOOKS

New York   London   Toronto   Sydney   New Delhi

G

Gallery Books
Division of Simon & Schuster, Inc.
1230 Avenue of the Americas
New York, NY 10020

First Gallery Books trade paperback edition September 2014

GALLERY BOOKS and colophon are registered trademarks of Simon & Schuster, Inc.

For information about special discounts for bulk purchases, please contact Simon & Schuster Special Sales at 1-866-506-1949 or business@simonandschuster.com.

The Simon & Schuster Speakers Bureau can bring authors to your live event. For more information or to book an event contact the Simon & Schuster Speakers Bureau at 1-866-248-3049 or visit our website at www.simonspeakers.com.

Interior design by Joy O'Meara
Cover design by Regina Starace
Cover photograph courtesy of the author

Manufactured in the United States of America

10 9 8 7 6 5 4 3 2 1

Library of Congress Cataloging-in-Publication Data

Theall, Michelle.
Teaching the cat to sit : a memoir / Michelle Theall.
pages cm
Summary: "Theall seeks to baptize her four-year-old son, a mixed-race kid who was in an abusive home with unfit teenage parents before she and her partner of eleven years adopted him, and wrestles with where she came from, what it means to be Catholic, what her faith means to her in spite of the Church's stance on social issues, as well as coping with her own mother's unwillingness to accept her loving relationship with her partner. A mother-daughter story about being a mother when you still need a mother yourself."—Provided by publisher.
1. Theall, Michelle. 2. Mothers and daughters—United States—Biography.
3. Parent and child—United States—Biography. 4. Lesbians—United States—Biography. 5. Lesbianism—Religious aspects—Catholic Church. I. Title.
HQ755.85.T47 2014
306.76'630973—dc23
                                          2013032835

ISBN 978-1-4516-9730-8
ISBN 978-1-4516-9731-5 (ebook)

AUTHOR'S NOTE

Names and the identifying details of some of the people portrayed in this book have been changed. I have tried hard to reconstruct conversations, places, and events from photos, journals, newspaper clippings, letters, and emails in keeping with my own memory and perspective. This is my story and my truth. The name on the cover is my own.

For my family, the one I was born into and the one I made

And the day came when the risk
to remain tight in a bud was more painful
than the risk it took to blossom.

—ANAÏS NIN

CHAPTER ONE

"Rain is God's spit," Connor tells his grandmother through my iPhone. He turns his head sideways and puts his right eye close to the screen, as if she might be trapped inside it. "God spits. He really does."

My mom's sandpaper ex-smoker's laugh bursts through the speaker like a spray of gravel from a semitruck. With equal parts amusement and disapproval, she says, "Oh, Connor, I'm sure God doesn't spit." Connor flinches. Before Grandy can get out another word, he drops the phone on the kitchen counter, tucks his chin to his chest, and bolts from the kitchen. At almost four years old, he's already learning to navigate her sharp corners.

He may even be better at it than I am. My mother will be here in five days for Connor's baptism, and I'm too afraid to tell her it's been canceled.

As I retrieve the phone, my partner, Jill, edges by me with Connor's plate of pancakes in one hand and his sippy cup in the other, calls our son to the table, and taps her watch at me—a reminder that we're going to be late for school. I nod to her and shrug, mouthing the words, *I know but . . .*

"I can't wait to see that little booger," my mom says. "Where on earth did he learn that? The rain is God's spit, honestly."

"Where else?" I laugh. "Catholic school." I pour two to-go thermoses of coffee.

"So, did you get him the shoes like I told you?" my mother asks. "They have to be summer white to match his outfit."

Because Connor is too old to fit into a traditional Catholic christening gown for infants, Jill and I planned to dress him in a coat and tie. Hearing this, my mom opted for something a bit more sacred: a baptismal suit she won after bidding aggressively for it on eBay.

"Yes, I got him the shoes," I respond. I open my mouth to confess about the baptism being called off and then close it just as quickly. Like a kid hiding a bad report card, I think if I don't tell her, the problem won't exist.

A woman with more courage would already have told her mom that Father Bill has refused to baptize our son, perhaps before my mom bid on the suit or started buying holy items for Connor and having them blessed by their bishop in San Marcos. If not then, certainly before she and my dad drive two days and five hundred miles in the minivan and pull up into our driveway. And maybe I would have if the Catholic Church wasn't the paper clip holding our relationship together. Also, I like the grandmotherly doting and fussing. It's one of the few things helping me forget that nothing about our situation is normal, as much as I might want it to be.

"Michelle, are you listening? He can't wear Batman underwear because the black wings will show through the white pants." There's a thud, followed by my father swearing in the background. "Al, what in the Sam Hill?"

I shake my head and smile. "No Batman undies, got it."

In between her instructions about Connor's shoes and underwear, Mom yells at my father as he packs their suitcases, "No, Al. Honestly. The Purell goes in the outside pocket." Before she hangs up she says to me, "Make sure you get his hair cut. We want him to look good in the photos. Love you, sweetie, see you this weekend."

At the back kitchen door, I lift Connor into my arms and Jill yanks his rain hood up over his head before we dash to separate cars to rush him to school. I'll be staying at Sacred Heart for a meeting with Father Bill in a final attempt to make him change his mind about us. I buckle Connor into his seat and back out from the garage where the sound of thunder rattles our steel cocoon. "You think He's mad?" Connor asks.

"Who, God?" I look over my shoulder. "No, little man."

He puts his hand against the window and nods. "Well, something's going on with Him." He traces a drop of rain with his fingertip as if he can stop its momentum. "You'd never let me spit like that without a really good reason."

FIVE MINUTES LATER, JILL and I stand with Connor in the doorway of the Teddy Bear room at Sacred Heart of Jesus School, waiting for his classmates to finish morning prayers before we step inside. Beyond the glass-paneled door, a paint-chipped Virgin Mary cradles baby Jesus in her arms and candlelight flickers across the toddlers kneeling on their square ABC mats. Hands touch bellies and ears and noses in no particular order, in an attempt to make the sign of the cross that looks like baseball coaches calling plays from the dugout. After a chorus of amens, the teacher motions for us to come inside. I flick on the lights and settle Connor at a table with some other kids.

Jill helps the teacher distribute packets of crayons before she bends over and kisses the top of Connor's head. She walks toward me and places a hand on my shoulder. "Let me know what Father Bill says today." She taps a finger along my collarbone to make sure I really hear her. "I know you're angry, but this isn't about you."

"You could go with me," I say.

"Sure. We could hold hands, because that would make it better."

"The whole thing's ridiculous. I asked all the right questions ahead of time."

"Think of it this way, would you rather be right and have to explain to your mom that the baptism's been canceled? Or be wrong and have your mom standing with us at the altar next to our son in his little white eBay suit?" She gives my shoulder a squeeze, our equivalent of a good-bye kiss in public, and she is out the door, walking to her car.

I am leaning over to say good-bye to Connor too when the girl sitting next to my son asks me, "Why does Connor have two mommies?" Heat rises to my cheeks. Of course I expected this moment to happen at some point, but I'm still unprepared for it. How can I explain to her that I sometimes do my own double take? At home, I stare at our family photo above the fireplace—the one we took at Disney World—and I see two white, middle-aged women with their half-Cambodian son wedged between them and I think: *Who are these people?* I peer down at this tiny girl in an art smock and striped leggings, terrified that she will judge me.

I'm about to answer the girl, whose mother happens to be the school's director, when Connor's teacher, a married woman with five kids of her own, quips, "He has two mommies because he's lucky."

Connor takes a thick black crayon in his small fist and starts to color in a picture of hippos and bunnies heading two by two up a ramp onto Noah's ark.

"There are lots of different kinds of families," I tell the girl. I'm aware that the teacher is watching me, and a class aide too. I'm still so new to this mommy thing that I don't know if I can pass scrutiny from the real moms, the ones who know how to do this, the women who seem born to it. Plus, I feel like they might think I represent all gay parents, which means I have to get this exactly right. I continue, "Some people have a dad or a mom or both. Some are raised by their grandparents. And some have two mommies or two daddies."

"Oh," she says, then wrinkles her brow in confusion. "Well, which one of you does he call Mommy?"

"That's a great question. I'm Mama and his other mother is Mommy," I say, knowing full well that as two anxious, newly minted moms, we answer to just about anything: running water, the smell of open markers, items dropped into toilets, and anything that sounds like a head hitting the floor.

The girl places her palm over the drawing of Noah in front of her. "My daddy doesn't live with us anymore." She says this without emotion, as if she is explaining to me that Barney the dinosaur is purple. I look at her little hand covering Noah's face and kneel down next to her. She twirls a strand of wavy hair around her finger, which starts to turn white at the tip.

I unravel the hair from her hand, replace it with a blue crayon, and resist an overwhelming urge to sit down next to her and color for a few hours. "I'm sure your dad loves you very much," I say, placing my hand on top of her head. I hold on for a few extra seconds, trying to convey all the things I haven't said: *You will be okay. You are loved. And whatever is going on with your parents has nothing to do with you or anything you have or haven't done.*

I look at Connor, coloring intently, and wonder if he wishes he had a dad, if Jill and I will be enough.

I give Connor a quick kiss, and we touch noses. "Bye, sweet boy," I say and trail my hand across his bony spine. Even though he drinks a high-calorie PediaSure every morning, his shoulder blades jut from his back like broken bird wings. It's as if all the things he can't or won't say about the family he was born into—before he came to us— are written on his body anyway. *How much of his past will determine his future?* And, as for the immediate future: *What in God's name am I going to say to Father Bill to convince him to baptize my son?*

CHAPTER TWO

I CAME OUT OF MY mother's womb a half-answered prayer. My Roman Catholic mom and dad wanted a boy and had named the lump in my mother's belly Matthew, after the saint and apostle of Jesus. Since they already had a perfect little girl, my sister, Kathy, who had eyelashes as long as Elizabeth Taylor's and slept in a tutu, I couldn't really blame them. Who wouldn't want one of each? Plus, there was the whole legacy thing to consider. My dad was an only child, the last in a line of Thealls, and a son would carry on the family name. But because God has a sense of humor, I wriggled my way into the world, five pounds, five ounces of pink baby girl—clearly missing a penis—and already disappointing my parents.

Since my mom and dad could no longer name me Matthew, they did the next best thing for a couple in 1966; they named me after a Beatles song. Six months prior to my birth, "Michelle" won the Grammy for song of the year. My namesake was a "belle," a refined and beautiful French girl who probably wore a lot of stiff ruffled gowns and waltzed and sipped tea. And so my parents christened me with their expectations, never realizing that God had other plans.

•   •   •

"SIT STILL," MOM SAID, SEPARATING out a strand of my hair and working the comb through a snarl, trying to get me ready for fifth-grade picture day. I leaned away, pressing my hand to my scalp, and stared at the vials of perfume on her vanity table. The little rubber pumps attached to the colored glass bottles reminded me of the red ball on the horn of my Huffy bike, the pink one Santa brought me. If I still believed in Santa Claus, which I had until last year when I turned ten, my parents would have blown it with that bike. The real Santa would have gotten me a black one with fire decals on the sides.

My mom yanked my head toward her. "You're pulling too hard," I said.

"It won't hurt if you stop squirming and cooperate with me," she replied. I yelped and she held up both hands. She palmed my head like a basketball and turned it toward the mirror. She shrugged her eyebrows, then softened. "Honestly," she said. She squirted a few pumps of No More Tangles onto the gnarled nest and eased a comb through it. Like on every other picture day that had gone before it, I wiggled and she held on until we each gave up in our own way.

Our fifth-grade classroom smelled like French fries and grease and a boy who sat in the front of homeroom and never bathed. In the back row, Kevin, the school bully, tried to teach me how to glick, a process that involved placing one's tongue against one's teeth to project a miniature fountain of spit. Every time I did it, I drooled on my shoes, which made Kevin tip his chair over backward from laughing so hard. He was making fun of me and I didn't care. "Boys!" Mrs. Hover shouted to us without looking up from the piano. "Back in your seats now or it's swats."

I kicked my feet against Kevin's chair until he glicked on me, and the bell rang. We sprinted away from Mrs. Hover, banged through the double doors, and didn't slow until we reached the outbuildings alongside the cinder track and makeshift football field.

Coach Vance stood seven feet tall. He wore red nylon basketball shorts and his skin seemed too loose for his face. He blew his whistle three times to assemble all of us before announcing it would be a "free-play day." He couldn't know he'd be fired by the end of the week. It was what this free day would cost him.

We scattered and I ran up into the metal bleachers. Kevin and a girl named Frieda clambered up the stands. He chased her and she squealed. "Show me!" he yelled.

"What are y'all doing?" I asked.

"Wouldn't you like to know?" Kevin pulled at the neck of his T-shirt where a sweat ring had started.

"It's boys catch the girls," Frieda yelled, ducking between two of the seats and dropping to the ground below. "They catch ya, you have to show them something." She ran off in a storm of red dirt. By fifth grade, girls didn't run or play sports together anymore. They braided each other's hair. And ever since the day I'd challenged and beaten one of the biggest boys in an arm-wrestling contest, I'd been blacklisted from touch football or red rover with them. I was tired of being left out. I rested my hand on the hard edge of the bleachers and dared Kevin with my eyes.

"Now you," he said, pointing at me.

I dropped from the stands and sprinted toward one of the outbuildings they used for storing football gear. Kevin was slow but I heard him behind me. Because I didn't have brothers, I was curious about the anatomy of boys, so I ran toward the lean-to on purpose and waited for Kevin to catch up. Kevin rounded the corner. "Ha! You're caught."

"Whatever." I knew I didn't have anything up top he didn't have. Without hesitation, I untucked my shirt and lifted it to show him my flat chest. I counted to six to give him a good, long look.

His eyes bulged like hard-boiled eggs. I yanked my shirt down and smoothed it into place. I pointed to his pants. "Your turn."

"No way, Jose." He ducked out of the lean-to, then took off yelling, "I saw it! I saw it!" His words echoed off the back wall.

"You saw nothing!" I called after him. But he was out of earshot, and I felt cheated. That wasn't the way it was supposed to go.

An hour later, I swung my legs like pendulums beneath the lip of my plastic chair in the principal's office waiting room, alongside several other girls. I thought about how great it had felt, for sixty whole minutes, to be included—to be a part of something, even if that something was trouble. But now, I knew I was on my own. And because none of the boys was there with us waiting to be punished, I understood that because God had made me a girl, I was going to be in trouble a lot.

The principal's secretary called my mother at home. Dread weighed on me like bags of wet sand. I pictured Mom lying on the sofa, smoking a True cigarette and scratching the top of her head. I knew my mother would be angry before the secretary even said a word. It was two o'clock, and *Guiding Light* was on. Even I knew better than to interrupt Mom's stories.

Twenty minutes later, my mother arrived, thundering through the threshold, making heads turn, and leaving the smell of Estée Lauder Youth Dew in her wake. She yanked her circus-size purse free of the closing door. I stared at my Earth shoes, brown suede with thick rubber soles, and avoided my mother's eyes until the principal called her into his office.

When she emerged thirty minutes later, her lips were pressed into a hard, chafed line. Her red clip-on earrings and the silk scarf strangling her neck matched the shade of her mouth. Once we were inside the car, she unleashed on me. "Do you have any idea what you just put me through? Nasty behavior. I won't stand for it." She slapped her hand flat against the steering wheel and held it there. Her palm blazed with color. "You should be ashamed of yourself. Acting like that. Nice little girls don't do those sorts of things." She put her hand on her head, and dug at the itchy spot on her scalp. "What's wrong with you?"

"I didn't do anything." I crossed my fingers so the fib wouldn't count. "Why don't you believe me?"

"Oh really? Listen, missy, something happened, and you were involved in it, so don't lie to me. Running around like a wild heathen. Inexcusable. No daughter of mine . . ."

Little grenades of words exploded.

When we reached a stoplight, my mother grew quiet. She shook her head and reached toward me. I braced for a slap. She smoothed a few wisps of loose hair from my forehead and ran her fingers through one of my ponytails, which stuck out from the side of my head like the ear of a donkey. Her finger caught in a tangle. She recoiled as if she'd been bitten. When the light turned green, the other drivers honked at her. "Everyone will know what happened." She gave up in a thick exhale and eased her foot off the brake. "Do you really want to be remembered as the girl who got picture day canceled by showing boys her private parts?"

That night, I perched on the stairs above my parents, in the living room. I wove my fingers through my cat Mittens's fur. I let her walk serpentine around my hands, leaning in, pressing her ears and cheeks against me. I heard Mom tell my father that this would go on my permanent record. I buried my head in the soft pillow of Mittens's neck and wondered if there really was something wrong with me, something so bad that I could never change it. The world was a complicated place with an instruction manual I didn't understand. I had embarrassed my mother—no, worse—I'd made her ashamed of me. *I don't have any real friends*, I thought, my head pressed against Mittens's fur. *If my family gives up on me, where does that leave me? Isn't there an unwritten rule that your parents have to stick with you, no matter what?*

No more than two days after the incident on the playground, I was dunking an Oreo into a glass of milk, my face inches from the cast of *Happy Days* on our mini black-and-white television in the kitchen, when the front door slammed. "No child of mine—" my mom said. "Go put ice on it."

My sister, Kathy, rounded the corner, headed straight toward the freezer, grabbed a piece of ice, then a paper napkin, and turned toward me. Her lip was swollen to three times its normal size. She pulled out a chair and covered her mouth.

"Oh wow." It was all I could think of to say. Her bright blue eyes filmed over. She shook her head. Tears streamed down her cheeks. Her expression tightened as if she were constipated.

Mom's angry heels clicked across the kitchen floor until she stood over Kathy. "Let me see." She pulled away the wad of dripping napkins from my sister's fat lip. "Tell me exactly how it happened."

"I was just sitting there on the bus. Anita came down the aisle, stopped at my seat, and told me to get up. Said it was her seat. I just ignored her. Barry and me just sat there acting like we didn't hear her."

"Barry and I." Mom tapped out a single cigarette and lit it with a puff. "So Barry was there with you? He saw the whole thing?"

"Once we got off the bus, she was waiting there. Her friends held Barry up against the wall, and she said, 'I don't like your mouth,' and she socked me." Kathy removed the ice from her lip and looked at the wall. "I don't know why. I didn't do anything."

"Of course not." My mom put her hand over my sister's and brought the wad of ice back to her mouth. "Keep it there, honey. Thank God she didn't knock out any of your teeth. You're the only one who's not going to need braces."

I hid my overbite behind my glass of milk.

"Did you hit Anita back?"

"No!"

"Then they can't suspend you for fighting. This is ridiculous. They don't know who they're dealing with." Mom phoned the middle school, blew smoke against the wall, and waited for someone to answer. My mother would get this girl Anita suspended, maybe even expelled by the time she'd finished with her. And yet, I didn't think that the situation was being handled right. I turned to the television. Fonzie would kick Anita's butt. If I did something like that, Kathy would see how great a sister I was, and she would invite me to play with her and her best friend, Veronica. She would forgive me for stealing the reeds from her clarinet to make water skis for my Ken doll and for giving her a bloody nose when I was five because it was the only way I could get her attention. But I couldn't beat Anita up; I couldn't even leave the yard without permission.

That night, Kathy let me crawl into bed next to her and she showed me her fat lip. We listened to the sound of our mother downstairs, who sobbed and screamed at my father, "I just can't take it anymore, Al. Not another second."

We knew what that meant. *How many hours or days would we lose her?*

"You think she'll have a nervous breakdown?" I asked.

Kathy stared at the purple gingham checks on the canopy above her bed. "Might just take a Valium and sleep for a while."

Tears rolled off Kathy's cheeks onto the pillow.

Beneath the haven of my sister's canopy, we were finally more alike than different. While we couldn't share dolls or clothes or magazines, we had our mother in common.

"How big is it now?" she asked, pulling out her lower lip. "Do you think I can cover it with makeup?"

"It's already going down," I told her.

"Okay then," she said. Her raised eyebrows asked me to leave.

I rolled out of the covers. "You'll be back to normal tomorrow," I told her, certain it was true.

BY THE TIME MY FIFTH-GRADE photo was rescheduled, I convinced my mother to cut my hair. "I want to look like Dorothy Hamill," I told her and watched her bloom at the idea of me wanting to be like the cute and very feminine figure skater. But once I got that wedge cut and was alone in my room, I used a wet comb to slick back my short hair into a fifties ducktail. I threw on a jeans jacket—the one I'd begged for at Sears because it was the closest I could get to a leather one—and popped the stiff collar up around my ears. With no one else around, I could be the Fonz, and, if I kept it from my mother, perhaps I could even be me.

CHAPTER THREE

AFTER DROPPING CONNOR OFF at school, I step outside to regroup before my meeting with Father Bill Breslin, the pastor of Sacred Heart and the head of its school. The rain has passed. I take it as a good omen. I stare at the signs in front of the YWCA across the street: EMPOWERING WOMEN, ELIMINATING RACISM, and a totem pole next to the children's playground, MAY PEACE PREVAIL ON EARTH, transcribed in four different languages. In a place like Boulder, where environmentally conscious CEOs commute to work on skateboards and medical marijuana shops and lesbians outnumber Republicans, I didn't think the Catholic Church here would mind if two mommies wanted to baptize their son, especially since they hadn't cared when we enrolled Connor in their school.

I remember sitting in front of the director, who promised Jill and me that Connor wouldn't be treated differently from other kids at Sacred Heart of Jesus School or penalized in any way because he had same-sex parents. The only thing I hadn't been completely up front about was being a member of their parish. I claimed I belonged in order to move Connor to the front of the waiting list for enrollment. I did go to Mass at Sacred Heart—not every Sunday, but fairly regularly. *What constitutes "membership"? Was I supposed to sign something official or give a certain amount of money each year?* I didn't know and didn't ask. I figured after enduring eighteen years of Confraternity of Christian Doctrine Sunday school class, I'd earned a little preferential treatment.

Still, for the baptism, I covered my bases. Six months ago, I had gotten approval from the baptismal director. I specifically asked if there would be any problem with Connor having two moms. Even though I'd been out of the closet for years and had a family I couldn't hide, coming out to complete strangers still felt like driving forward with the emergency brake on. I hated that split second or two waiting for a reaction.

The baptismal director said she'd check for me and then called me back to say it was fine. So I took the classes. I selected a date from the ones they offered me. Then Father Bill had second thoughts. *How can he judge us when the director of his school is a woman who may be headed for divorce?* I try to channel Jill's even-keeled self-assurance and check my anger at the door. I have to make this baptism happen in five days' time as planned; it's as simple as that.

I step inside the parish center and Father Bill ushers me into his wood paneled, plant-barren office; I feel like I've been sent to see the principal. Sitting less than two feet from me, he relaxes in his chair and folds his hands in his lap. I want to be fair, but I see only his flaws: stubby fingers, fat from eating too many church-lady casseroles; thin lips; and the tattered edge of his black-and-white priest's collar where the rolls of flesh around his neck have worn the fabric away.

He doesn't speak, and so we stare at each other until I decide I want to get this over with. "We're really excited about Connor's baptism," I say, as if it still can happen.

"Yes, of course. It's a wonderful thing when a child gets baptized. But I'm not sure we have much more to talk about."

"My parents will be here in five days. They're driving from Texas—they bought him a baptism suit."

He scoots forward in his seat and fixes his gaze on me. "How do you reconcile your homosexual lifestyle with your Christian beliefs?"

I balance on the edge of my chair, my leg bobbing up and down like a sewing machine needle. That single question has taken me almost forty-two years to answer, and I think about the different responses I might give: *God doesn't care that I am gay. He made me this way in the first place. It's not a lifestyle, it's who I am. Why do I need permission to worship God?*

Instead, what comes out of my mouth is: "It doesn't matter what I think. Yes, Jill and I are gay, but we're pretty sure Connor isn't." I tap my fingers on my thigh and say, "I promise, you won't be letting another one of us in." I try for levity; he seems to get the joke, his lips widen slightly, so I continue: "Father Bill, Connor didn't choose his parents. None of us does. Without us, he would have been an orphan."

At the word "orphan," Father Bill looks at his feet and blushes. It's an odd reaction I can't quite read. *Is he embarrassed? Hiding something?* He rubs the palm of his hand against his forehead. "I'm just trying to figure out where I stand on all of this," he says.

On the off chance that he really is still confused about the matter, I scroll through my iPhone to show him photos of Connor. In one, Connor is just fourteen months old and dressed as a fuzzy lion for his first Halloween with Jill and me. In another taken a year later, on his adoption day, he wears a little navy blazer, khaki pants, and a red-and-blue clip-on tie. As I swipe at the screen, I watch Father Bill's eyes. This man of the cloth, with no children of his own, nods and says, "Yes, yes. I see." And I wonder if he can.

When I reach the end of the photos, Father Bill stands and says, "I'll let you know what I decide."

A million thoughts run through my head—decades of history I can't unravel for him in a few minutes. "My mom is going to be his godmother. You won't find a more devout Catholic." I clench my hands over and over into fists as if I'm trying to squeeze blood into a heart that's stopped beating. "We want our son to know God. How can that be a bad thing?"

He turns me toward the door. He nudges me, his thick hands on my shoulders. Before I can stop myself, I turn to him and say, "You know what? I honestly don't care if you think that being gay is wrong. I'm not trying to convince you otherwise, but Connor is innocent in all of this." His eyes soften, so I take a deep breath to calm myself. "You'd be lucky to have him," I say. As soon as the phrase is out of my mouth, something shifts inside my chest. The words repeat inside my head, *You'd be lucky to have him,* and I realize that it sounds like I am giving my son away and I have to wonder: *Is that what I'm doing?*

This morning Jill had said, "This isn't about you." And she was right. It wasn't. It wasn't about me or Jill or even Connor, but shouldn't it be?

SIX HOURS LATER, CONNOR GALLOPS through the back door of our house, hugs each of our three dogs in succession, dives through my legs, and makes a beeline for his *Star Wars* Legos in the living room. In the kitchen, I kiss Jill and boil water for pasta.

I tell her everything about my meeting with Father Bill and before I am done, I am teary. "I just feel so stupid. They don't want him. Why am I fighting so hard for Connor to join a church where he isn't even welcome?" I toss a pot holder onto the counter, defeated. Though I already know the answer, I want to hear someone say it out loud.

Jill moves behind me where I stand at the stove, wraps her arms around me, and says into my ear: "Sweetheart, you know exactly why. Because Jesus doesn't sit at the right hand of God. Your mother does."

Steam curls around our hands and shoulders, and in that moment I know why we've stayed together for eleven years. Jill squeezes me before going to uncork a bottle of Cabernet.

"You know your role in all of this, right?" she asks.

"What do you mean?"

"Well, don't take this the wrong way, but you've kind of created this whole thing. It's more than just a baptism. It's like you're trying to get away with something." She moves around the counter and puts a glass of wine in my hand. "You think if you can get the Catholic Church's blessing, you'll finally get your mom's too. And I understand it, I really do."

I shake out my right arm and knead the muscle to try to get the muscle spasms to stop. "That's not it. Not entirely anyway."

Jill puts down her wine glass and beats on my bicep with karate chops. I think about the rock that Jill has been, how she never even flinched when I was diagnosed with multiple sclerosis back in 2003. She could have walked away. As far as I know, it never even occurred to her.

"Aren't you due for an MRI?"

I shrug. I know it's been a couple of years, but nothing my neurologist says will make me do anything differently. And it's too alarming to me to see images of my brain eaten away like Swiss cheese.

"If you keep worrying about this, you're going to have an exacerbation," Jill says. "It's not worth it. Why don't we just call it off? We'll get him baptized in a different church, one that accepts us completely."

"Petey," I say, using the random nickname we call each other from the dog in the old kids' series *The Little Rascals*, "I appreciate you trying to give me a way out, but leaving the Church will hurt my mom way more than Father Bill canceling the baptism." I take my arm away. "Plus, the Church is wrong about this. I think Father Bill will see that. You can't blame a child for who his parents are." I kiss her on the cheek and drink my wine. "I bet he'll call me tomorrow. You'll see." By the time I get to the second glass, I almost believe it too.

OVER THE NEXT THREE DAYS, I call Father Bill several times, but he never responds. I don't let that stop me. Jill and I clean the house from top to bottom. I pretend that the baptism is happening because it has to; my parents are only a few hours away.

I cut fresh flowers and put them in the bathrooms. I take my daily dose of Prozac and consider doubling the amount given the anxiety I feel. I hang clean bath towels, washcloths, and hand towels, trying to find sets that match. In the guest bedroom where my parents will stay, I hook up a TV, clear out the closet and dresser, and find reading lamps for both sides of the bed. It's a relief that I no longer have to "de-gay" the house for my parents, as I did in my twenties. In those days, I removed anything that suggested I was a lesbian: photos of friends who played softball, Indigo Girls and k.d. lang CDs, Rita Mae Brown books, the Picasso print of the naked woman that used to decorate my bathroom.

While Jill vacuums, I head to Safeway to purchase items we'll never use but that my parents have to have. I'm in aisle 5 grabbing Nestlé Coffee-mate fat-free hazelnut creamer when my cell rings.

Father Bill sounds busy, as if calling me is an inconvenience. "I've decided that we will go ahead with baptizing Connor. But I need to see if you are flexible regarding the time on Sunday."

I punch a fist of triumph into the air. A man grabbing a packet of tofu stares at me.

Father Bill continues talking. "After our meeting I really wanted to do the baptism myself. As it turns out, I'll be out of town, and the priest who usually celebrates Mass when I'm away is less than delicate about situations like yours. But if you don't mind the baptism being done later, I have another priest who is available at four thirty."

"What do you mean when you say less than delicate?" I ask.

"Well, he might say to the congregation, 'What do we have here, two mommies? Now I've seen everything.' Or something like that. He definitely wouldn't be subtle."

I grip a package of Wonder bread and leave a handprint in the loaf. This isn't the time to argue. Father Bill is allowing the service to take place, and the last thing I need is for a priest to berate me in front of my mom and an entire congregation of people. I flash back to a few years ago when I joined my parents, sister, brother-in-law, and niece at Disney World, and a man on a tram commented, "Good thing you brought your family here today. Yesterday, they had Gay Pride Day at the park. Homosexuals prancing around everywhere waving rainbow flags. I swear it's the end of everything decent." My mother shielded her stomach with her denim Mickey Mouse tote as if she expected him to punch her and said, "Well, you know, as long as they keep to themselves and aren't hurting anyone." It was the best she could do, and I was proud of her for saying anything.

"Absolutely; let's change the time, Father," I say.

"Good, good. I just want it to be a lovely occasion for all of you," he says. "Father Alan is really wonderful. And once this is all over, I'd like to meet again to discuss another related matter."

"Sure," I say dismissively, scanning the shelves for Folgers half-decaf coffee and NutraSweet. "So four thirty at Sacred Heart with Father Alan. Thank you so much, Father Bill."

Three hours later, my father honks in the driveway. Seeing them is what I imagine childbirth would feel like: immense joy numbing the

pain that came before it. My father unfurls his six-foot frame from
their Dodge Caravan and I throw my arms around his neck. He says,
"Ah me, that was a long drive. How're you doing, sweetheart?"

My mother emerges from the passenger side, and I hug her
rounded shoulders. Her head is even with mine. She plants a kiss
on my cheek. "I'm about to kill your father. Where is that little boy,
my sweet Connor? Michelle, honestly, you look too thin. Aren't you
eating anything? Tonight I thought we'd treat you to Ruby Tuesday
if you have one of those around here. Then tomorrow night I'll make
pasta for dinner so we don't have to go out. I'll make extra sauce so
you can freeze it. Are you still just eating fish and vegetables? You can
pick out the meat, right?" A little dust tornado trails behind her as she
heads toward the house. I haven't even said hello yet.

Connor peers over the half railing outside the back kitchen door
and falls to the ground as if shot by shyness. "There he is!" Mom
walks to the gate, leaves her bags for my father and me to handle, and
scoops up Connor in her arms.

Connor scrunches up his face. "Grandy, your breath smells," he
tells her. "Where's Papa?"

"What do you mean? That's not nice. For goodness sakes, I just
had a Big Mac with onions. I brought you toys," she says, bribing him
to like her more.

"Papa!" Connor runs to his grandpa and jumps up and down in
front of him. My dad sets down the bags in his hands and laughs.
"Okay, okay. Hello, Master Connor, sir."

I grab the luggage. "I've got everything. Just go in and get settled."

Jill comes outside as they try to go in, and my mother gives her a
hug and a kiss on the cheek. My father sets Connor down and does
the same. "Howdy, chief," he says to her.

"How was your drive?" Jill asks.

"We hit a heck of a storm in Lubbock," Dad says.

"What the heck," Connor says.

"We don't say that," I tell him.

"Well, that's stupid," my mom says. "Why can't he say 'heck'?"

"We don't say 'stupid' either," I say.

She rolls her eyes at me and walks past Jill into our house.

"Lots of lightning," my dad says. He puts a hand on my back and guides me toward the path of least resistance.

While Mom and Dad unpack, I sit at my desk in the loft upstairs, adjacent to our master bedroom. I pull out the last three issues of *Women's Adventure*—the magazine I started back in 2003, sold in January of 2008, and have continued to run for the new owners for the past two years—along with a feature I just landed in *Health* magazine. I boot up my Mac and launch iPhoto to show my parents images from the press trips I took to Costa Rica and Iceland.

"Don't you people have any real soap?" My mother climbs the steps to the loft and holds up a bar of organic oatmeal soap, round and flat and the size of a hockey puck. I go into our bathroom and grab a bar of Dial from beneath the sink and hand it to her. She turns to walk away.

I say, "Here," and hand her the magazines, like a kid fishing for praise for a macaroni self-portrait, "I thought you might want to read these. I have a feature in *Health* this month." While she thumbs through an issue, I say, "The piece I did on the leatherback turtles just won a North American Travel Journalist award, and I got one for the polar bear piece too."

"That's wonderful, sweetie. But who reads your magazine? I never see it at our Barnes and Noble."

I don't know why it hurts so much, but it does. Maybe because I still feel like a child around her sometimes, hoping she'd be so proud she'd tack my work up on the fridge and prompt me to tell my father about it when he came home for dinner. After all, she's the one who always said I should be a writer. Another part of me knows I'm still trying to make up for being gay, as if my getting an article published or being a great mom or owning a big house will give her something she can brag about. I feel silly for caring.

"It's doing okay," I say quietly.

"I'm not trying to be mean, I just wondered." She stares at my by-line on the page and looks wistful. "I should write something besides our church newsletter."

"I could assign you something in the magazine. We really need more pieces at the front."

"I'm too old. It wouldn't be any good."

"You've been saying that for ten years." When my mom gradu-ated at the top of her class in the 1950s, she aspired to be a working woman or mystery novelist like Agatha Christie. Instead, with the exception of a few teaching and temp jobs, she did what other women of her generation did—she got married and stayed home so her chil-dren wouldn't be latchkey kids.

"Plus, I don't have any spare time."

"You're retired."

She sighs as if her words are too heavy to hold. "I've got book club and Bunco. We're getting the kitchen redone and your sister has us watching the kids sometimes."

"Okay," I say. She walks down the steps holding the magazines in one hand and the railing with the other, slump-shouldered and un-steady. I turn back to the computer and stare at an image of me roped up and wearing crampons while climbing a snow-covered volcano in Iceland. I hit the sleep button and the screen goes black.

THE NEXT AFTERNOON, FOUR HOURS before the baptism, my mother sends my father out to gas up the car. She asks Jill for an iron and ironing board. When my father returns, she sends him back out for spray starch and brand-new white socks for Connor—because she tells us the ones we have are too dingy, and honestly, can't we get the boy some new socks—and then has my father stop at McDonald's to get us all lunch.

"We don't eat fast food," I tell my mother. "Connor has never been to McDonald's, and I'm a vegetarian."

"For once, could you just do something I ask? Would it kill you?" She goes to her room and returns with wrapped packages, silver and white with angels, presents for Connor. She sets them on the kitchen counter close to the back door so they won't be forgotten. "Every army has to have a general," she says, turning to my father, who is waiting for more orders. "Al, why are you standing there?"

Dad leaves, and Mom opens a can of Diet Coke. She puts a glass under the ice dispenser and selects the crushed setting. She stares at the refrigerator door, which has Connor's picture of Noah's ark that he brought home from school. "Couldn't Connor use some other colors?" Black scrawls of crayon obscure the outline of giraffes and elephants heading in pairs into the boat.

"Black's his favorite," I say as if I'm proud. I don't admit how much I worry that Connor's paintings reflect his anxiety or anger, or how desperately I want him to draw a house with two mommies and three dogs and a rainbow.

Mom pours the can of Diet Coke into the icy glass and it fizzes. She runs a hand over the picture. "Well, even if he wants to use black all the time, he still needs to learn to stay inside the lines."

SOON, MY FATHER RETURNS with burgers and fries for us and a Happy Meal for Connor that indoctrinates him into an American rite of passage we wanted to avoid. I fix myself a peanut butter and jelly sandwich. Jill, who has been on a diet, shrugs at me and devours her Big Mac and fries.

After lunch, I head out for a run, a form of meditation I hope will allow me to remain calm for the rest of the day. As I hit the trail across from our house, my mind and body get lost in the rhythm of my footsteps, my breath, the wind, until I am praying, as I always do: *Thank you, Father God, for all of these blessings. For my health. For Connor. For my soul mate, Jill. For my family. Help us to be good parents and for Connor to feel You at work in his life. Make him kind and good-hearted. Fill him with love. Help us get through today without any problems. Amen.*

When I get back to the house, my father is shaving and Connor is watching him with great interest. I head to the kitchen, dripping with sweat, and chug an orange Gatorade. My mother finds me. "Oh, Michelle, you're so red. How can you go out in the heat like that? Didn't the doctors tell you not to get so hot?"

"I run, and eat right, and watch my stress. I'm doing just fine. I'm on it," I assure her. I don't tell her that lately my left leg has been going numb when I bend my neck and that I sometimes have trouble seeing out of my right eye.

"Maybe you should get back on the medications."

"Why? They're poison. Seriously. There's been no progression for six years. Stop worrying."

"It's what mothers do. We worry." She puts a hand on my back and rubs it in tiny circles before walking back to her room. She calls over her shoulder. "I'll get Connor dressed. You and Jill just get ready." I am basking in her love and concern for me when she adds, "And for Pete's sake, wear a dress." As she closes the door to her room, I think that my mother is just like the interferon drugs I used to take: She heals and destroys me all at the same time.

Thirty minutes later, I jog down the steps, my hair still damp from the shower. I'm dressed and putting on earrings. Connor runs past me and hides behind my legs. He wears his blue pajama bottoms with a pair of tighty-whities on the outside. His chest is bare. "Connor, what's up with the underwear?"

"I'm Batman," he says and holds up a picture from his coloring book. Sure enough, Batman does wear his underwear over his tights.

My mother yells from the other room, "Connor Theall, you get in here right this minute!"

"Batman needs to fly to his room to get dressed for church," I say. I lift him up with my arms beneath his torso and he extends his hands and hums the *Batman* theme song. I set him down next to my mother.

"You sure you don't want me to help?" I ask.

"Just take care of yourself," she says. I walk out of the room, but instinctively wait by the door, listening. "Connor, get over here now," my mother says. "You're going to make us late." I hear Bumblebee, his Transformers robot shooting rat-a-tat-tat and saying, "Enemy attack." I am about to go back into the room to help when I hear my mother say to my son: "Honestly, is this the way you act before going to church to pray? Listen here, mister, if you don't get that baptism suit on this minute, Jesus won't love you."

At first, I'm too stunned to say anything. I wait for her to say she's just joking, but she doesn't. I stomp into the room and start yelling. "What's wrong with you? Do you ever listen to yourself? Just once, could you think about what you're saying before the words come out of your mouth?"

She ignores me and wrestles one of his arms into the sleeve of the white suit.

"Connor," I say to him and wait for him to meet my eyes. "Jesus doesn't care what you wear; He will always love you."

My mother stops fumbling with his outfit and glares at me. "Oh please, I'm just trying to get him to cooperate." The edge in her voice, sharp as a razor.

"Really? And you're going to be his godmother?"

Mom stands and our faces are six inches apart. Connor sits between our feet, still tangled in his suit. She says, "Don't you ever question my dedication to the Catholic faith." Her voice lowers to a growl. "Of all people, you should talk."

Jill appears in the doorway. "We're not going to do this today. Both of you, knock it off. Michelle, go upstairs and finish getting ready. Phyllis, do you need me to take over here?"

My mom says, "No, I was doing just fine. She criticizes everything I do." I start to respond, and Jill pokes me in the ribs. I wander off. Within minutes, I start to feel guilty for the way I spoke to my own mother and embarrassed that I'm reduced to adolescence with just a few sentences between us.

At four thirty inside Sacred Heart, my father, mother, Jill, Connor, and I form a semicircle around the baptismal font and face Father Alan. My sister, Kathy, and her two kids, my teenage niece Madison and nephew Dylan, arrive. Though I know it wasn't intentional (the kids' school activities prevented them from taking an earlier flight), my sister has conveniently avoided all the chaos and conflict traditionally associated with Theall family events, and her husband, Eric, was smart enough to stay in Texas and golf instead. I wave and smile at them as they shuffle into the front pew, sweaty and rumpled from rushing to get here in time. My sister rubs the tip of her nose like she's petting a pony, a nervous tic akin to my chewing and peeling the skin from my thumbs. While my hands are ragged and ugly from it, my sister's incessant nose rubbing has smoothed out the pores and made the point more turned up and perky than it already was. Despite the fact that she is in her forties, she's still beautiful—huge blue eyes, an hourglass figure, dimpled cheeks, and a wide smile like Mom's that she actually uses.

Kathy will always take my parents' side when forced to choose, but I'm relieved she's here. She gets along with our mom in a way I never could and makes it seem easy. And because that's something I've always wanted, I would never ask her to give that up for me.

She just wants us all to get along, and I can't really blame her for that.

Father Alan looks like Santa Claus, with wire-rimmed glasses, a white beard and mustache, and apple cheeks. Light fractures over us from the late sun splintering through the stained glass windows. Since the baptism is being held at four thirty, aside from my sister's family, the church is completely empty except for a woman we do not know who is just there to sign paperwork for the parish.

Throughout the baptism, Connor stands between Jill and me wearing the little white suit embroidered with delicate crosses that his Grandy toted all the way from Texas. Connor behaves through most of the prayers, until it is time for him to be lifted over the font.

Jill and I try to hold him as he flaps his arms and arches his back away from the holy water. During the struggle, he kicks off one of his patent leather shoes, and I grimace. It rolls off the edge of the baptismal font and lands on the altar. Father Alan ignores Connor's flailing and raises a pitcher over a leaf-shaped receptacle that looks more like a birdbath from Home Depot than something sacred. While he says something about the Holy Spirit, my mother's chiffon-draped arms swoop in underneath my own on their way to grasp the back of Connor's neck. Though she means well, her ornate metal bracelets scrape against my forearm. I pray the scratch isn't bleeding so it won't leave a permanent stain on Connor's special white suit.

Because Jill is five ten and stronger than my mother and me, she holds the bulk of Connor in her arms. The fact that she manages to do so in a classic flowered skirt and white blouse while smiling reveals a fierce capability that is as frightening as it is beautiful. Her knuckles turn white from gripping our son, but she remains poised, her tall frame, blond hair, and fair, Scots-Irish skin looking like she might just as easily participate in the Miss America pageant (like her sister did) as keep a group of her Italian in-laws and our half-Cambodian son from getting out of hand at this christening. Even as I am wrestling to keep Connor's foot from kicking me in the ear, I think about how Jill will make me laugh later about the tarnished green smears my mother's bracelets have left on my biceps and the farting sound Connor's shoe made when it hit the rubber-covered seam on the rug of the altar. Like God's grace, I am counting on it.

Through all of this, my father stands a few steps removed from us with his hands clasped in front of him. On his index finger, he wears a fresh neon Band-Aid from some wound he quietly suffered this morning and doctored on his own. It's the kind of thing that would normally make me feel sorry for him, except that he chose to get into this boat on his own when he married my mother. He should never have assumed I'd be the kid to help him bail water instead of putting more holes in the bottom.

In the end, it takes my mom, Jill, and me to get Connor to submit to God, and patches of sweat seep through our clothes like we've just performed an exorcism. As with any function where my family is involved, the real miracle is that we get through it still speaking to one another.

After Father Alan gives the final blessing, we hand our cameras to the woman who is there from the parish to document the occasion. We assemble in front of the font for a group photo, and Connor slips away from me. He runs serpentine around the candles and chairs and lectern. He rolls across the floor and tries to crawl beneath the draped altar. His white patent leather shoe catches on the tall candleholder, and it wobbles before crashing over. I fall to my knees to catch it before it can hit the dry carpet and catch fire. When I rise from the floor, Jill holds Connor and says, "Let's try this again." We reassemble. The shutter clicks, and as it does my mother says, "I can't wait to come back for his First Communion."

CHAPTER FOUR

In my CCD Sunday school class at St. Mary's, my teacher said that Jesus was about thirty-three years old when he died. I pictured him at my age—ten—with sun-kissed curls and sandals. Hard as I tried, I could only imagine a serious child Jesus, one who taught in temples and squares and hung out with adults instead of kids. If he laughed or played tag, there was no record of it. Still, by the time he was a grown man, he'd made at least twelve friends. I was just praying for one.

One scorching night in June, as I was getting ready for bed, I overheard my parents talking about me downstairs. My sister and I weren't allowed to close the doors to our rooms—my mother didn't like secrets—so I caught my name drifting through the gap. I yanked on my pajamas, stiff with retardant because my mother worried I'd burst into flames while sleeping, and tiptoed to the top of the stairs. I took two steps and hopped over the baby gate my mother put up every night so that my thirteen-year-old sister and I wouldn't accidentally tumble down the steps. I perched on the third riser to eavesdrop.

Over the sound of Ed McMahon introducing Johnny Carson, Mom discussed the new neighbors, the Crandalls, with my dad.

"There's a story there. Mark my words. It goes well beyond them letting their child go around so unkempt."

"Phyllis, I know where you're going with this. Just because they've both been divorced doesn't mean they're bad people. I'm sure they're fine."

"I was hoping Michelle would be able to play over there. But now, I just don't know."

"They're divorced. They didn't kill anybody."

I grabbed a fistful of the shag rug carpeting the stairs. I'd glimpsed the little girl my parents were talking about: straw gold hair and jutting elbows, throwing rocks at the curb in front of her house, a crocheted rainbow cape around her shoulders. I didn't care that she wasn't Catholic or that her parents had once been married to other people, even though my parents had told me that divorce was a mortal sin. I was more afraid of being alone than I was of anything going on over at the Crandalls'. Mittens ran up the steps toward me, purred, and groomed herself with her noisy cactus tongue. I threaded my fingers behind her ears and listened.

"Don't be naïve, Al. I met the mother today. It's a mess over there." A match hissed as Mom lit a True cigarette. "The boy is hers from a previous marriage. The girl, Holly, is his, but he has full custody, Gillian said. Not sure how that all works. And I don't know where the child's real mother is."

Twisting ice trays creaked. My father poured two Coca-Colas. "He can't be a bad guy if he got full custody. That's something."

"Mmmm." This meant Mom wasn't so sure.

"Honey." Dad's tone dropped to a serious low octave. "I saw Michelle teaching the cat to sit."

"When?" my mother asked, a worried hitch in her voice.

"Yesterday afternoon."

Mom exhaled. "She's lonely, Al."

"She can't catch divorce. It's not contagious." My father's joke fell flat with my mother.

"Mmmm," she replied.

"She needs a friend, Phyllis—the kind without fur and a litter box."

THE CRANDALLS' HOUSE SAT DIAGONALLY across from ours, like it was watching the other houses on the cul-de-sac and waiting to be picked for kickball. Exterior paint, a distinct shade of booger green, bubbled up and peeled off the siding like a sunburn that wouldn't heal. Two old cars convalesced in the driveway; a third idled in the garage with its hood open.

I knocked just once. Holly Crandall swung open the front door, left it bouncing against the doorstop, and reached out with both arms. This scarecrow of a girl, with hair my mother said looked as though it had never been brushed, stood on the other side of the door like she'd always been waiting for me.

Without a word, she grabbed my hand between two of her own and pulled me through the den to the back door and into the backyard. Once the door closed behind us, she leaned against it as if she were holding back monsters. "Whew," she said and let go of my hand. "I'm supposed to be grounded." She shrugged. "Whatever."

The backyard was an exact rectangle enclosed by a six-foot fence, all lawn with no flowers or bushes or anything but a giant maple. In the center of the yard, tied to the tree, was an emaciated German shepherd named Bongo. He choked against the tether, strangling the trunk until it bled sap.

"Can we turn him loose?" I asked.

"I did it once. I won't do it again," Holly said, jutting her chin toward the garage where her father worked on one of the cars. A fierce clang of metal punctuated her words.

We slid our backs down the wall of her house and took turns

tossing rocks into a rusted Folgers can that was half filled with nails. The wood siding shuddered with the beat of drums blasting from the second story. A KISS album blared, "Rock and Roll All Night Long."

"My brother, Danny, thinks he's Peter Criss," Holly said. "Plays those stupid drums every single day for hours." She lobbed a stick toward Bongo, who devoured it in seconds. "Stepwitch won't let me play my stereo above three, but she lets Dipshit bang the crap out of those things."

Holly was a head shorter than me, but her cursing made her tall. I waited to hear what would come out next.

"I don't know why Dad married her. She's such a bitch." Sweat dripped from the tip of her nose. She sniffed and ran the palm of her hand in an upward swipe. No one I knew wiped a nose that way. It seemed counterintuitive, like rubbing velvet against the grain.

"She hates me."

"You think that?"

"Hell, yeah. Stick around and you'll see." She grinned wide, a big toothy smile and pink gums. "I'm God-danged Cinderella."

By the end of my fifth-grade year, Holly was my best friend, and sometimes, aside from Mittens, my only friend. While my mom was sleepy and sad much of the time, Holly was there for me. But my mother had been right to worry about her family.

On the first day of July in the middle of an angry Texas summer, Holly and I spent the morning in the strip of woods separating the end of our cul-de-sac from the freeway. We caught two lizards, tried to figure out if they were male or female, named them Tarzan and Jane, and left them in a Mason jar wedged inside a John Deere tire so they could mate. After that, we built an obstacle course out of empty

Schlitz cans, a car bumper, and part of a velour sofa dumped off the highway. By midafternoon we were resting in the branches of an oak tree when a crack of lightning scarred the sky and sent us scurrying toward her house. We raced each other there, getting drenched on the way. In Texas, it was impossible to outrun a storm.

Holly's house smelled like cigarettes and engine grease mixed together and stuffed into an old sock. Crumbs lingered in couch creases; dishes soaked in rotten food juices in the sink; no one ever ran the vacuum.

"Anybody home?" I asked. Holly put her finger to her lips. From the garage attached to the house, an engine sputtered and died.

"Just Dad," she said. "Danny's at his father's house and Stepwitch went to Walmart."

We bounced up the stairs to Holly's room. There was a new hole in the wall just below her Peter Frampton poster. She saw me eyeing it and said, "I got pretty pissed off about Bongo." A week ago, Holly's dad said he couldn't take Bongo tearing up the yard anymore. He loaded both the dog and his shotgun into his truck, but came back with only one of them. I spent two days convincing Holly not to run away from home. "I mean, the yard's all dirt and grass anyway," she said. "Nothing for a dog to tear up. It's not like we live at the Houston Botanical Gardens for Christ's sake."

"Hell yeah, like we do at my house," I said. I chewed on the swear word to see how it tasted.

Holly tossed me a green Bic lighter. "Found this under Danny's bed. He's been smoking."

"So put it back."

"No way, man." She slid the lighter in her back pocket. "You're soaked." She pointed to my shorts and T-shirt. "Borrow my stuff and we'll toss yours in the dryer." She went to her dresser and pulled out a T-shirt that said GONG SHOW REJECT and a pair of jeans shorts with tattered cuffs and her own inked graffiti scribbles across the back pockets. "Designer jeans. You're in luck," she said as she threw them to me and took mine downstairs to the dryer.

I stepped out of my shorts and pulled hers on quick. The fit was tight. I sucked in my stomach to yank the zipper up.

Holly yelled to me from the bottom of the steps. Standing in the den, she unfolded a Twister mat and I joined her on the carpet. We played for fifteen minutes before her father came into the room.

"What are you girls doing?" Holly's dad stood behind the couch and grinned at us before moving to sit cross-legged next to the board. "I'll spin for you." His face was creased and tan, etched like the hide of a football, and his angular limbs folded down to sharp edges with ropy tendons and thick threads of blue veins.

Mr. Crandall hit the spinner, looked at it, and then did it again. "That one didn't count because it hit the palm of my hand by accident. We've got a do-over," he explained. When the needle landed on blue, left hand, I had to reach under Holly's leg and all the way across the mat. Stretched out and bowed in the middle like an old mule, I started to fall. "Hurry, spin, spin!" I yelled at him. He took his time. I collapsed onto the mat.

"You keep losing because your shorts are too tight. Hell, just take 'em off. No one cares," he said. "You could have reached across there if you'd just had on your underwear."

Before his words had time to register, Holly shoved me off the white plastic and started folding up the mat. "I'm bored," she said. "Come on, Michelle, let's go do something else." She stuffed the game back in its box. I lay faceup on the filthy carpet where she'd rolled me, about to get up, when her father walked over on his knees and straddled me. "I know a game," Mr. Crandall said.

Mr. Crandall wrestled my shorts and cotton underwear down to my ankles. His face grew red and sweat beaded up across the bridge of his nose. His thick hands were rough, dry, like cracked earth, raw and rubbing. I wanted to leave, but he told me to relax, whispering it like he was trying not to wake me.

Even though my body was pinned beneath Holly's father, my mind could go anywhere it wanted. I thought about the dirt clinging to the bottom of the Crandalls' drapes. About Holly, who looked at me as if what her father was doing to me was normal, while shredding bits of cardboard from the Twister box into a pile beneath her hands. I thought about the neighbors who lived on this cul-de-sac and how they must know, as even a fifth-grader did, that he beat Holly, even if they didn't know about this. I felt my stomach heave and swallowed the bile rising in my mouth. I thought about Jesus on His crucifix. Certain that He wouldn't have wanted the worst moment in His life to be what people remembered about Him. That the Easter Jesus or the Christmas-manger Jesus should be the one we put up year-round and wore on chains around our necks.

Mr. Crandall grabbed my wrists. My shorts and underwear ensnared my ankles. Instead of saying no or stop, I said I was sorry— over and over again. Pain pierced me from the inside out, surprising and sharp and final, like touching the coils on a hot stove. And I disappeared again, because it was no longer a choice to remain present. I did not know how long I had been gone when I smelled the smoke. Something was burning. Mr. Crandall noticed it too, and jumped off of me yelling, "Jesus Christ, what the hell?"

Sitting on the couch, Holly held Danny's Bic lighter in one hand and a flaming Twister box in the other. In a calm voice, she said to me, "Our house is on fire. Go on home before you get hurt."

I ran from the room, grabbed my clothes from the dryer, and changed as quickly as I could, leaving Holly's GONG SHOW REJECT T-shirt and tiny shorts in a heap on the floor. On the way out the front door, I glanced back toward the den. Holly was gone. Her dad doused the box she'd left burning on the couch with two glasses of water. I went home.

When I opened the door to our house, I found Mom on the couch napping. My sister was at her best friend's house one block away. I headed to the powder room off the kitchen and pulled down my pants to pee. Red blood was smeared across the crotch of my white underwear. The shock of it stopped me cold and I skidded like Alice in Wonderland down a rabbit hole of memory.

I am six years old, all alone in my parents' house, trying to reach a shoe box on the top shelf of my mother's closet. My fingertips graze the edge. I rise up on tiptoe. The chair kicks out from under me and I fall, straddling the back of it. I cry and run to the bathroom. My pee burns. The toilet paper has red on it, but not much, and soon it is gone.

When my mother gets home, I tell her how I hurt myself. I expect her to pull me into her arms and hold me, to tell me everything will be okay. Instead, she yells at me, "I asked you to do one simple thing. Now look what you've done." She puts down the box of valentines she has purchased for me to share with my first-grade class. "And here I was trying to do something nice for you. Why can't you just do what I ask?"

She makes me lie down on the bed and spread my legs, and then leaves me there to dial the phone. Five minutes pass. One of our neighbors arrives. I am told to hold still, and when I try to cover my-self, my mother grabs my wrists. I turn my head to the side, and stare at the wall. Fingers probe and move my skin, while my mother asks this woman's opinion. She is afraid that I have broken something—but she does not call a doctor. Evidently I have injured something that cannot be fixed.

I thought about telling my mother what had happened at Holly's house, but this memory coupled with the incident on picture day made my decision easy. My mother had called me a liar. *Nasty behavior. No daughter of mine*, she had said. I just wanted it to be over, and if I told her, it would never be over. I considered the red in my underwear, browning at the edges like an old photograph. I decided I had gotten my period. It required no discussion or disclosure. It was as simple as I made it.

I took ginger steps up to the bathroom I shared with Kathy. I rigged up a belt and pad, washed out my underwear, and hung them in the back of my closet to dry. I put on a new change of clothes. I tried to remember what I would normally do in my room, but normal didn't exist anymore. *Was there a way I could still be friends with Holly after this?* If there was, I couldn't see it, and that made me saddest of all.

I didn't bleed the next night, or the next. On the fourth night, I woke at 2 A.M. and remembered that Holly and I had left the lizards in the woods, trapped inside a jar and wedged inside a tractor tire. I thought about running out there to get them, but I knew by then I couldn't save them. They were already gone.

CHAPTER FIVE

CONNOR SPRINTS ACROSS OUR LAWN with two kids from Sacred Heart and one of our three dogs, a Shiba Inu named Biscuit, trailing him. Connor's bare feet kick up grass, and the children chasing him scream at a decibel level only achieved by boys and girls under the age of six. Connor grimaces. He's thrown off by the commotion and laughter and also desperate to be a part of it. I want to believe his anxiety with other kids is just a phase. I want him to have friends even though no boys or girls his age live close to us. If I'm honest with myself, I know there's something else going on. While I want to forget all the terrible things that happened to him before he came to us, I know they are there: in the way he reacts to loud noises and doesn't sleep through the night and licks his lips in circles until they are raw.

Today we're celebrating his fourth birthday and Connor wears a pirate hat, an eye patch with a skull, a striped bandanna, and a plastic hook on his left hand. In his right hand, he holds a sword. Watching him dart around the backyard, it occurs to me that he very seldom chooses to be the good guy. In fact, aside from his Batman cape, Connor without fail will pretend to be the villain: Captain Hook instead of Peter Pan, Darth Vader instead of Luke Skywalker. It's as if he already believes that the bad men hold all the power, and though we tell him that the hero always wins, he isn't buying any of it.

Reese, a girl from Connor's class at Sacred Heart, arrives in a pink sundress with French-braided hair, towing her mom, whom Jill and I have never met. As Reese runs off, we introduce ourselves to Deb, and offer her a margarita. While I pour her drink, Deb explains that her partner, Sarah, got called in today and couldn't make it. Both women are physicians.

We knew that a child in Connor's class at Sacred Heart had two moms, but we never had the chance to figure out who they were. We want Connor to know that there are other kids who have gay parents, but in all honesty, we've been too busy deworming the dogs and unclogging our gutters to make much of an effort.

While Jill hangs a pirate piñata off one of the beams on our porch, I ask Deb if her girls were both baptized at Sacred Heart, and I tell her about the meeting I had with Father Bill prior to Connor's baptism. She stops me when I get to the part about Father Bill changing the time for the service.

"So, you had a closet baptism too," she says. A boy on the porch whacks the pirate across the face several times with Connor's *Spider-Man* bat, but nothing happens.

"What do you mean?" I wince into the sun and the next child steps up to the piñata. She raises the bat above her head and comes straight down with it on top of the pirate's hat. One of the parents says, "Is that thing made of steel or what?"

Deb says, "Connor wasn't baptized with the congregation there, right? Neither were our girls. They do it later so it won't take place at the regular Mass. It's in secret so none of the other parishioners will know about it."

"No," I say. "That's not right. He told me if he had been in town, he would have done it at Mass."

"He was in town for ours, and he still held them at different times." Deb scoops up some guacamole and crunches a chip. I walk away from her without another word and head toward the porch. I cut down the piñata and lay it on the deck. I take the bat from a frustrated little girl. I pummel the pirate until its candy guts spill out all over the porch. The children dive toward the candy. I drop the bat and go inside for another beer.

As soon as the guests leave, I tear up the house looking for Connor's baptism certificate and go online to look up Father Alan Hartway. I want to know if the man who performed our service is even a real priest. I scroll through the faculty bios at Naropa University, where he works, until I see Father Alan's photo. Beneath it, I read that he is in fact an ordained Catholic priest in something called the Society of the Precious Blood.

Jill finds me at my computer and scans the blurb over my shoulder. Raised Baptist, she was taught that all Catholics were going to hell because of their idol worship of Mary, coupled with the fact that we drank, danced, and gambled. "What on earth is the Society of the Precious Blood?" she asks. When I tell her I have no idea, she says, "Man, your religion is weird." I want to agree with her, but I can hear my mother saying, "Once Catholic, always Catholic," and I wonder if it's somehow true, like she's initiated me into a prison gang and I can't get rid of the tattoo.

From my desk I watch Jill go into our bedroom to put on her boxers and T-shirt and brush her teeth. With toothbrush in hand she comes back into the loft and asks, "Why are you so angry about this?"

"Really?"

"Yeah, I mean, what did you expect?"

"He had his chance to cancel it, and because he didn't do that, I expected to be treated like everybody else. I didn't think he'd go out of his way to hide us."

With her free hand, Jill smooths the middle of a couch cushion that has developed a crater from the consistent burrowing of Daisy, our Jack Russell terrier. Her effort doesn't make a difference. "Yeah, but wasn't a closet baptism better than none at all?"

"I don't know. When he looked at those photos of Connor, I really thought I'd changed his mind about us." Jill pulls my hand away from my eyebrows where I'd been unconsciously tugging, and tiny black hairs drift from my fingertips like falling ash.

"You thought the Church would change? The Church will never change. Look, if you're that pissed off about it, send him an email. Tell him off—it's not like your mom will ever know anything about it."

I choose to ignore the comment about my mom. I'm a grown woman, after all. "What good would that do? It's over. Why would I want to engage him in a debate I won't win?"

"Because it's not about winning."

AN HOUR LATER, I PUT my fingers on the keyboard and type out a few lines to Father Bill before highlighting and deleting them. I leave my desk and crawl into bed next to Jill. I try to sleep, but my thoughts careen like bumper cars. Jill and I both wanted Connor to be baptized, but she didn't care about the denomination, and neither did her family. We knew my mom would care. We decided to have Connor baptized Catholic, as a reward for how far my mother had come. At the time, it had seemed such an easy call to make. I pull the pillow tight to my ear. *Let it go. It's done.* But it doesn't feel done. There will be First Communion, and Confirmation, and a million other times I'll have to pull this off. It feels the opposite of done.

I count backward from one hundred. Nausea swims through my gut, and even though I know it's psychosomatic—an obsessive-compulsive gift from my mom's side of the family—I can't stop it.

My stomach roils. I go to the bathroom and swallow a blue pill, the one I take a few times a day at the first sign of stomach cramping. Then I swig the cherry-flavored Emetrol for nausea and check under the counter to make sure there's a new bottle on reserve. I slip back under the covers and say the alphabet backward until the medicine takes effect.

Hours go by in bed as I twist around in the covers and rub my feet together like a cricket. Jill knows I am not sleeping. She finds my hand beneath the sheets and holds my fist inside her palm. She says, "He can pretend we don't exist as much as he wants, but he can't unbaptize Connor." As I watch the shadows of trees reach out like arms, I wonder if I want him to.

THE NEXT AFTERNOON I SIT in the loft. I boot up my computer and before I lose my courage, I type:

Father Bill,

I met another gay couple who had both their daughters baptized at Sacred Heart and also had what they called a "closet" baptism (separate from the rest of the baptized, who have a ceremony all together after the 10 A.M. Mass). I'm hoping that you reconsider letting children of gay parents be included in the regular ceremony with the others.

No matter what your parishioners think about who a child's parents are, the child is innocent and the parents should get at least a little respect for deciding that the child should be baptized in the Catholic faith (rather than never baptized or brought up agnostic or otherwise). I see it as your responsibility to educate the other priests and your parish to welcome the baptism of all children into the Catholic faith. Holding

*separate baptisms is sneaky and doesn't serve to educate your
community. Thanks for listening.*

I read the email twice. It is not very bold or angry, but I am particularly proud of my use of the word "sneaky." I hit send. I don't wait
for a reply.

HOURS LATER, I WEDGE A bag of groceries under my armpit, lock the
car with a dangling hand, and hold my cell phone with the other, re-
playing the message I just missed. "Hey, baby, it's Mom. Why haven't
I seen any photos from Connor's baptism or birthday yet? I couldn't
open the ones you emailed, so you'll have to mail me prints. And
what's this about wanting me to join FaceSpace? I don't even know
what that is." There's a pause and a crackle as she leans away from
the phone and says, "Al, are you okay up there? Well, what was that
crash?" Then she is back. "Say a novena, sweetie, we've got squirrels
or something in the attic and I've got your father up there trying to
see what's going on. He'll probably get the hantavirus. Or is that just
from mice?" There's the splintering sound of something breaking.
"Jesus, Mary, and Joseph, I hope he didn't fall through the ceiling.
And why don't you ever answer your phone? We could be dead and
you wouldn't know about it. Honestly. Call me."

I unload the groceries and yell to Jill that I'm back before heading up to the loft to get on my computer. I boot up iPhoto and open
my son's baby book. I print off and add the photos of his baptism and
birthday party, writing notes in the margins. As I go I make a pile of
four-by-six copies for my mother.

Connor wanders into my office, holding a snack in his hand. He
crawls into my lap and asks, "Can boys eat Girl Scout cookies?" I
tell him yes, and he takes a bite of a Thin Mint. Because Jill is from

Lexington, Kentucky, and I am from Texas, our American-born, half-Cambodian son speaks with a drawl. The word "cookies" has four syllables. I add the last of the new photos and then, as I always do, I flip back to page 1 to marvel at how small Connor was when he came to us at just thirteen months.

Connor loves to look through his baby book. I thumb through the pages until I get to the back of the album, the place where I keep photos of his biological parents, Tara and Brian, two people Jill and I have never met. Most of the photos we received from the caseworkers are double-exposed and hazy, images of ghosts. Connor drops black crumbs onto one of the pages and I brush them away. He points to a photo.

In the shot, Brian and Tara sit next to each other against an institutional white cinder-block wall with Connor between them and their arms around him. They are an unlikely trio. Despite the fact that it is the coldest month of winter, Connor's feet are bare and he is dressed in shorts. Even though he is only four months old, Connor seems to realize that these people cannot take care of him. He leans away from his mother and does not smile. Sandwiched between his biological parents, Connor has his legs crossed like an adult's. There's a fretting old soul peering out from his almond eyes.

Brian is a wiry four-foot-eleven Cambodian teenager, clean shaven, with short black hair except for an eight-inch tail left hanging in the back, and a large diamond stud in his left ear. With his curry-colored skin, honest dark eyes, and a movie-star grin, he is a tragically handsome street kid. He looks like he has just realized that he has become a father.

Tara is nearly three hundred pounds and a foot taller than Brian. Her blond straight hair rests on her shoulders and she stares into the camera, twisting her broad, childlike face into a confused, affable expression. She wears a black T-shirt with white tigers on it that does not fully cover her stomach. Her blue sweatpants strangle her waist even with the drawstring untied.

I'd seen so many girls like Tara over the years—in foster-care training and while volunteering as a court-appointed advocate for abused and neglected children. This is what I came to know about family: No matter what a parent does to his or her child, the child still seeks their unconditional love and acceptance. We all want to know that we mattered to the people who gave us life—that we were wanted—which is why I smile at Connor over his baby book even though inside my head I scream: *These are not your parents or your mom or dad. I am your mom. Jill is your mom. Sex might make a baby, but it doesn't make a mom.*

And yet, mostly I've felt sorry for Tara and Brian. How could they parent a child when they never had parents of their own? Who was there to rescue them? I keep their record in a file for Connor; it is typed out and smudged and assembled by numerous caseworkers over the years and condensed into narrative form.

Connor's dad, Brian, was nine years old when he was found in an orphanage in post–Khmer Rouge Cambodia by an American woman who decided to adopt him. She brought him to America and kept him until he turned fifteen, at which time she decided she couldn't control him. Brian suffered from depression and posttraumatic stress syndrome. He couldn't "unsee" nine years of land mines and genocide, trafficking, starvation, and the atrocities of war. Those things came back in his behavior in school and at home. He was diagnosed with bipolar disorder. His mother gave him away to the state of Colorado, relinquishing her parental rights. Brian was set adrift, an orphan again, but now in a new country, where he still spoke Khmer better than English. He ended up living on the streets of Denver and met Tara there.

Tara had an IQ of seventy. She had been shaken as a baby, sexually and physically abused. She lacked the ability to make basic decisions or hold a job. She never found a permanent home. Not with parents. Not with Brian. Not with Connor.

In 2005, Connor was born. Tara and Brian collected welfare and obtained housing through social services. But the drugs Brian took to control his anxiety and mental illness left him catatonic and unable to work. He disappeared for days and weeks at a time, leaving Tara to care for Connor by herself. But she couldn't.

Within his first year of life, Connor was starved, physically abused, malnourished, and hospitalized twice. At two months old, he sustained several bumps to his head because Tara propped him up in a corner before he could hold himself up. He kept falling over onto the concrete floor. A few months later, a social worker showed up to check on Connor and found Tara watching television. When she asked Tara where Connor was, Tara kept her eyes on the television and pointed toward the hallway. She said, "He's taking a bath. He cries when he's done." Connor was five months old. The social worker found him submerged and drowning. Social services placed Connor into foster care and tried to work with Tara and Brian to see if they could safely parent Connor.

After Connor was returned briefly to Tara and Brian's care, a social worker found him playing with an open light socket. His gaunt naked body had a rash, his diaper was overflowing, and he had a swollen and tender knot on his forehead. The social worker asked Tara when she had last fed Connor. Tara told the woman that she had just tried to feed Connor an apple. Connor, who had no teeth yet, "refused" to eat it. On other visits, the social worker watched Tara ignore Connor wailing from his crib, deaf and unmoved by his cries. After months of not being held, Connor's head was misshapen, and his skin oozed, raw in places from being unbathed and left to sleep in his own filth.

By the time he was placed in foster care the second time—after being released from the hospital for pneumonia—Connor's eyes were glazed over. He was unresponsive to cooing or stuffed animals or arms reaching out to hold him—a lost baby who would eat anything his caregivers put in front of him, including a fully loaded pizza, peppers and all. He couldn't trust when he might be fed again.

Now Connor stares at the images of his biological mother and father, and I wait for him to ask me questions. Sometimes, when we get to those pages at the back of the album, he asks: "Did you get me from the pet store?" "Was I a stray like Winston?" "Did you know I'd be this cute when you picked me out?"

Other times, he asks questions about them, the strangers in the photograph who gave birth to him. "When do they get me back?" "Can we go see them yesterday?" "Why didn't they want me?" These questions are never easy to answer. So sometimes I tell Connor he's a star that fell from the sky and landed in the wrong belly. Other times, I remind him that Jesus, Santa, Luke Skywalker, and Superman were all adopted. More often, I explain that the woman and man he was born to were just kids, not old enough yet to be parents, so God brought him to us. When he is ready and wants to know, Jill and I will tell him the truth. We will give him all the case studies and files, and even a scribbled note his mother wrote to him before she gave him away.

I close Connor's book and he slides out of my lap. He stares just past my computer at a vase with withering gerbera daisies, and I steady myself for one of his tough questions. His brow furrows like mine. He says, "Aw, Mama, your flowers are sick. They threw up their petals," and he touches the fallen leaves like he is petting a wounded animal. I nod because I cannot trust myself to speak.

After Connor goes downstairs, I email my mother a few of the baptism shots along with instructions on how to open them. I especially like the one of my mother feeding Connor with a silver baby spoon, mine from when I was an infant, that my mother brought for him to keep. I drop the prints in an envelope addressed to her. It's then that I see the reply posted from Father Bill. I print it out to read it—hold it in my hands like a precious text.

Ah, Michelle, we do not do "closet baptisms" unless the parents request a private service, which must have been the case for the couple you mentioned. I hope Connor is feeling the effects of his baptism. Also, as I mentioned a few weeks ago, I'd like to set up a time when we might discuss a related and delicate matter. It's important, so please let me know a convenient time and day for you. God bless you, Jill, and Connor always.

I crumple his lies inside my palm. I have no intention of meeting with Father Bill. *What's so important? What could we possibly have left to discuss?* I consider leaving Sacred Heart and yanking Connor out of its school. *But wouldn't that be admitting we've done something wrong? What would my mom think about the sudden change?* Coming back to the Church is what brought her back to me.

I smooth out the email. Father Bill is just one man. I learned a long time ago that priests are just people. He's not the Church. He's not God. I read the email one more time. I want to be surprised or enraged, but in the end, all I feel is pity.

CHAPTER SIX

I CARRIED A BOX LABELED FRAGILE: MICHELLE'S MEMORIES through our empty dining room and felt the contents shift. Inside, my mother had bubble-wrapped my childhood: my Raggedy Andy doll, Etch A Sketch, First Communion veil, and kindergarten report cards were bundled together, preserved for our move to Dallas for my father's new job as regional manager of a plastics company. I came back to grab two more cartons and mouthed off to Mom, "You sure keep a lot of crap." She pinched the skin on the back of my arm. "Listen, missy, you'll thank me one day. That junk will be worth something to you." She twisted my flesh and released it. My father wadded up newspapers on his knees three feet away from us. He raised one eyebrow at me as if to say: *Please, you know your mom's nervous. Why are you making it worse?*

At thirteen, I was skinny but tough, and eager to show how much more I could carry than my family. I grabbed three boxes at a time even though my mother warned me it was too much. When I dropped one, she yelled, "You girls are just worthless. I told you to make more trips." My sister, who since her early puberty had burst into the body of Marilyn Monroe, glared at me from the back door. Her enormous boobs rested atop a single box as if they were tired from all the work, and she yelled in the direction of our mom, "What did I do?"

Mom stood in the foyer and checked off items on a clipboard. The typed sheet contained a list of everything the movers had taken, along with the breakables and personal items she wouldn't let them handle, which we packed and shoved into every last recess of her car.

In between loads, I took a break out on the driveway next to Mom's new Plymouth Fury, a white ship of an automobile with embroidered blue seats and a steel hull meant to protect us from disaster. I leaned against the chrome bumper and stared across at the Crandalls'. My sunburn peeled like the paint on Holly's house, and my shiny pink shoulders dripped sweat onto the pavement. I rolled layers of my flaking skin between my thumb and forefinger like rubber cement, wishing I could slough off my old skin and start over— praying that Dallas would be better than Meeker.

Around noon, my family crammed into the Fury. We said our usual round of Our Fathers and Hail Marys, and my mother kissed a St. Christopher's medal before setting it in the glove compartment.

We pulled away from the place we'd lived in for thirteen years. Holly's house quivered, like an apparition, in the wake of the Fury's exhaust. After what happened with her father, I never went over there again. I abandoned her like I was fleeing a hit-and-run, and since then, I'd missed her like crazy.

Maybe moving would help me forget about her and the truth I'd finally allowed myself to see: While her father had abused me once, I knew he did it to her all the time. If I had told someone, anyone, they might have helped her. But I didn't. I was too worried about my Mom getting angry with me—blaming me. And in the dead of night when I couldn't sleep, that made me as guilty as her father.

For most of the five-hour ride to Dallas, I wiggled my fingers through the holes in Mittens's crate and tried to pet her. The rest of the time, I crossed my arms and held myself tightly. I didn't cry, but Kathy, who was about to turn seventeen and was miserable about leaving all of her friends behind halfway through her junior year, sobbed while my mother dabbed at her own nose with a Kleenex.

A few hours into the ride, after the tears had subsided, Kathy and I shoved Mittens's kennel between us, arguing for more space, until a stinky sulfur smell invaded the car.

"Kathy farted," I said.

"I did not, you freak," she said.

"Honestly, girls, we don't say 'fart.' It's not nice."

"What should we say, then?" I wasn't trying to be smart-mouthed; I really wanted to know. My mother paused. Kathy and I waited.

"You say, 'Please excuse my toot,'" she said without turning around.

Kathy and I looked at each other. Her eyes widened and her cheeks puffed. Two seconds later, we exploded with laughter.

"Oh, yes, please excuse my toot," Kathy said in a British accent, placing her hand across her chest.

"Yes, of course, oh, my goodness, that one got away from me," I said. "Ta-ta now. Must go find a loo."

My mother pursed her lips, trying to contain herself, and was soon laughing freely with the rest of us. As we headed into uncharted waters, I figured that I might be aboard the *Titanic*, but at least my family was still in the boat with me.

JUST BEFORE DUSK, MY DAD parked in front of our new home. I unbuckled my seat belt. I studied the solid, sterile, symmetrical brick ranch with its crisp landscaping and bay windows. Our new house on Ambassador Lane looked like all the other houses on Ambassador Lane. In fact, it looked like every house we'd passed for the last fifty miles, each with a tidy, vacant yard on an empty street. In Meeker, the houses had shrugged and given up. The houses here whispered a warning: "Everything on the outside is in its place. Keep it that way." I knew that this order, the surface perfection of it, pleased my mother. We sat in the Fury, as if we were lost or casing the joint, until my mother said, "Shall we?"

My father unlocked the front door. Kathy and I rushed past him to pick out our rooms. Kathy veered left, so I darted right. I found a room with a built-in desk, wood paneling, and a small bathroom with a shower stall. It was meant to be a study, so it was separate from the rest of my family, sequestered on the opposite side of the house. "Mine!" I yelled. I caressed the shelves. All I needed was a smoking jacket, a pipe, and an inkwell with a feather pen.

Off the kitchen, outside my room, I unlocked a heavy door that led to a two-car garage on the back side of our house. I pressed a button and the doors squealed open. I stepped forward a few paces and blinked my eyes. All Saints Catholic Church, a single-story brick building that looked more like a courthouse than a church, sat directly behind our house, about the same distance as the Crandalls' had been from us. Positioned where it was, the church's crucifix would be visible from almost every room of our new home.

My mother found me in the driveway gaping like a fish. "Isn't it wonderful?" she asked. I turned and watched the hard lines of worry around her mouth soften. The valedictorian of St. Agnes's had bought a house with God Himself living in her backyard. It should have been my first clue that things here would be just a little off, like a table needing a shim. I sighed. *Was this an omen?* It seemed like it was, that instead of friends my age on this street, I'd have Jesus. What's more, I'd never again have a good excuse to miss Mass.

• • •

"YOU WILL NOT WEAR THAT to church, young lady." Mom tapped her rosary beads on the kitchen table. "Al, tell her."

"Please put on something more appropriate." Dad lowered his glass of orange juice to look at me.

I left my Cocoa Puffs to bob in their bowl. "I don't think Jesus cares what I wear," I said. I dodged to avoid my mother's swatting outstretched hand and ran smack into the gold Formica countertop with a grunt.

"See, God punishes," Mom said. I hobbled to my room and wondered: *If that was true, was I her punishment or was she mine?* Upstairs, I shed my Wrangler blue jeans and black Camaro Z28 T-shirt. I put on the only skirt I owned, the one I called my Sunday Jesus Skirt. When I came back into the room, Mom told me how nice I looked. I liked hearing her compliment me, but I didn't feel pretty. I felt like I was playing the role of "pretty" on her Broadway stage.

An hour later, my mother led us up the aisle to the front of All Saints and genuflected at the fourth pew. Father Rudy Kos, our new priest, had a *Magnum P.I.* mustache, which was too dark and thick for his hair color and texture and looked straight out of a costume shop. He opened his arms, which were draped with colorful vestments, and said in the voice of an orator, "Peace be with you," to the congregation.

The parishioners replied, "And also with you."

"Lift up your hearts," he said.

"We lift them up to the Lord."

We sat and stood and kneeled at the exact same times, as we had done in St. Mary's Catholic Church back in Meeker and in every Catholic Church I'd ever been in. We knew the prayers, the hymns, the refrains. If I closed my eyes, nothing had changed at all, which was comforting and terrifying all at the same time.

When Mass ended, my mother introduced herself to Father Kos, who greeted people just outside the entrance of All Saints. A baby-faced boy about my age stood next to Kos; the teen's dark brown eyes peered at me from beneath a shag of bangs that he did not bother to push away.

Mom was saying, "—and this is my other daughter, Michelle. She'll be finishing eighth grade at Hilltop." My mother ran a knuckle down my back, and I adjusted my posture. Father Kos took my hand in both of his own and said, "Great meeting you. My son Jason here goes to St. John's." I nodded at the boy. My mother said, "Mmmhmm," before she could gather herself enough to say, "Yes, lovely to meet you," and then tripped in her espadrilles on her way to the welcome table. There was no mistaking his words. Our celibate Catholic priest had a son.

I followed my mom. I wasn't going to miss this. She approached a woman inside the vestibule and stood in front of her. Mom's eyes twitched at the corners. The woman at the table looked up and held out a church bulletin. My mother waved it away and placed her fingertips against her breastbone. She whispered the delicate question: "How did Father Kos become the parent of a thirteen-year-old boy?"

"Oh, that," the woman said, dismissively. She explained that up until a few years ago, Father Kos hadn't even been Catholic. When he felt the calling to the priesthood, he left an unconsummated marriage, had it annulled, converted to Catholicism, joined the seminary, adopted Jason, and then became a priest. I needed a flow chart to follow her, but the woman smiled as if this was normal.

"Where do they live?" Mom asked.

"In the rectory of All Saints," she said. "Where else?"

Father Kos and his son Jason were our new neighbors. My mother nodded and seemed satisfied. On the way back to our car, she said, "Such a selfless example of faith, don't you think?" But I could tell by the way she said it that she wasn't asking me.

When I returned from Mass, I ditched my Sunday Jesus Skirt and put my T-shirt and jeans back on. In the garage, I unpacked boxes, trying to find my Nerf football and *Indiana Jones* whip and fedora. Across the alley, Father Kos emerged from the rectory. He wore blue jeans and a Hawaiian shirt, open at the top to reveal coarse sprigs of dark, curling chest hair. I wondered what Jason called him: Father Dad or Father Father, or maybe something else. Father Kos waved at me, hopped into a red Mustang, and drove off. I had one thought as I watched him speed away: Father Kos was absolutely, unequivocally cool.

MOM INCHED THE FURY INTO a parking space at my new school, then backed up, turned the wheel, cut too sharp, and repeated the maneuver. I rolled my eyes. "Be nice to your mother," she said. "I have bad depth perception." I slumped in my seat until she turned off the engine. "Ready, sweetie?" She twisted sideways and used two hands to secede her Texas-shaped purse from the vinyl armrests between us. I clutched my Trapper Keeper notebook to my chest and slid out the passenger side.

Classical music tinkled out of the open doors of Mercedes and BMW sedans as parents in suits dropped off kids who looked like birthday cakes, dressed in pinks and greens with tasseled loafers and pastel-colored ribbons for belts. There were no Trans Ams with AC/DC pulsing from the windows. No bumper stickers saying, SIMON SAYS YOU'RE AN ASSHOLE. Gone were the boys with corduroy 4-H baseball caps and Wrangler jeans with their faded circles on the back pockets from tins of Skoal. Likewise, there were no girls here with long bangs feathered and shellacked into crisp, Farrah Fawcett wings—the way I had done mine that morning.

My mom and I walked to the front entrance. I looked at my clothes. In an effort to please my mom and to redefine myself at my new school, I had worn what my mother had suggested, a pair of red pants with a white cotton shirt that had buttons down the front and a huge embroidered parrot on the left pocket. My mother insisted that the red feathers of the parrot would color-coordinate with the red pants to make a stunning first impression. I finished off the look with a gold herringbone belt clasped with a metal heart and some tan suede double-toned saddle oxfords.

"I feel sick," I said. "I should go back home."

"Don't be silly," Mom answered. She opened the door to the front office and nudged me inside. I willed myself invisible, tucking my chin to my chest and curling my body in on itself like an armadillo in the middle of a highway. I wanted my mother to rescue me, swoop in and grab me with those sharp, red-painted talons of hers and drop me safely on the other side of the road. But that wasn't going to happen. Because in her mind, this *was* the other side of the road, where girls joined orchestra and tried out for dance team, and became National Merit finalists. My mother said, "How lovely" and "Delightful" to the woman wearing pearls behind the counter, who suggested to my mother that I join something called the Newcomers' Club.

The entire day, I did my best to disappear, which was impossible with a twelve-inch parrot over my left boob. Still, no one spoke to me. The only person who paid direct attention to me at all was an odd-looking boy with a large head who appeared to be wearing eyeliner. He slipped me a note in Language Arts class. It was elaborately folded into what looked like a stork or crane of some sort. In tiny, precise letters, he wrote: CURTIS MORGAN AT YOUR SERVICE. I tucked the piece of paper into the pocket of my pants and stared ahead. When I didn't acknowledge the note, he clucked his tongue like a dripping faucet and crossed his legs at the knee so I could see his shiny penny loafers wiggling in rhythm in my peripheral vision.

At lunch, when students headed to the cafeteria, I found a

wooden bench outside, away from Curtis, who appeared to be stalk-ing me, and the hive of girls who giggled and pointed at me behind the glass doors. Under a breezeway, I ate my Vienna sausages out of the brown paper sack my mother had packed for me. Inside, on a napkin, she had printed a note to me: GOOD LUCK, SWEETIE XOXO, MOM. I wiped the beads of sweat from my upper lip, tucked my hideous shoes beneath me, and waited for the day to end.

And so it went. Every afternoon when I got home from school, my mother begged me to join an activity: band or choir or the newspaper staff. And every day, I hid in my room and created a fantasy world. I called in dedications to KISS FM and made up people to receive them. I'd say, "This is Michelle. Please play 'With a Little Luck' by Wings for my boyfriend, Alex, who is trying out for football tomor-row," and then wait hours just to hear the DJ say my name. I taught Mittens to roll over and fetch a pair of my tube socks, and convinced myself I'd enter us in the eighth-grade talent show where my class-mates would discover how cool I was for training a cat. When I got bored, I smuggled my parents' art book, *Michelangelo: The Painter,* into my room and studied all the naked bodies—penises, buttocks, fleshy and pink. Draped in blue, Mary's perky breasts curved out and up like two water slides at a pool. Even Jesus was half naked. I wor-ried I'd be struck blind from looking at them. So the next time I went to Mass, I plunged my hand deep into the holy water, crossed myself lightly, and saved some drops for a few moments later when I non-chalantly tucked my shirt into my Sunday Jesus Skirt and put some of that holy water down to a place where it would do the most good.

But it was worse than that. My body was changing and my mind went places without my permission. It wasn't the kind of thing I could talk about to anyone, except maybe God, or Holly if we had stayed friends. I was certain something was terribly wrong with me—be-cause I kept fantasizing about being raped. I thought about boys in my class forcing me to have sex with them, and my excitement rose along with my fear. Did that mean I had wanted what Mr. Crandall had done? If Holly and I were still friends, I would ask her if she was as confused as I was, because she was the only person on earth who might understand. She would ask the question I couldn't: Had her father broken us in ways that might never be healed?

But Holly wasn't around, and I thought about whom I might turn to for answers. My parents never spoke about sex, preferring to discuss private parts by saying "down there," and simply telling us to "keep our pants zipped." Though they must have had sex at least twice in order to get my sister and me, they seemed sexless, like department store manne-quins. After watching my mother navigate my sister's adolescence, there was no way I'd talk to my parents about all the feelings I was having.

When Kathy had turned thirteen, my mother refused to take her to the mall to have her ears pierced, opting instead to have our ninety-year-old pediatrician do it in a more sterilized environment with some rubbing alcohol, a sewing needle, and hands that shook against my sister's earlobes like he was dismantling a bomb. When Kathy needed a bra, my mother drove her to Foley's and enlisted a female salesclerk to go into the fitting room with her. The old lady's arm skin wagged as she measured my naked sister across the nipples and around the rib cage. When my sister had her period and wanted to swim in the hotel pool on vacation, Mom paced and fretted in front of the queen beds while my father, sister, and I watched. After much discussion about whether or not one could lose one's virginity from tampon usage, my mom and sister stowed away in the hotel bathroom with a lavender-scented box. My father and I stared at the wood pan-eling, terrified to look at one another, and turned up the U.S. Open. We pretended not to notice thuds, crying, and occasional laughter coming from behind the bathroom door. "Terrific rally," my father would say. "Outstanding," I'd echo.

Despite making it over those hurdles of puberty, Kathy was still more naïve than I was, asking my advice instead of the other way around. Case in point: Within just a few weeks of our move to Dallas, she already had a new boyfriend, though she wasn't quite sure what to do with him.

She came to my room and sat on my bed, the one my mother had recently decorated, transforming it into a giant replica of a Crayola box, using a forest green and gold comforter with the word "nontoxic" falling about where my private parts would be when sleeping. My sister scooted to the edge of the mattress next to the built-in sharpener, clutched an oblong red crayon pillow to her chest, and asked, "Do you think tongue kissing is wrong?"

She was in my room, asking my advice, like we were just a couple of teenagers hanging out and talking about guys.

"Gross, but not wrong," I told Kathy.

Kathy considered my answer. "I think I'll ask Father Kos." She bit her lip and turned from me. "Because if you think it's okay . . ." She pointed toward hell. "It's probably not." I flung a pillow at her head. She strutted out of the room.

After confession the next Saturday, I waited in Kathy's room for her to come home. Maybe this would be a beginning for us; she might think of me like the teenager I was now. And if so, maybe it wouldn't be so scary for me to talk about the disturbing thoughts I'd been having. "Well, what did he say?" I asked.

She breezed past me to her bathroom and reapplied her mascara in the mirror. "How many times have I told you to stay out of my room?" She blotted her lips against a tissue.

I slumped, gripped the white bedpost of her canopy bed as if she might pry me from it. "I don't think he said that. Seriously." I would not leave until she made me.

She huffed the answer to my question. "He told me that French kissing was more serious than regular kissing because it was an invasion of another person's body. But that it wasn't really a sin." She smeared gloss on top of her lips with a fingertip. "Why are you still here?"

I swallowed my sadness and disappointment, but couldn't eat my anger. I became as childish as she saw me. "You're going to see David now, aren't you?" I kissed my forearm and made smooching sounds. "Taking a trip to Paris with him? Oui, oui! "

"Get out!" She slammed the door, but I made sure she heard me making sucking noises all the way down the hall. The next morning I woke with my arms covered in hickeys.

UNLIKE KATHY, I DIDN'T MAKE Father Kos my confidant—at least not yet. Because even at church, I felt invisible. The All Saints youth group was mostly comprised of boys who tagged along after Kos and his son, Jason, like a Cub Scout troop. Other than formally announced gatherings, like the upcoming Search Retreat my mother insisted I sign up for, I never knew how or when these impromptu meetings were going to happen. So I missed out on them.

But something was going to have to give soon. I couldn't believe that no one could see what was going on with me, how desperate I was becoming—how insignificant, weird, and confused I felt. Puberty exacerbated all of it. In an effort to get attention, I started banging my ankle against the metal frame of my bed, trying to break it. I'd seen a girl on crutches at school; kids buzzed around her with fat-tipped markers trying to sign her cast. But no matter how hard I slammed my leg against the steel, I couldn't get it to snap. Pain was a relief, until it faded. Because even though I kept kicking the bed frame, the dresser, the shower tile, my body got used to the abuse. The bruises faded; my skin and cartilage hardened. My mother never noticed me limping along, which is when it finally occurred to me that she was having problems of her own.

In the months that followed our move, I often found my mother, dressed for the day in brightly colored clothing, asleep on the black vinyl couch next to a pitcher's mound of cigarette ash. Her makeup was fresh, her brows tweezed and sharp, and she wore a scowl of lipstick across her mouth. No one but me would guess she'd been attached to that black vinyl upholstery for most of the afternoon. She didn't go anywhere or do anything. When I asked her about this, she emptied her ashtray, flipped on *Guiding Light*, and said, "I'm here for you. You girls don't know how lucky you are. You've no idea what it feels like to come home to an empty house."

Off the couch, her spirits were no better. She obsessed over dirt and germs. Imaginary illnesses metastasized inside her. One week she had breast cancer and the next swine flu. She also raged over simple things and spoiled for fights, even with complete strangers. She didn't get the right table at a restaurant, so she screamed until the manager kicked us out. She reduced a hotel maid to tears because our room didn't have enough toilet paper or towels for a family of four. A man cut her off on the highway, so she got out of her car at the next light to yell at him and pound on his window. I was afraid some lunatic might kill her, until I realized that she was the one acting crazy.

Because my dad traveled a lot in his new position and my sister had already joined band and had a boyfriend, the fire of my mom's anger landed on me. I was a raging teenager myself, so I fed her fury like dry timber—arguing, sassing, and shouting back at her.

Her yelling led to crying. *It was my fault she was screaming.* Crying led to Valium. *My fault she took tranquilizers.* Valium led to sleeping. *My fault she couldn't get out of bed.* How did I know? Because sometimes, in the middle of the worst of it, her hands trembling with rage, she would open the green bottle, swallow a Valium, and yell, "See? See what you've made me do?"

Her volatility became the skipping record of my adolescence. When I wasn't afraid of her, I was afraid of what was happening *to her*. I still needed her to be okay, and perhaps more than that, I didn't want to be the reason she wasn't.

I finally accepted the fact that I was alone and would have to solve my own unhappiness, which I traced back to that day at Holly's. Everything began and ended there. I considered the cause and effect: *Was I different because Dale Crandall attacked me? Or did he attack me because I was different?* My mom always said "God punishes." Was my loneliness here payback for abandoning Holly? I was certain that Holly would have answers for me. But I'd blown it. I had all but thrown away the one real friend who accepted me without question, the one I had prayed would come into my life. Hell, I hadn't even said good-bye.

I thought about this one afternoon in my room, twisted my Rubik's cube in my hands until the colors aligned and an idea came to me. In a few weeks, we'd be going back to Meeker for my grandparents' fiftieth wedding anniversary party. I could apologize to Holly. Just because we lived in different cities didn't mean we couldn't write or call or be best friends again. I had broken this, maybe I could fix it. I put down the cube, picked up my Magic 8 Ball, shook it, and asked, *Will Holly be my friend again?* "Ask again later." I shook it harder. "Don't count on it." I went to the garage and came back with a hammer. I pounded that plastic ball until the blue gel oozed out. It fell onto my bathroom floor, and I let it stay there for a solid week so it could say, "Outlook not so good," to the linoleum instead of to me. I didn't need anyone's help or advice. I would save myself.

CHAPTER SEVEN

CONNOR GNAWS ON THE SLEEVE of his white turtleneck as I try to dress him for a holiday music recital at Sacred Heart. Like kids who suck their thumbs, he seems comforted by the habit. At first Jill tried to stop him, even threatened to spank him for ruining all of his shirts. But I convinced her it was normal and something he couldn't help, in the same way that I mindlessly chew on and peel at my thumbs until they bleed, or grind the plastic caps off of my pens with my molars. It doesn't matter to me if all of Connor's shirts are stretched beyond repair with tiny holes from his sharp baby teeth, and the right sleeve of every shirt he owns hangs lower than the other, like a home economics project gone awry.

I stand in his room surrounded by Legos and stuffed animals and move his wrist away from his mouth so I can pull a red Christmas sweater over his head. The crew-neck sweater, a gift from my mom, is a rich berry red, thickly woven, with reindeer arranged in a pyramid across the chest. Without a doubt, it is the cutest sweater Connor has ever owned, as long as you don't look at it too closely. Because my mother views bargain shopping as a sport, Santa has ten reindeer instead of eight, and the one at the top of the pyramid has a red bow in her fur instead of a nose that glows. Regardless, it is exactly the kind of gesture she would make for my sister's kids, and this is the measuring stick I use to gauge her fairness.

Connor starts singing "Rudolph, the Red-Nosed Reindeer." I wrap my arms around him and he nestles into me, the buttery skin of his neck against my cheek. I sniff him like a mama bear, snorting and nosing at him until he erupts in giggles and begs me to stop, and then begs me to do it again. I lean in and say my favorite line from the book I read to him almost every night, *Where the Wild Things Are*, "'Oh, please don't go. I'll eat you up, I love you so.'" To which he responds, "One of the beasts has human feet," and then as an afterthought, "I love you, Mama."

Jill and I drive Connor to Sacred Heart, take him to his classroom where the other children have assembled, and file into the auditorium to find a seat. Because I am videotaping, I stand to the side in full view of the stage. I am so excited to see Connor perform, I keep testing the camcorder to make sure it's working right. While I'm fumbling with it, Father Bill sidles up to me and taps me on the shoulder. "If I didn't know better, I'd think you were avoiding me," he says.

"Hi, Father," I say. "They looked so cute lining up out there, I can't stand it."

"If possible, I'd love it if we could chat before the holiday? Perhaps next week sometime?"

I nod. "I'll have to check." I put the camcorder to my eye and pretend to focus on the empty stage. Father Bill walks away. I shake off my irritation. I won't let him ruin this for me.

The children shuffle in and position themselves on the risers. Connor is in the front row, smack in the middle, as if he is the star. Onstage, each child has a set of jingle bells to shake during the first carol. I point the video camera at Connor and wave with my free hand, but he doesn't see me. The children start to sing, "Dashing through the snow." Connor shakes his bells once and his eyebrows knit together. He grits his teeth in a fake smile, and wrinkles his nose as if the preschooler next to him has bad breath. He beats his bells against his thigh and winces. Because it is cute at first, a few parents chuckle.

Connor gazes out at the audience and shakes his head from side to side as if the people he sees are water in his ears that he can expel. Because they do not go away, he clamps his eyes and lips shut, and clenches every muscle in his baby face to keep out the entire world. I lower the video camera and look across the sea of parents to try to find where Jill is seated. I want to ask her: *Are you seeing this? Is he okay?* But I can't find her.

A minute passes. With his eyes still closed, Connor relaxes his face until he looks like he is sleeping standing up. It is as if he has left the room in his mind, simply vanished in a way that reminds me of documentaries I've seen of autistic children—and I think, *What if I cannot get him back?* The children on either side of Connor stare at him while they sing but keep going. I have never experienced so many emotions at the same time: love, anguish, laughter, fear, pride, hysteria, and sadness. My eyes brim with all of them. After they finish the song, the audience claps and Connor reappears. He sets down his bells and seems fine. I unravel my fingers from the camcorder and wiggle them until I can feel the tips again. But the recital is not over.

Each child picks up a tiny wrapped package from the floor, and they begin to sing "Feliz Navidad." The boxes have sand inside them so the kids can shake them to the beat. Connor grimaces and grips the gift between his hands with clenched teeth bared to the room. He squints his eyes to tiny slits and presses the fist of one hand against his eye before banging the present against his forehead with the other.

I step to the foot of the stage, say his name twice, and he sees me. His face relaxes. I mouth to him, "It's okay. Sing. Sing." And he does for a while with his eyes locked on mine, singing only to me. But a child drops her bells, and a teacher runs across to hand them back to the girl, and Connor looks away from me. Staring at the crowd, he makes claws with his hands and scratches them down his cheeks before punching himself in the head several times. Just when I think he can't take any more, the song draws to its end. Connor recovers a bit. He joins the other children and sings the last line, ". . . I want to wish you a Merry Christmas from the bottom of my heart," and in tandem with his classmates, he draws a heart in the air with his hands.

I clap with the other parents, simply proud that my son made it through the situation as best he could. I try not to stare at the red marks on his sweet face. I watch him step down from the riser. He picks up his bells and his wrapped package. Before he reaches the wings of the stage, he turns to face the audience full on. I grip the camera and hold my breath. He leans out over the edge of the stage, and in his best villain cackle, above the waning applause, he yells a huge and reverberating "Ha!"

That night after we put Connor to bed, Jill and I flop onto our sofa. We face the fire, drinking Malbec, and stare at the mountains lit up by a full moon. Headlamps from rock climbers dot the Flatirons like rogue embers. Tonight I am inching my way through darkness too. I take a long swig of my wine and wait to disappear into it.

Jill turns sideways and slides her feet beneath my outstretched legs. "I think we should take him to play therapy," she says.

I groan. I knew this was coming. "He's four years old. It was just stage fright," I say.

"Here we go," she says. "I don't think we should ignore this."

"I'm not saying to ignore it, but we don't need to overreact either."

"Says the woman who has MS and refuses to see her neurologist."

"Can we stick to the point?" I rub her calf, next to my thigh, and give it a quick squeeze.

"I saw you trip the other day—on nothing. And last weekend, you were so tired you couldn't get out of bed."

"I'm fine."

"Oh, don't think I'm saying this because I love you. It's selfish really. I'm older than you, so I have to keep you healthy enough to push my wheelchair when I'm eighty."

I raise my palm like a traffic cop. "Please focus. We're talking about Connor."

"Listen, I'm a good problem to have." She touches my cheek and I lean into the cup of her palm. Just as quickly, she's on to solving the next problem. "Okay, now Connor. He doesn't sleep through the night. He chews on his sleeves. And tonight"—she shakes her head— "wasn't normal."

I rise from the chair and head to the kitchen to refill my empty glass. "He's been speaking in full sentences since he was two. There's nothing wrong with him."

From the other room, I hear her say, "I didn't say he wasn't smart. He's too smart. He's already starting to try to deal with things he can't understand on his own." I pour the Malbec and enjoy the weight of the wine as it steadies my hand. She says, "Why are you so resistant to getting him help?"

I come back into the living room, but I don't sit down. "Because I'm not sure he needs it. What if a psychologist brings up stuff that makes it worse?" I want him to forget the things that happened to him before he came to us. "Maybe he'll grow out of it," I suggest.

"We both know it's not getting any better," she says. "Problems don't go away just because you pretend they don't exist."

"I just want him to be okay."

"That's why we're going to help him. Otherwise he'll find his own ways to cope, and I doubt they're going to be very healthy for him."

I lower myself onto the couch next to her and set down my drink. "I hate this part," I say. "What if we screw him up?"

"You're kidding, right? All parents screw their kids up. Hell, I started saving up for therapy the minute we got him." She takes my hand inside her own. "We're just going to do what all mothers do: We're going to say a million prayers, and then do the best we can."

LATER THAT NIGHT, I WAKE to screams. "Mama, Mama!" I run down the flight of stairs to Connor's room. He's lying in his blue race car bed, the one that replaced his crib. His head drips with sweat, hot with terror. He flops against me as I lift him, shell-shocked and worn out. I carry him upstairs and lower him onto Winston's dog bed, the one Jill and I layered with blankets and pillows and put on the floor of our room for this nightly ritual. Winston, our one-hundred-pound wolfhound, never used the bed and half of the time he sleeps in Connor's race car. Does letting our son sleep on a dog bed make me a bad mother? I'll be damned if I know, but it seems to help him feel better.

I kneel next to Connor on the floor of our bedroom and tuck his *Pirates of the Caribbean* blanket around him. He rubs his lips against his stuffed Lamby like he is whispering secrets to her. He's just a little guy, still so small. I push his matted hair away from his forehead and kiss him. He gives a shuddering sigh. I curl up next to him, but I do not sleep. I say a little prayer that God will make him better and will tell us what to do to help him. I watch over Connor until light breaks across the room. Jill is right. Of all people, I ought to know that pretending everything is okay doesn't make it so.

• • •

WITH CONNOR STILL SLEEPING soundly on Winston's bed, I go to my computer and play around on Facebook, looking up people I used to know. I love the voyeuristic distance it provides. Without ever contacting people, I can connect with them through "likes" and "shares." I upload a photo of Connor in his reindeer sweater. My phone vibrates atop my desk in the loft. Before I can say hello, my mother says, "Sweetie, check your email. I'm doing my Christmas shopping and need to know if you girls want something I saw on an infomercial last night. I think they're really neat. It gets so cold where you live, I think they'd be cozy."

I look at my email and scroll to the image of a woman wearing something called a Snuggie—a bright blue fleece blanket with sleeves.

Jill peers over my shoulder on her way down to get coffee. She whispers in my ear, "Please, no. Do not let your mom waste her money on those."

I wave Jill away, open up iPhoto, and download the rest of Connor's recital images and videos onto my Mac while my mom keeps talking. If my mom wants to buy us Snuggies, so be it. *Why should I hurt her feelings when it's the thought that counts?*

"Your father just wants money from you and Kathy this year to go toward his Knights of Columbus uniform at church. It comes with a real sword. You know how uncoordinated he is. He'll probably stab himself."

I scroll through the photos of Connor while my mom tries to convince Jill and me to leave earlier and stay longer on our upcoming trip to Texas for the holidays. In each successive image Connor looks more tortured than the last. I accidentally mouse over the video. My speakers play a chorus of four-year-olds singing "Jingle Bells." I punch the mute button, but I'm too late.

"Was that his recital? How did that little toot do? I bet he was cute as the dickens. Send me that video, and some regular images too. I want to blow up one to put in the living room next to the ones of Madison and Dylan when they were little."

I consider telling her about Connor's meltdown and the other things we've noticed. I want nothing more than to ask her for advice. I know how she used to feel about psychiatry—though over time, and frankly, out of necessity, her views have evolved. But it's more than that. I can't trust that she won't blame what's going on with Connor on me or Jill. On us. As much as she accepts Connor now, her reaction to the adoption still festers inside of me—raw and sore—like a splinter beneath my skin.

FIVE YEARS AGO, WHEN JILL and I began to discuss having kids, we thought it was just our hormones talking. But the idea wouldn't leave us. I told Jill I had no desire to carry a child myself. Jill declared her eggs too dusty to risk it. My relief surprised me; I'd been hiding the truth from myself. I knew it was going to be difficult enough to get my mom on board with the idea of Jill and me raising a family without tossing in the idea of artificial insemination, and without acknowledging it, I'd been keeping some giant balance sheet in my head when it came to my mom. On one side I listed my virtuous deeds, on the other the gay stuff. *Why was it so important that I prove myself?* Because it seemed to me that if the person who taught you to say your prayers, and share your toys, and always flush for the next person thought you were going to hell, there was a good chance she was right. Kids don't come out of the chute saying please or apologizing for their mistakes. Our first knowledge of right and wrong doesn't come from God—it comes from our mothers.

Some part of me knew that adopting an orphan was a very good thing, something my mother would eventually not find fault with, if for no other reason than that it would make *her* look like a bad person to turn her back on an innocent child. I had it all figured out.

When the tsunami hit Thailand, a friend of ours brought back photos from an orphanage there, and we set our sights on international adoption. We applied online with the Adoption Alliance, wrote our first check of what we estimated would be around $30,000, and found ourselves in a cramped office in downtown Denver across from a placement worker in high-heeled shoes and an expensively tailored pin-striped suit. The woman explained that gay couples came to their agency all the time. As if it was no big deal, she said, "One of you adopts as a single parent and in some cases signs an affidavit stating that you are not a homosexual."

"But I'm not a single parent," Jill said. "And also, I'm gay." Jill pressed her shoulder into mine.

The woman waved her hand. "Semantics. Look, do you want a baby or not?"

We nodded.

"Okay, so Russia and Guatemala are really your only possibilities. China recently figured out the gay loophole and won't allow many single-parent adoptions anymore."

There was a gay loophole? Okay. But Russia was out. Jill and I had heard stories about missing and switched babies at Russian orphanages. That left Guatemala.

"So in Guatemala, I'd be able to go with Jill so we could pick up our baby together? I could go as a friend, right?" I asked.

"No. Too risky. Even phone calls would be frowned upon."

We had to lie to start our family. In the end, we weren't willing to do it.

There was another option. Unlike some states and cities in the U.S., Boulder County not only allowed, but openly recruited lesbians and gays to adopt. We assumed that an affluent, liberal town like

Boulder wouldn't have a huge need for foster parents and that we'd be waiting forever for a placement to come up. But at orientation, our social worker said, "It's five days away from Christmas. I've got fifty-six kids and no homes to put them in." We signed up that day.

For our foster care certification, Jill and I completed more than sixty hours of training, much of it covering the effects of early childhood trauma. The primary message seemed to be that there were more ways to be damaged in life than there were therapies to heal from them. After a particularly disturbing video on something called oppositional defiance disorder, Jill hooked her arm through my own as we walked from the social services building to her car. "I want an infant," she said.

"Are you crazy? We'll never get any sleep," I said. "And we'll be waiting forever because everybody wants a newborn."

"I don't care. I want a baby that will bond with us out of the chute. The less trauma they'll have been exposed to, the better."

As we walked along, I thought about that. My mom had had me from my very first breath and yet we couldn't be what each other needed. I'd often said it was like she'd hatched out a baby bird instead of a little girl. I had no idea how to be the child she wanted, and she had no way to teach me to fly. Yet I also knew I'd been born with an undiagnosed hole in my stomach. My parents wrapped me up and took me home from the hospital, where I rejected everything my mom tried to feed me. My constant vomiting left her sour, weary, and frustrated. And while that defect eventually healed on its own, I wondered if all my puking during those formative child-parent bonding months had stolen something essential between us.

"You're right," I told Jill. "We'll get a newborn."

We finished parenting classes, got fingerprinted and trained in CPR, and had our financial and medical records scrutinized. We filled out fire evacuation plans, sent in dog vaccination records, and baby-proofed the house. As the last step in the process, we received "the list," the one we had to fill out for social services, marking "yes," "no," or "depends" next to the attributes we'd be willing to accept in our hypothetical child. We sat on our deck outside and tried to navigate the forms together.

"Would we take a fecal thrower?" Jill said, holding a corner of her checklist by her fingertips.

"Please tell me that's not a real thing," I answered. "How about a head banger or a heroin baby?"

"Yes to heroin, but no on fetal alcohol."

"It feels like we're ordering sushi," I tell her, putting a mark of "yes" next to heroin and "depends" next to physically handicapped before leaning over to touch my forehead to hers. We went through several pages of possible negative behaviors, disabilities, and drug exposures, terrified by all of them. But we also believed God wouldn't give us more than we could handle, so we checked two-thirds of our boxes with "yes" or "depends." We knew that no baby would be perfect, even if one of us had given birth to it.

I waited until Jill and I were certified before I told my sister and parents about our decision. I knew the influence my mom had over me. If Jill and I weren't far enough along in the process, there was a chance I could back out. When I told my sister, she said, "Well, I just don't know. Parenting is really hard, have you thought about that?" She paused. "When are you telling Mom?" I knew what she really wanted to say was: *Why are you doing this to me? You know I'm the one who'll have to put Mom back together again.*

The next call was to tell my parents. I asked my mom to take some time to digest the news before responding to it. I told her not to say anything she might regret or couldn't take back. In my head, I willed her into saying something neutral like, "Okay, honey. Keep us posted." But, without a moment's hesitation, she unleashed on me. "It will never be our grandchild. Not ever. Not like Madison and Dylan are to us. We will never accept that child as part of our family." An avalanche of words. *Why had I expected she would react any other way?* "It's a huge mistake," she said. "You have no common sense. You never did. Why would you ever put a child in that position?" I didn't ask her to clarify the word "position," because I couldn't bear to hear her definition. *Was I putting a child in the position to be rejected by his grandparents simply because he wasn't their flesh and blood? Or, was she implying that a child would be damaged more by being raised by two women than it would be from having bad parents or none at all?* Instead I asked her, "What could possibly be wrong with me adopting a child who needs a home?"

She skirted my question. "I thought we were in a good place. Honestly, why do we have to constantly tear a scab off of this wound?"

"This isn't about you!"

"The baby will have something wrong with it. Attachment disorder or brain damage. Plus, you've not been in good health and you're not getting any younger."

"Why can't you just tell me it will be okay? That you'll support my decision?" I tilted my chin up to take in more air and to stop my throat from closing. "You know, when most people announce they're having a baby or adopting one, people are excited for them. They say, 'Congratulations.' They send stuffed animals. Is it so fucking hard for you to be happy for me?" I didn't wait for her response. I hung up on her. I buried my head in the crook of my arm, splayed out on the floor, wracked with the kind of sobbing I hadn't done since I was five or six years old. My skin sucked into my ribs and my windpipe shuddered in spasms that made it hard to catch my breath. When Jill heard me, she came running up the steps. After allowing me to cry, she sat next to me on the floor.

"Either you can tell them, or I will," she said. "They'll either be in our child's life one hundred percent as grandparents or not at all.

I won't have our baby be abandoned by its biological parents and them too. So, if they're going to walk away, they can do it now." She kissed me on the cheek and stood. "They have a choice. It's on them to make it."

After Jill left that afternoon to get her car washed, I sat at the kitchen table and stared at the crossword puzzle in the newspaper in front of me. Jill had drawn some horns and a goatee on a real estate agent's photo on an ad in the corner, and at the top of the page, where she knew I'd see it, she drew a heart with an arrow through it. I wouldn't allow Jill to give my parents the ultimatum about being grandparents, because it was important to me that she stay on my parents' good side. I was too scared to give them the news by phone; so I emailed them. I never received a reply. So when we got that first call for a baby, not for Connor, but for Jeremy, the infant we would lose, I never even told them.

Even though it's been years, I can clearly picture Jeremy's face, with his curious algae-colored eyes and the ears that stuck out from his head in an attentive way, like he was trying to understand us.

He was twenty-one days old and had been removed from his mother at the hospital because he was born drug-positive. Mom was an eighteen-year-old addict. Dad was thirty-six and had disappeared. Social services had placed the baby back in the home with his mom three times in three weeks, with no success.

The minute they told us about him, Jill called each member of her family. She held the phone between her ear and shoulder and paced the halls of our home like a new dad handing out cigars at the hospital. Less than an hour later, we drove to social services and left in the rain, instant parents, with an infant sleeping in his car seat. Jill drove while I sat next to Jeremy in the backseat, unable to take my eyes off him, smoothing the blanket he came with. We passed a Walmart and Jill ran inside to get some of the things we'd need while I waited in the car. Jeremy moved his mouth in circles, his tongue white with yeast from a thrush infection that had recently developed. I used my cell phone to dial the number the case aide had given me for the People's Clinic, a place where foster care children on Medicaid could be treated. Jeremy slept through cracks of thunder.

Jill returned with three bags, her eyes wide, as if she'd been struck by lightning on her way across the parking lot. "I was beginning to think you'd gone out for a pack of smokes and left us," I said. It was an old joke between us, but she didn't laugh. Her earlier excitement seemed squashed by reality. We left that Walmart parking lot with our new baby waking in the backseat and a full-on rainbow in front of our windshield. I took it as a message from God. I was in love. Jill was in shock. And, because Jill had no idea how many diapers a baby might go through in a day or a week or a year, Walmart was now out of Pampers.

The first night, Jeremy didn't sleep. He was inconsolable, and we had no idea how to make his world right. He cried for so many hours straight we thought he might hurt himself. We called Jill's three sisters, then her mother, Ellen, for advice. I stayed on the phone with Ellen for an hour. She reassured me. Convinced me we couldn't break him. Promised she'd be there by the weekend to help us with her new grandson.

Jill and I rocked him, tried different brands of formula, checked his diaper, dangled toys in front of him, and sang. We ruled out fever, rashes, and colic. We put him in bed with us and took turns laying him on our chests. I understood my mother in that moment, when she had relayed a story to me once about getting so frustrated with me when I was sick as an infant that she'd literally thrown me into my crib, and then felt so guilty about it that she cradled and kissed my clammy, crimson face for the next twenty-four hours straight. I was furious with my mother now. She should be here. And yet, I hadn't even given her the opportunity. I blamed her for that too.

In the morning the social worker called to tell us she'd be picking up Jeremy for a supervised visit with his mom. When she asked about our night, I told her that it was miserable for all of us. Her answer was shocking and simple: "He's going through withdrawal," she said. "Cocaine, PCP, and meth." She explained that on this visit with his birth mother and every one thereafter Jeremy would breast-feed, even though his mother's milk was still testing positive for all three drugs. The baby would suffer from withdrawal every time he was away from her. No secret ingredient in the Nestlé's formula could compete with meth. *How could we bond with a baby who was literally addicted to his mother?*

"It's the law. She has the right to breast-feed her child," the social worker said.

One week later, Jill and I were at the People's Clinic with Jeremy when my cell phone rang. I rocked Jeremy's carrier with the toe of my shoe and listened. The social worker explained: Our baby had an aunt. She wanted to adopt Jeremy. We were to keep Jeremy for a few more days and then take him to social services and leave him there.

In the car, Jill and I drove without speaking while Jeremy slept in his seat behind us. A deer darted in front of us and Jill swerved. She slammed on the brakes. I reached across and banged on the horn to warn oncoming traffic. Three cars in rapid succession crushed the animal like a battering ram. His bones snapped and parts of his body separated and flew into the air alongside our windshield. I don't know if we screamed, but we pulled over to the side of the road. Traffic poured by us. Jill grabbed the wheel with both hands and put her forehead against it. I slumped against the dash. Jill gutted out words between sobs. "Why is this happening? I don't understand."

I moaned into my hands. "We didn't want him enough. God did this because we didn't want him enough. He took him away."

We went through the motions for the next two days, loving a baby we knew was no longer ours. I memorized his smell, and read to him, and covered him with kisses. Jill's mother, Ellen, flew in, and went with us to social services, sat with us in the office as we said our good-byes to Jeremy, and held on to us as we left empty-handed.

For several days, Jill and I didn't talk. We circled each other in our grief. Ellen stayed with us, counseled us. And because I knew she was a devout, born-again Christian, I asked her why God had allowed this to happen to us. We sat on the couch in the loft, side by side. She said, "Well, honey, maybe this wasn't about you at all. Maybe it was about Jeremy." She pulled me toward her, leaned my head against her shoulder. "God knew that the two of you would provide him with a safe and loving place when he needed it most. Maybe it's as simple as that."

Ellen didn't leave until it seemed we could stand on our own again.

IN THE LOFT AFTER I hang up the phone with my mother, I stare at my computer and choose the same photo I posted to my friends on Facebook of Connor in his red reindeer sweater, one we took before we left for the recital. I send my mother this shot of her smiling grandson, legs crossed at the ankles, a normal and happy little boy. Afterward, I go downstairs and find Jill in her office. She is on the phone with her mother too. I sit down next to Jill and she pushes the speaker button so I can be part of the discussion. Jill's mom's voice joins us in the room. Ellen is a therapist, and Jill is asking her what we should do to help Connor.

Ellen's voice is slow and thoughtful, with a grandmotherly lilt at the end of each word. She talks about play therapy and what she's seen work to lessen a child's anxiety. I look at Jill, relaxed and at ease, trusting her mom to guide her, that bond never lost between them.

Ellen has always called me her daughter and sends me birthday cards signed "Love, Mom." When we told her we were going to adopt, her very first words were, "I'm holding that baby in my arms right now." I'd be lying if I said I hadn't wondered what it would be like to have grown up with a mom like Jill's. Still, I'm not jealous. Because of Jill, I get three more sisters and another mother out of the deal. And yet, sometimes I feel disloyal, as if by loving Jill's family or allowing them to love me, I'm abandoning my own in some way.

I sip my coffee in Jill's office and she mentions Connor's nightmares to her mom. Ellen says, "I think you need to cradle him in your arms like he's a baby, if he'll stand for it. Look him in the eyes as you rock him. When he was born, he didn't get that and he never felt safe enough to fall asleep. He cried and no one came. Instead of starting him off in his room where he is terrified, maybe you could let him sleep in your room indefinitely. Get him used to feeling safe, with his parents right there to take care of anything. See if you can get him into a regular pattern of uninterrupted sleep. I'm sure you all need it too."

It seems so logical and simple that I wonder if it will work. *Is it possible to rewrite the past—to get what you never had from the people who are around you now?* I think about the many times that Ellen has asked me to call her Mom. I can't bring myself to do it. *Do we ever stop needing our mothers?* I wonder if part of me will always be the little girl who grew up on a cul-de-sac, going in circles, unable to see the way out.

CHAPTER EIGHT

THE FURY FLEW DOWN INTERSTATE 45 toward my aunt and uncle's house in Houston where my mom, dad, sister, and I would stay over the weekend for my grandparents' anniversary party. My father hummed, but his fingers gripped the wheel. My mother cracked the window and angled her cigarette toward the gap. She blew smoke against the dash. Kathy sprawled next to me and sculpted the tip of her nose by rubbing the dip between her nostrils in nervous repetition. I peeled the skin on my thumbs. Today, I would see Holly. I would tell her I wanted to be her friend, and that I was sorry I hadn't helped her. That none of what happened was her fault. Words from billboards shouted at our passing car: IT'S A CHILD, NOT A CHOICE. And GUNS DON'T KILL PEOPLE. PEOPLE KILL PEOPLE. We were almost home.

As we neared the exit to our old neighborhood, my mother picked at her scalp. "Why hasn't she visited?" Mom asked my father. "I mean, they've been through Dallas twice since we moved."

"Well, sweetheart, your sister didn't visit us that often when we lived in Meeker, less than thirty miles from them."

Mom scowled at him. "Sure, take their side."

I was too young to understand the dynamics between my mom and her only sibling, my aunt Carol, and had been told little about how they'd grown up, except to note that Carol was seven years older than my mom. The last time we had seen my aunt had been at my Catholic Confirmation just before we moved. My mom wanted something from the relationship that Carol wasn't willing to give, and I had to believe there was more to the distance between them than the gap in their ages. My own sister lounged three feet away from me. She thumbed through an issue of *Cosmopolitan*. Biology might determine whether two people looked alike, but it couldn't determine what they might become to each other.

The thick pines passed in a blur and I practiced in my head. Here's how it would go: My parents would drop my sister and me off at Veronica's, Kathy's friend's, house, while they ran errands for the party. Under the guise of wanting to take a walk through the old neighborhood, I would break away from Kathy and Veronica and head to Holly's. I would knock on the door. I would be brave. I wouldn't care about Mr. Crandall being there. I would avoid him. And if anything happened, I would kick and scream and fight like my life depended on it. I would pull Holly out of the house. This time I would save her too.

Mom flicked ashes out the window of the Fury. We exited and crossed the six lanes of traffic where my father used to say, "They've opened the floodgates," and I'd really thought that a wall of water was coming for us. When we pulled up in front of Veronica's, my mom tapped the face of her watch. "An hour, girls," she said.

Kathy and Veronica disappeared into Veronica's room, as I knew they would. Veronica's mom set out some Oreos and a glass of milk for me. I sat at their kitchen table while she cooked something, answering her polite questions about my new school and house and neighborhood. I watched the kitchen clock, an owl with huge eyes that moved right to left with each second. No one was making me stay. The Crandalls' house was one block away. *Tick. Tock.* I was stalling. I drank the last bit of milk like it was a shot of whiskey, and Veronica's mom gave me permission to walk over to our old house.

One block never felt so far. My shoes dragged along the asphalt, and I jumped at a squirrel that darted by me through a hole in a fence. I stood at the corner of our old street. I hooked my thumbs into my front pockets. Nothing looked any different than it had before. We hadn't been gone long enough for anything to change—least of all me. The Crandalls' front door was one hundred feet away. But it might as well have been Dallas. My eyes burned. I walked backwards, up the curb behind me, and into the woods where Holly and I used to play. I found our tree with a pink ribbon tied around its trunk, a bulldozer parked nearby. I swung myself up onto the lowest branch and willed Holly to come out her front door and meet me in that tree.

An hour later, we were back in the Fury on the way to my aunt's house. My sister sulked in her seat with tears swimming in her eyes. Mom twisted in her seat to look at her. "Honestly, girls. I know you want to spend more time with your friends, but we're here for your grandparents. Fifty years is a huge milestone. Tell them, Al."

"It's a long time to be married," my father said, staying safely in his lane.

"Besides, you can use the phone the whole rest of the day. Call whomever you want; it's not long distance. Just stay out of our hair so we can get work done."

Why hadn't I thought of it before? I could call Holly. I wouldn't have to see her dad or their house. That was something I could do. I wrung my hands together and peeled my thumbs trying to figure out what to say. God had given me yet another chance. I wouldn't waste this one.

My parents parked the Fury in my aunt and uncle's driveway behind their Thunderbird, Cadillac, and Lincoln. Dad honked like a hillbilly, and Mom whacked him with her Gucci knockoff. My parents joined my aunt and uncle in the kitchen to go over plans for the party and drink iced tea. I sat alone on a waxy leather couch waiting for Kathy to get off the phone so I could use it—afraid with each passing minute I'd lose my courage. I had already ratted on her once, telling my parents she was hogging it. My mother shook the ice in her glass as if she was trying to make a toast and said, "You should be ashamed of yourself. You only have one sister. One day when we're dead and gone, all you'll have is each other." I hoped my aunt heard my mom as clearly as she'd intended.

I stared at the deer, wild boar, and moose heads mounted high on the walls of the living room and curled my bare feet into the wool of the sheep's hide beneath the table in front of me. Kathy twisted the coils of the phone cord around her wrist and giggled.

A half hour later, she sauntered into the living room, and the phone was free. I stared at the yellow receiver, dial tone humming in my hand. *What would I say? How's it going? And what if her father answered?* It didn't have to be my first call, right? I could warm up to it.

I thumbed through the phone book at my feet and called Terry, a linebacker of a girl who had threatened to beat the crap out of me on the day I first met her at Meeker Middle School. Terry had shared my homeroom class, so I asked her if she would pick up the yearbook I ordered and gave her my new address.

"Anyone you want me to have sign it?" she asked.

"I don't know." I named a few kids before adding Holly to the list. My pulse beat into my hands.

Terry paused and said, "You didn't hear? Holly ran away a month or so ago. Her family didn't even bother looking for her."

I stumbled through the rest of the conversation with a dull buzzing in my ears. *Where would she go? How would she survive?* I should take the Fury and try to find her, even though I'd never driven anything, not even a go-kart. My face grew hot. I knew crying would lead to questions from my parents that I couldn't answer. It was too late. I stared into the glass eyes of a deer above my head and wondered if he felt relief now—if being dead was somehow less exhausting than being prey.

Hours later, I trailed behind my family into the reception hall, scowling, and trying not to land ass first on the slick tile. I found a folding chair in a corner, clasped my hands in my lap, and crossed my legs at the knee so I wouldn't show my geriatric relatives the built-in cotton crotch of my L'eggs panty hose. Because my mother insisted my Sunday Jesus Skirt was getting too ratty, I wore a white chiffon dress with little purple flowers, and Candies pumps with one-inch heels that made me stumble.

My sister tossed her Toni Tennille hair and swayed in the center of the room, looking effortlessly feminine and happy. She was as at ease here as she had become in Dallas, adjusting quickly to our move, making friends and becoming a half-time twirler and JCPenney model. I wanted to kill her, but the distance was too much for me to cover without risking an accidental plunge into a tray of cold cuts.

Across the room, the band played "Somewhere Over the Rainbow," and my grandmother held on to my grandfather's arm. She had been suffering from Alzheimer's for more than a decade, and she likely didn't remember anyone in the room, with the exception, I hoped, of my grandfather. He led her to the buffet table, pushed her hair back from her face, and fed her peel-and-eat shrimp. After each bite, he wiped the corners of her mouth and chin with his handkerchief. Next to the buffet table, I saw the photo of them on their wedding day. In the black-and-white shot, my grandmother gripped a bouquet of Shasta daisies and wore a wide-brimmed hat. My grandfather stood next to her, rigid, with his hands at his side. They both looked scared to death, and somehow resigned. I wanted what they had. I wanted someone who would promise forever to me. But when I looked at that photo and tried to see what the future held for me, I could only envision myself dressed in a pair of my nicest blue jeans with an empty spot where the groom should be.

My grandfather led my grandmother away from the cheese tray. He spoke to her, even though she no longer said real words or sentences back to him. It was as if they had created a new language, and they were the only two people in the world who knew it. I felt silly for thinking about Holly while I watched them, but she was the only person I'd been even half that close to. I thought about the times I'd seen her upset, how her cheeks trembled and the scar above her lip turned bone white. She never cried. Ever. Because she told me, "That means they win." I didn't have to ask who "they" were; I just knew.

When it came time for the toast, I walked across the room. My dress itched, my stockings sagged like a loaded diaper, and I had to point my toes outward like a penguin in order to stay upright. I grabbed a plastic glass and dipped it beneath the champagne fountain. My mother spoke first. She talked about how blessed we all were to have such an example of steadfast love and commitment and about the importance of family. At the end, the room echoed her. "To devotion!" we said. I filled my glass again and drank. "To love!" I did this five times until it warmed me. I counted five more. It felt good. Like floating. I couldn't control anything going on in my life, but I had found a way to make myself feel better by feeling nothing. No one seemed to notice a thirteen-year-old girl on her way to her seventeenth glass of Asti Spumante.

Hours later, I woke up in a strange bed. Beneath the sheets, my clothes were gone. I was in my bra and underwear. "Here's your dress, darlin'." Pauline, a spinster relative of mine who lived close to the reception hall, swept into the room and draped it across the bedspread. "I cleaned it for you. You got a little sick. You want some coffee? Wait, kids don't like coffee. Water maybe?" Her eyes were kind, but I couldn't look into them for long. I said, "No thank you," and she left.

I got dressed. I faced the mirror and licked my index finger to clear the smudges of mascara and blue powder from beneath my brows; my eyes looked like they might bleed. It was like science fiction. I had apparently said and done things, moved from one place to another, even thrown up—but I had no recollection of it. None. A piece of my life had gone missing completely. The last thing I remembered was counting that seventeenth glass of sparkling wine. For those missing hours, I hadn't cared about anything. I even stopped feeling sorry for Holly. Running away was easy; staying was what was hard.

The doorbell rang. "I believe you have a child of mine," my mom's voice sang from the other room. I walked around the corner but said nothing. My parents ushered me to the Fury. I hopped in the back. The second it was in reverse, I remembered that I'd left the purse my sister had loaned me shoved beneath one of the catering tables at the reception hall. I told my parents. Dad took a right and a left and we were there. He walked in with me, and I squatted beneath a skirted table and grabbed the little white handbag. As we headed out the door again, my father cut the lights to the room and said, "Mom doesn't know about tonight. And we don't plan on telling her. We're not going to let you ruin this for her." I waited a beat in the dark. He said, "You were tired, so we took you to Pauline's. That's the story. When we get back to Dallas, you and I will have our own talk about it." The door latched behind us and I headed to the car.

In the backseat, my sister slapped me on the thigh and mouthed the words, "What's wrong with you? How could you be so stupid?" My mother hummed to the radio before twisting around in her seat to smile at me.

In my cousins' guest room, my sister laid into me.

"Why would you do something so dumb? Unbelievable."

"Keep it down."

"If Mom knew, she'd disown you."

"Just tell me what I did."

Kathy paced in front of the bed. "Where do I even start?"

"Sarcasm," I said. "Not helping."

"I'm so mad at you I could spit. Maybe I shouldn't tell you any-thing." She sat on the bed next to me and wiggled her feet. Her high heels dropped to the floor one at a time. "You were outside the recep-tion hall running up and down the sidewalk. All dressed up. Ruffles going everywhere. When I tried to get you to stop, you climbed up one of the metal poles under the breezeway and started crying."

"Did I say anything? Please, tell me I didn't." I sat on my hands to keep them from trembling.

"You kept wailing, 'No one gives a shit about me. I screwed it all up. I don't have a home.' So to get you to stop screaming, I said, 'Okay, just come down and I'll take you home.' But you just climbed higher, saying, 'Where is it? You don't know, do you?' and started sob-bing again."

"Oh."

"You think I'm not sad we left Meeker? You think this is harder on you than it is on me? I can't even graduate with my class—all the friends I've grown up with. You don't see me pulling something like this. Seriously, what were you thinking?" She was angry again, but crying as well. "You're not going to bed until you tell me."

"You wouldn't understand."

"Bullshit. Don't tell me I wouldn't understand."

Kathy never swore; I knew she was serious. "It just comes easy for you."

"What does?"

"To be what everyone wants. Everyone likes you."

"Give me a break. You don't think it's hard on me, having a little sister who doesn't have to crack a book and gets straight A's?"

"Yeah, but you never get into trouble. You already have new friends. You're pretty. Mom and Dad tell you all the time what a good girl you are—a beautiful girl."

"They also say I'm stupid. That I got brain damage from some high fever I had when I was ten. Grow up, Michelle."

There was a painting across the room with a man in a boat in a storm. Her words rocked against me like that sea. "So, how did I end up half naked at Pauline's house?"

Kathy sighed. "You started throwing up. I got Uncle Andrew to help me with you and we propped you up next to us on a bench alongside this wall so we could lean you over toward the grass every time you hurled. Still, all these old people kept coming over to say good-bye as they were leaving. We just told them you were tired. Occasionally, we'd even raise your hand for you to give a little wave."

At this, I drew my mouth into a tight line. I was trying so hard not to laugh that my shoulders and head started to bob. I thought Kathy was going to slap me, but instead, she started to laugh too. "God, what am I going to do with you?" she said. Sitting on that bed together, I thought about the handful of nights when we were little kids—how I snuggled next to her on her four poster canopy bed listening to *CBS Radio Mystery Theater* with her. She'd set her red transistor between us like a barrier I couldn't cross, and I tried to pretend I was braver than I really was. Those were the moments I thought things might be different between us. Now, in one more year, Kathy would be leaving me for college.

Before we drifted off to sleep, Kathy said, "Just because I laughed doesn't mean I understand why you did something so screwy." She rolled away from me and took the covers with her. I tried to yank them back, but I should've held on tighter in the first place.

• • •

IN DALLAS, AFTER WE'D UNPACKED, my father stood in my doorway. He wrung his hands and scratched his jaw and said, "I guess we need to talk about the champagne." His face sagged, worn, like a boxer who had gone ten rounds and lost. My father was the kind of man born for raising daughters. He whistled around the house, alerting us of his presence, bought the Tampax we added onto the grocery list, and lifted my sister and me up above the waves off Galveston Island. There was not a violent or mean-spirited bone in his body, and at times, he was the only evidence I had that men could be good. I was not afraid of my father, only of disappointing him.

"I'm not going to give you a huge lecture." He stared at his loafers. "I figure getting sick like you did was punishment enough. I'm just trying to understand why you did it."

I shrugged, my eyes tearing up. When I didn't answer, my father sighed. He came over to the bed and sat down next to me. He pulled me to his chest and let me cry against him. "Sweetheart, it will get better. We moved when I was about your age and I remember I had a terrible time with it. It's hard making new friends in a strange place. I know you're lonesome. But we love you." He tilted my chin up to him. "You're creative and talented and smart. You'll find your niche. I promise you."

I wiped my nose on my sleeve and looked at the wet spot I'd left on his pocket. "Sorry," I said. "I snotted on your shirt."

He squeezed me tighter. "You've got the Search retreat this weekend. If you can't talk to me, maybe you can talk to Father Kos. You know, you don't have to go to confession to talk to a priest . . . Think about it."

FATHER KOS'S RED MUSTANG SPED down I-75 and I glanced at him as he drove. Father Kos's son, Jason, and the others had caught the bus—the one I had missed—so it was just me and my priest. It felt serendipitous, like God himself had arranged my ride. I could say anything I wanted and no one else would hear it.

Father Kos wore Levi's with a black short-sleeved shirt and white priest's collar and smelled like Polo men's cologne. His biceps rippled as he gripped the wheel.

I cleared my throat. "So, anything I say to you, you have to hold in confidence, right, like a lawyer?"

Father Kos stared out the windshield. "Yep. I'm bound by my vows, unless you're about to hurt yourself or someone else." He turned down the radio. "What's on your mind?"

"Well." I opened my mouth and nothing more came out. So I said, "Why do we have to confess to a priest if God is the one who forgives us?"

"That's what's on your mind?" He raised one eyebrow.

I nodded.

"Okay. Because when we sin, we don't just sin against God. We sin against our brother. Against the community of Christ." Father Kos smoothed down his mustache. "You may not be able to go to everyone you've wronged. The priest is God's instrument on earth. We intercede. We help you make amends to God and man."

"Good answer."

"Thank you. What else you got?"

"Why can't priests get married?"

"There's a Scripture in the Bible that allows for it. Says that it would be better for a man not to marry, to completely dedicate himself to Christ. But that God understood that this might not be possible. He allowed men of God to marry, but it wasn't His preference. The Catholic Church follows His highest intent. Priests are married to God."

"Why can't women become priests?"

"That's a good one. Doesn't make sense to me either." Father Kos laughed. "Why? You thinking about joining the priesthood?"

"I don't think they'd take me."

"Why's that?"

I ran my chewed nails down the ridges of my jeans. "I got drunk at my grandparents' anniversary party. So drunk I don't remember anything." I could see him out of the corner of my eye, but I couldn't look at him directly.

"You're not the first kid to have a drink," he said.

"Yeah, but it's wrong."

"I'm more concerned about why you're drinking than I am about the drinking itself."

"So it's not wrong?"

"Remember the story of the wedding at Cana? It was a big party. So big that they ran out of wine. Typically, at that point in an event like that, they break out the cheap wine because everyone's had so much that they don't notice the quality of it anymore, meaning they're all a little drunk by then. Mary comes to Jesus and asks Him to make more wine. So He turns the water into wine. And the Bible says it's the best."

"So everyone was drunk and He gave them more."

"Yep."

"I still don't feel better."

"Michelle, why were you drinking?"

I took a deep breath. "It's a long story."

"I've got time," he said.

I TOLD FATHER KOS ABOUT Mr. Crandall and Holly. I told him about my mom, and the couch, and the Valium. Father Kos asked me if I believed in God. I told him that I did, that I'd never felt completely alone in the world. Still, it was the same God that I thought of every time I couldn't get the things that had happened out of my head, and it all seemed to start that day at Holly's house.

Every day, the news reported that some kid had been abused or kidnapped, and every day I was reminded that I'd joined a group of lost girls who would never be the same. If God had a reason for everything, I asked Kos, then what was His reason for this? Father Kos pulled the car onto the shoulder and came to a stop. "Michelle, here's what I think. You have so many holes in you, you've become porous, like a sponge. No wonder you wanted to drink to fill up those empty places. But, if you let God, He can fill them up too. I don't believe God punishes us. I believe He teaches. Just talk to Him and be ready to listen."

I thought about this as Father Kos pulled back onto the highway. I was damaged, he'd said so himself. But this man of God hadn't judged me; he didn't even tell me I had to quit drinking. Instead he offered me advice. I trusted him. We all did.

CHAPTER NINE

"I NEED TO TALK TO you, today if possible." Father Bill's voice. A low rumble in my ear. "It's become quite critical now. It can't wait."

I will say no or hang up. "I've got a ton going on. Can't we just talk about it over the phone?"

"I'm afraid not. I'd prefer to handle this face-to-face."

FATHER BILL MEETS ME IN the Parish Center and walks flat-footed, leading with his gut, taking me back to his cramped, stale office. Settling in a chair, he rests his folded hands atop his belly, and just like the last time I was here, he makes me wait in uncomfortable silence until I start the conversation. "So, I'm here like you asked," I say.

"Ah, yes, Michelle." He nods his head while saying, "I wanted to ask your opinion." He brushes something off of his black slacks with his chubby fingertips. "I've been doing a lot of thinking since our last conversation surrounding Connor's baptism. You brought up quite a few good points and I've been praying about them in earnest."

For a moment I think, *Maybe I have been wrong about Father Bill.*

"I'd like to ask you some personal questions, if you're okay with it."

I nod.

"You mentioned in our previous meeting that your parents were devout Catholics. How have they dealt with the fact that you are a lesbian?" I crinkle my nose up at the word "lesbian," a label that sounds like a disease requiring penicillin. *Ms. Theall, you have a case of lesbian*—as if it were gonorrhea or syphilis.

"My mom accepts us, which isn't the same as saying that she approves of us. Acceptance and approval aren't synonymous." I think about my mom and the efforts she has made to remain in my life. "She's come a very long way in her feelings about Jill and me and our relationship. Though I'm sure she still believes it's wrong."

Father Bill bites his lower lip. "I think if you take an honest look at it, you'll find that acceptance and approval are more closely related than you think. I'm not sure you can truly have one without the other. Your mom can't accept you if she doesn't approve of you."

I sit stunned, jiggling my leg like he's Tasered me. Who is he to judge my relationship with my mother? "We've struggled with this for forty-three years. It's not something so simple that you can just wrap it up in a few neat sentences." My voice sounds watery. My body buzzes.

"I'm sorry if I've offended you. You're right that I don't know what you and your mother have been through. But I am, in a way, the parent, if you will, of Sacred Heart. I'm trying to decide what's best for it."

"I'm not sure I follow."

"What should I tell the students and parents at our school when they ask me why a child has two parents of the same gender, when the Church teaches that these relationships do not honor God?"

"Tell them that those types of families exist. As do single-parent families. Lutheran families. To ignore the fact that gay people with children exist in our world is to lie. I can show you Connor's birth certificate if you want proof." My voice is shrill and I lower it and try to smooth out the jagged edges.

Father Bill is calm. "Yes, but if we teach children that it is wrong to be gay, we are telling a child something bad about his or her parents, and we don't ever want to put an innocent child in that position."

"Why would you teach kids that being gay is wrong as if it's something they can help? My parents were straight, and Catholic, and look how I turned out." I smile at my own self-deprecating humor. "Being gay is who I am, not something I do. I'm gay whether I'm in a relationship or not. It's something I can't change."

"Yes, but the fact is that you are in a relationship. You haven't *chosen* to be single or celibate. You have a life partner and a child. By merely accepting gay families into our schools, we are implying that your family unit and lifestyle are acceptable choices to make. And they aren't. The Church is clear on this. We teach that marriage between a man and a woman is a sacrament. And we can't ignore the teachings of our faith simply because they aren't popular. The laws of man and the laws of God are two very different things. For example, it may be legal to have an abortion, but it is not moral."

The soles of my feet heat up like they are on fire. I know I need to calm down, that this isn't healthy for me, but I can't stop. "I'm glad you brought this up, because there's a sign outside the church, the one etched in stone with the Scripture, 'Before I formed you in the womb, I knew you.' You can't have it both ways. You can't believe that every life is of equal value and then tell me mine or my son's is not." I pause and gather myself, and at the risk of getting someone fired at Sacred Heart, I say, "You know what? I know exactly how your teachers should respond to questions about our family because they already did." I tell him the story about the director's daughter asking me why Connor had two mommies and the teacher's response of "Because he's lucky." By the time I'm finished, Father Bill is wincing. I realize I've likely only reinforced his position.

He looks at his hands and taps his foot. He is done with me now. "I've asked Denver's Archbishop Chaput to weigh in on this issue, but I haven't heard back from him yet."

"On what issue? How Sacred Heart should respond to same-sex families or whether or not it should be taught in schools?" I stuff my hands in my front pockets, afraid to let them loose. "Father Bill, the fact is, we adopted a mixed-race, traumatized toddler whose parents had abused and neglected him. In your ideal world, some Catholic, heterosexual couple with a perfect marriage would have adopted Connor. But they didn't. We did. Are you telling me he should have stayed in foster care for the rest of his life rather than have us as his parents?"

Father Bill answers with a sigh. "I understand that. Really, I do. But it doesn't change things." He pulls on his priest's collar as if it's too tight. "I'll get to the point. I see that Connor is registered for the new semester. Will you be keeping him at Sacred Heart?" he asks.

"Are you telling me we can't?"

"I didn't say that. It's something I haven't decided. That's what I'm waiting on. I want to hear back from the archbishop first."

"Connor's not going anywhere! You think you have God all to yourself, is that it? That you get to say whether or not God can love us or we can believe in Him?" I stand up to leave. "I'll happily let God judge me, but I'll be damned if I let you."

Father Bill rises from his chair and stumbles forward before catching himself. "I didn't say—"

"I can't believe you're somehow presenting this as something that's in the best interest of your school's kids. Do you even read the papers? Just this morning the *New York Times* said that when Pope Benedict was a cardinal, he could've done something about priests who were molesting kids, and he looked the other way." I grab my down jacket and crumple it in my fist. "Connor doesn't need to prove himself worthy of the Church. The Church needs to prove itself worthy of him."

I stomp to my car and lower the top of the convertible. I don't care that it's winter—I want to feel the punishing cold against my cheeks. I need air and time and distance, because Father Bill's condemnation feels familiar to me. Somehow, Father Bill has reached into a long-forgotten place inside of me and yanked something loose. I suddenly don't want to be gay or in a relationship or be a parent. I want to run away. I feel like a bad person. Unlikable. Rejected. Unworthy. Immoral. Without value. Depraved. Perverse. Electric shocks course from my palms to my forearms, making my hands twitch as I grip the wheel. I just want to disappear.

On instinct, I drive up Boulder Canyon and take a left up Magnolia and speed across miles of rutted dirt-road switchbacks that jolt my bones and rattle the car and send dirt into my lungs. I don't take my foot off the accelerator until I am four thousand feet above where I live now and staring at my old home, the place where I felt closest to God—the place that healed me. I park the car along the side of the deserted road and the quiet settles around me. I zip up my jacket and realize I am shivering. I hadn't bothered to put on my gloves and can't feel my fingertips.

People say, "No one can make you feel bad about yourself. You give them that power. You decide to feel that way." Bullshit. People can totally rip you apart whether you want them to or not. We're not fucking Teflon. The words we say to other people inflict real damage. I will not have this man destroy my faith, because God has not rejected us even if Father Bill has. I sit and listen to the quiet of snow, the way it absorbs everything around it. I breathe the smell of metal and water and rust, the clean bite of winter, and before I know it, I am praying: *Father God, thank you for giving me the courage to say what I needed. Help me to remember that there are good people in the Church. Help me to stand up for my son, even when it's difficult. Open Father Bill's heart. Guide me. I don't always see the way to go, but if you show me, I'll get there. In your name, amen.*

By the time I get back to the house, I am peaceful. I know that

God has a plan and that all of this is happening for a reason. Just maybe, it has nothing to do with Jill and Connor and me, and everything to do with Father Bill and Archbishop Chaput.

It's late afternoon. The dogs greet me with pushy muzzles and slapping tails, yipping and crying as if I've made it home from a long and treacherous journey. The wind picks up, promising snow in the next few hours. Storm clouds gather above the Flatirons and their heavy bottoms sag. I see Connor in the backyard, dressed in his snow parka and gloves, playing on his swing set, determined to get in some outdoor time before the sky dumps on us.

Jill yells from the kitchen, "We're having pancakes for lunch. Smooches, please."

I shed my jacket and boots. Grab Jill around the waist and give her a kiss on the cheek. I find the griddle under the stovetop and spray it with Pam. Jill moves the mixer and takes the flour from the lazy Susan. We orbit each other, and as we do, I tell her about my conversation with Father Bill. With each sentence, I watch anger form in the tightness of her jaw.

"So Tara gets to have a baby she can't take care of and we're the bad guys?"

"I know. I told him off. Screamed at him. Even cursed, I think." I take down the baking powder and orange zest and cinnamon. "But what does it matter? He can't say we aren't a family. No one can. Legally, Connor has two mothers. Period. So who cares what he says?"

"I do!" Jill lines up the *Star Wars* molds atop the griddle, and metal grates against metal. "All of this is changing and you're blind to it. It started with him balking about the baptism and it's spiraling from there. I know you don't want to hear it, but I think we should take Connor out of Sacred Heart."

"I'm not giving in to that man. The parents and teachers don't care that we're gay."

Jill turns on the mixer as if she is trying to ignore what I'm saying.

When it's quiet again, she says, "I'm really pissed off, like done pissed off."

I take the syrup out of the pantry and heat it in the microwave. Without a word, she strides away from me and out the front gate. I hear the mailbox door slam and she returns, slapping several envelopes and a small package onto the kitchen counter.

"We're not taking him out of Sacred Heart," I say.

"You don't get to speak for both of us," she says.

My chest tightens. We rarely argue, and I hate it when we do. "I'm upset about it too, but it's not like they teach that stuff at school. They let children whose parents are divorced or not even Catholic go there. They need students and they like the money."

"You sure about that? We're not in the classroom. Maybe that's why Connor's so anxious that he can't sleep at night and chews on his clothes." Jill scoops out some of the batter and pours it into a mold of Darth Vader's face. Her voice softens. "You know, Michelle, taking him out of Sacred Heart doesn't mean you don't love God or your mom or that you're not a normal part of society. It means you stand up for your son."

I can't help myself. I yell at her. "I *am* standing up for him by leaving him where he rightfully belongs." I take the package in front of me, the one addressed to Master Connor Theall from my parents, and open it.

"Don't give me that. This isn't some cause for you. You're afraid you'd have to tell your mom why you've pulled him out of Catholic school. That's what this is about. Do you really think you've changed what she thinks about us? Hell, just read your mother's Christmas newsletter." She unfolds a green sheet of paper, scans it, and shoves it at me. "Do you see my name in there anywhere?" Batter pops like firecrackers. "Eleven years of mentioning her son-in-law's latest golf scores and her new baby grand piano, but not me. She writes about the vacation we all took to Scottsdale and specifically mentions every person in the family but me. It's like I don't even exist. I'm not being petty. I'm pointing out a way bigger problem."

"She asked you on vacation, didn't she?" I take Connor's package, thick with packing tape, and slice into it with a pair of scissors, nicking my hand. Winston comes over to my bar stool, nudges me with his nose, and I soothe myself by petting him.

Jill says, "She's ashamed you're gay. She doesn't validate our relationship, which in the end will hurt Connor. Even if you could somehow get the Pope to make you the first ordained female priest, it's not going to change her mind."

"She might be uncomfortable, but she's not ashamed of us, and she adores Connor." I read a few lines of the Christmas letter before shoving it over to her. "He's in there, isn't he?" I pry open the box my parents have sent to Connor and out pop two figures from a Happy Meal promotion. I place them on the kitchen table where Connor will eat his lunch, as if Alvin and his chipmunks have made my point and so there is nothing more to discuss.

"Prove it, then. When we get to Texas, ask her why I'm never in the Christmas letter. I bet you're too afraid of her to even do that."

Jill uses a spatula to scrape Darth Vader pancakes onto a plate. She walks to the back door and yells for Connor to come into the house. The sun angles low across the Flatirons, melting the ice into fangs along our eave.

CHAPTER TEN

RAIN PELTED MY FACE, sharp like nails, driving into me and slowing my pace. But I didn't care, because I was running. I chewed up the track ahead of my teammates. With my arms pumping at right angles, I lifted up onto the balls of my feet, a superhero, flying. Coach Sparrow blew her whistle and signaled to us to take one more lap. The girls groaned because of the extra work, but I didn't. I wanted to run forever. I splashed through the ruts in the cinder until I reached the finish line. The girls ran by me toward the locker room. "Where's lightning when you need it?" one of them said. Another: "I thought we were going to drown." When I was sure they could no longer see me, I jogged to the orange cones. Without being asked, I collected them for Sparrow and trailed behind her across the football field toward the equipment cages inside the gym.

Sparrow wore gray-striped, nylon track pants and baby blue Nike running shoes with bright yellow waffle patterns on the soles. Instead of a Polo or Izod shirt (clothes I'd come to think of as our school's unofficial uniform), Sparrow wore a simple T-shirt with a graphic of the sun rising up over a mountain, and a clear plastic rain slicker over it. Though Sparrow was fifteen years older than me, she was youthful and optimistic in the unhindered way of single adults without children. She was beautiful and fresh-faced, like the Bionic Woman, and she moved with a confidence I envied. Aside from a black Casio sports watch, she wore very little jewelry and kept her fingernails blunt and unpainted. Her hair was long, straight, and unpretentious. She didn't wear makeup and didn't need it. She wasn't trying to impress anyone, and in Dallas—a city of debutantes, face-lifts, BMWs, and boob jobs—being around someone like her was as beautiful and rare as seeing snow fall in Texas.

Inside the gym, Sparrow took a key from her pocket and unlocked the cage. She waited for me to set the cones in the corner, and motioned for me to come out before she padlocked the gate. She tossed me a towel so I could dry myself off. "What's the verdict from your mom?" she asked.

I thought about giving her an evasive answer, but decided to tell her my mother's exact words. "Since I agreed to try yearbook staff and the Newcomers' Club, my mom said I could join the track team, but she also told me that sports hold no value for girls in the real world. And that my ovaries are going to fall out."

Sparrow patted my shoulder. "Well, that would be a first."

We walked through the heavy gym doors and into a breaking sun. Steam rose off the parking lot. Our reflections in the puddles shimmied, like two girls moving inside a fun house mirror.

I wiped rolling sweat from my cheek with the back of my hand. "My mom can be difficult. But I love this. Probably more than anything I've ever done." I stared down at my skinny ankles. "I've never been part of a team. Actually, I've never been part of anything, really."

The air was thick enough to chew. In front of her car in the parking lot, Sparrow held her keys for several minutes as if she was weighing them in her hand. Maybe she'd forgotten something and would send me back for it. Instead, she steadied her keen blue eyes on me. "Well, from now on, you are," she said. She opened the door

to her silver Honda Prelude and tossed her duffel bag into the passenger seat. She cranked down her window and draped her arm over
the side. "You've got talent, but you also have something the others
don't—motivation. Trust me; running is going to come easy for you."

I slogged home with squishy shoes, unable to absorb anything
else. I wanted someone to understand me—to really see me—and
with that one sentence, I felt like Sparrow had. But I tried to be re-
alistic. We weren't going to hang out or have lunch in the cafeteria or
see movies together. Even if a miracle happened and she could see
me as more than just a student, there were only three months until I
graduated on to high school, at which point I knew I'd never see her
again. I kicked rocks along the sidewalk and prayed for St. Jude, the
patron saint of lost causes, to put in a good word for me.

As the weeks ticked by, I pushed myself through every drill, storing
up every bit of Sparrow's encouragement. I studied her, driven by questions I was too shy to ask: *How could I get my hair shiny and straight
like hers? Did the simple pearl-drop necklace she wore have any meaning? Who gave it to her? Where did she grow up? How did she get
involved in sports? Did her parents support her decision to be a coach?*
She didn't divulge any information, but before school she let me spend
time with her in her office thumbing through her issues of *Women's
Sports* magazine, a publication she told me had been started by Billie
Jean King at the same time a law passed called Title IX giving women
equal funding in sports. It was historic and reading it made me feel a
part of something larger than myself. Sparrow's office also became a
great place to hide from the amorous advances of Curtis Morgan, the
boy with the large head, who had been unrelenting in his pursuit of me
since his origami note on my first day of school.

Curtis wore crisp, pink, button-down Polo shirts and starched
khakis and sat behind me in Language Arts and Biology classes.
When he wasn't staring at me and appearing unannounced behind

my locker door or outside the girls' restroom, he carved our names into his desk using a paper clip. I was so tired of him bugging me that when he approached me after dissecting a frog in lab—wearing more makeup than I did and hands clad in latex gloves—and asked me to accompany him to the play *Jesus Christ, Superstar* with his mother as a chaperone, I said yes. My mother thought it a lovely idea that I spend time with Curtis, whose mother was on the PTA and involved in something called the Junior League.

At the musical, Curtis held hands with his mother—and for the next two hours, they sang every word to every song. I thought about Norman Bates in *Psycho*. At the restaurant afterward, I waited for Curtis to stab me with his fork.

The next day, I explained to Curtis that we weren't a couple. I liked him as a friend, but that was all. He said he was fine with this, and yet he kept giving me expensive presents, usually presented with a flourish of balloons or confetti. Pearls from Neiman Marcus were the final straw; I told him I couldn't be his friend anymore. While he never spoke another word to me, I could hear him behind me in class, carving deep furrows into the wood of his desk with the edge of his ruler until my name was slashed beyond recognition.

The semester rolled along and I forgot about Curtis. I focused on trying to get Sparrow something she might keep to remember me by once school was over. I bought a pair of baby-size Nike sneakers and gave her one shoe from the set. The next time I spotted her Prelude in the parking lot, it was hanging from her rearview mirror. Knowing that something I'd given her was right before her eyes every day made me float like a buoy in a storm. I tied the remaining shoe of the pair by its laces inside my gym locker. I imagined the matching sneakers connected us.

At dinner one night after my parents, sister, and I had said the blessing, my mother doled out meat loaf and green beans, my father sipped his iced tea, my sister studied sheet music and played her butter knife like it was a clarinet, and I started in energetically about track and Sparrow.

"Coach Sparrow really pushes us," I said. "But you know, she doesn't yell at us. She believes she can get the best from us with positive feedback."

"Please don't talk with your mouth full," Mom said. "Did the yearbook get printed? When will it be out?" Mom spooned out mashed potatoes.

I swallowed the bite of food in my mouth and chased it down with chocolate milk. "This week," I said. I needed to stop talking about Sparrow and track, but I couldn't. I was an overfilled balloon. "I have to work on my form. My arms are everywhere and she says it's costing me energy. I have a real shot at winning the four-hundred-yard dash in district."

"Be sensible, you haven't won a single race yet," Mom said. "I think we've heard enough about track and Coach Sparrow for tonight." Mom stirred her iced tea until it created a hurricane inside the glass. "It's nice you're excited about something, but you need to concentrate on your finals. That's the problem with our education system in this country. There's too much emphasis on sports."

I buried a spoon into my mashed potatoes and watched it fall over slowly. I mumbled, "I have straight A's. Besides, I'm going to major in phys ed in college and coach track when I graduate."

Mom slammed her iced tea glass onto the table. "You will not waste your college education to be a coach. I've had enough of this. We won't pay a nickel for you to do something so foolish, so you can forget about it, missy."

"Fine. I'll pay for it myself."

"Oh, I'd like to see you try! Al, are you going to let her talk to me like that?"

My father pointed at me with his fork. "Watch the mouth," he said.

I was a tethered dog being poked with a stick. I broke free from the table and threw the door to my room closed with enough force to rattle the frame of the house.

That night, I heard my mom yelling at my father.

"Honestly, Al. Are you going to put up with this nonsense?"

"Phyllis, it's the first time she's been happy in a while. And her grades are good. What's the harm in it?"

"She's not even that good at it. Maybe if she loses too many times, she won't want to keep doing it."

Nice. My own mother wants me to lose. Rage all you want, I thought. *Take a million tranquilizers. Sleep forever. I don't give a shit. I'm not quitting. And I will coach.*

After my mother went to bed, my father knocked softly on my door. I pulled the Crayola box covers over my head, not wanting him to see that I'd been crying. The bed dipped from his weight on the edge.

From beneath the sheets I asked, "What's so wrong with me wanting to be a coach or liking track? Why does she hate everything I love?"

He folded back a corner of the bedspread until my tear-stained face poked out. "Sweetheart, she just has bigger dreams for you than that. We both do. You could be a lawyer or doctor."

"Sure, like her sister's kids. Does it matter what I want?"

"Don't worry about it right now, okay? Just get some sleep. It'll all be better in the morning." He kissed my forehead before leaving.

"I'm not giving up track," I called out after him. "And I don't want you guys coming to my meets anymore, acting like you're supporting me when I know you're not. I know you want me to quit."

I curled up into a ball and clutched one of those oblong crayon pillows to my chest. I was good at running, and in time I knew I'd only get better. No one could take that away from me.

"WOULD IT KILL YOU TO spend a little time with your family?" My mother heard the front door open and asked me to come into the den where they were watching TV. Back from a track meet across town and dropped off by a teammate, I rounded the corner to find a familiar scene. Mom stretched out on the black vinyl love seat with her hair spiked up where she'd fingered the scab on her scalp. Dad's six-foot-two frame wedged in the La-Z-Boy, his black loafers kicked off beneath it, damp sweaty socks airing out into the room as he wiggled his toes without thinking. Kathy was on the carpet, laid out on her stomach and propped up on her elbows, her face less than a foot from the television. Unbelievably, they were watching *Three's Company*.

"Thought we weren't allowed to watch this show," I said and sprawled out next to Kathy. She gave me a look—the one that said *Shut up or you'll ruin it, stupid.*

"Your father and I decided that because it's a platonic relationship between Jack, Chrissy, and Janet, it's not really living in sin," Mom explained. "Otherwise, of course, a man living with two girls, or even one, without being married would be immoral and unacceptable." She tapped the tip of her cigarette into her ashtray. "We still don't condone it, though."

"Honey, it's supposed to be a comedy," Dad said.

"Sure, take their side."

Jack Tripper answered the front door in a pink ruffled robe, pretending to be gay so the landlord, Mr. Roper, would allow him to live with two female roommates. I watched Jack prance across the screen and flirt with Mr. Roper, who mocked him and pursed his lips in response. But Jack just hammed it up even more, lisping and swishing over to shake Mr. Roper's hand with a limp wrist. Roper wrinkled his nose in disgust, withdrew his hand, and called Jack "Tinkerbell."

I had been taught absolutely nothing about gay people at home or in church. My mother had never uttered the words "lesbian" or "homosexual." It would be like saying fart, ass, shit, or worse. For a woman who never wore white after Labor Day, such vocabulary did not occur to her. My father was a man who felt sorry for silverware that didn't come clean during the rinse cycle. He'd pull out a dirty fork and say, "This one didn't make it," before putting it back in the dishwasher. Yet he had once turned to me after passing a pair of effeminate men on the street—one wearing eyeliner and the other with a fuchsia boa—and told me that they made him physically sick.

So I chose my words carefully. At the next commercial, I asked, "What if Jack Tripper was really gay?"

My mom leaned forward on the sofa. "He's pretending. Just being silly. You know, like Richard Simmons and Liberace. It's all an act."

"But what if he liked guys?" I asked. Sparrow was in her thirties and unmarried, which either meant she couldn't get a man or didn't want one. But could girls be gay? I'd only seen gay men on television, usually in dresses and makeup. Perhaps that was just a guy thing. They couldn't have sex together; the parts wouldn't work.

"Our biology teacher says homosexuality is a psychiatric disorder," my sister said.

"Yes, those kinds of people are sick in the head," my mom said. "It's unnatural and perverse."

"But what if God made people that way?"

Mom smashed out her cigarette butt and went to the kitchen sink. She washed her hands, scrubbing them for several minutes, flipping the soap over in her palms, inspecting her nails, until I thought maybe she hadn't heard me. With the knob toward its hottest point, her hands pulsed red like traffic lights. "You want to know what God thinks about two men or two women together? I'll tell you. AIDS, that new plague that's killing all those men, that is God's wrath against gay people." She turned off the tap. "I don't want to hear another word about it. Got it?"

I watched Jack pull the plush collar of the pink robe taut against his neck. "I'm not that kind of girl," he told Mr. Roper. And he sashayed to the bathroom with canned studio laughter trailing behind him.

Late that night, I jolted out of bed to the sound of a chorus of boys screaming, "Michelle Theall has a dick!" outside my window. Handfuls of pelting rocks slammed against the house and echoed like shotgun spray. Shadows moved. Shoes slapped sidewalk pavement. Again the boys yelled—louder this time—"Michelle Theall has a dick!" I lay in the bed clutching my ribs as if I'd been punched. Their words stole my breath. *Oh my God, this can't be happening. Why would someone do this?* I crawled to the window. The silhouettes scattered. On my knees, I ducked beneath the sill and listened. I heard thumping and a shudder and it took me several minutes to realize that the noises were coming from my chest. *Was this because I hung out with Sparrow? Was I so stupid to think that no one saw how much time I spent with her? Or had I said or done something to deserve this?*

Five words. That's all they were. But they took the part of me that couldn't trust anyone and fed it. I thought about Curtis, how angry he'd been with me for refusing to be his girlfriend. *Was this his way of getting back at me?* But there was more than one boy. *How had he recruited the others?* Shame seared my face like a brand. When I was certain the boys were gone, I rose up and rested my hands on my thighs. Their screaming had been loud, but the shrieking in my head was worse. At best, I was someone's idea of a joke. At worst, I felt like the victim of a drive-by shooting. I had let down my guard—had started to forget that those around me might still see me as an easy mark.

In the dark, I tiptoed to the door of my room to listen. *Please, God, don't let my parents have heard them.* My mother's heels clicked across the foyer and the hinges of the front door squeaked as she opened it. I heard the door close and the double bolt latch, and she said, "Al, what was that? Go check on Michelle." At the sound of my father's footsteps across the kitchen linoleum toward my room, I jumped into bed and pretended to be asleep. He pushed open the door quietly, peered in, and walked away. I tried to hold still and stop shaking. I hugged one of the crayon pillows to my chest like a body, exposed and unable to put a name to what I'd done to feel that way. I had no idea if they'd come back again and felt powerless to stop them if they did.

The next morning, my family dressed for church. We showered and brushed our teeth. We piled into the Fury and drove it fifty yards to the church parking lot. We filed into All Saints and acted as if everything was the same as it had been the day before. I would never know if my mother had heard what the boys screamed, though I know she heard them yell my name because she'd sent Dad to check on me. I sat in between my mother and father, wearing my old Sunday Jesus Skirt, picking at the tattered hem.

My mother prayed the rosary. She gripped each bead, holding it for several seconds. Her lips moved with each Our Father and Hail Mary, and when she returned the beads to her purse, clearly embossed circles remained like stigmata on her palms. I could only guess what she was praying for, but I had my own words for God that morning. *God, smite those mean bullies—those cowards.*

But God didn't. The boys kept coming. Their visits were random and shocking and loud. Always, they screamed the same thing: "Michelle Theall has a dick." My anxieties grew in tandem with their assaults. I had debilitating panic attacks at restaurants and other public places, where my throat seemed to close up and I'd start to sweat and think I might throw up. I finally complained to my parents about nausea and stomach pains so much that they took me to a gastroenterologist. I swallowed three strawberry-flavored barium shakes for an ulcer test, convinced they'd still find that hole I was born with if they used a really strong X-ray. When the results came up negative, I tried to put my fist through the wall of my room. The only things that made me happy were running in circles around the track and the remaining dwindling days I spent with Sparrow. But before I knew it, the school year was over.

ON THE LAST DAY OF SCHOOL, I hopped from one foot to the other in Sparrow's office. I waited for the other girls to leave so I could have her sign my yearbook. By the time it was my turn and we were alone together, my hands were slick with sweat. Sparrow opened my book to the faculty section where her photo was and I read over her shoulder as she wrote: "It's been a great honor to have had you as an athlete and friend. You've got exceptional talent and I hope you continue to excel in sports. Lots of luck in your endeavors and keep in touch." She set down the pen. The word "friend" pulsed like a beacon. She left my yearbook open on her desk, and hugged me good-bye. Even though I knew I'd likely never see her again, I took comfort in the certainty that she hadn't called any of the other students her friend or held them this long in her arms. I had been special to her in some way, which was all I had really wanted. When I left her office I read the inscription over and over, and a million birds took flight from somewhere inside my chest.

SUMMER BOILED AND DID NOTHING to cool the heated adolescent war with my mother. In an attempt to get out of the house and stay in shape for track, I landed a job across town at the President's Health Club. My parents loaned me the Fury to get to and from work. I shoved my learner's permit in the glove compartment next to my mother's St. Christopher medal and left at five each morning to navigate the streets of Dallas. At the club, I answered phones, checked in guests, and flagged down sales reps to upgrade or sell new memberships. I enjoyed getting paid, but the best perk was that after my shift, I got to use the club for free and work out with my new friend, a woman named Wink.

"Keep your hips down," Wink said. "Don't bounce it off your chest, or you'll crack your sternum." Wink, a lanky ex-professional women's basketball player in her early thirties, hovered just above and behind my head as she spotted me on the bench press. She worked at the club as a trainer, and every day at two, we lifted weights. I added another ten-pound plate to the bar, secured the collars, dropped back onto the bench. I took a breath and released it with each repetition, feeling the bar sink into my leather gloves. After a month of employment at the club, I could bench-press eighty pounds. I measured my biceps and quads to track their growth. I was proud of what my body could do, and being strong made me feel safe and capable. "One more, all you," Wink said, and guided the bar back onto the rack.

At six foot three and as an elite athlete, Wink might have been imposing or intimidating; instead, she reminded me of a baby giraffe, goofy, loping, and circus happy. Her enthusiasm was childlike. She said what she thought. And though Wink was skinny, she wasn't frail or dainty. She didn't hunch her shoulders forward or slump to apologize for being tall. She didn't pretend to be something she wasn't and never would be. Wink was just Wink: boyish, with braces and short hair, and flat sinewy muscle where her breasts should have been. I adored her. So when she invited me over to her house one day, I phoned my mom immediately to ask her permission. I didn't lie to my mom, but I let her make her own assumptions. Likely, she believed that a girl with a name like Wink was a teenager like me with acne and a Walkman she played too loud, who hated algebra and was saving up money for weekends at the Six Flags amusement park. I was too afraid that if my mom knew the truth—that Wink was a woman in her thirties who coached high school basketball during the winter months—she would take my car keys away.

No more than twenty-four hours after Wink scribbled out the directions for me, I idled the Fury by a wood-carved mailbox with blue ducks and stars painted on it and wondered if I had the right place. Wink and her roommate, a woman named Sharon whom I had not yet met, lived thirty minutes from the health club in a tidy suburban neighborhood that looked very much like my own neighborhood, except that their street had a pulse: weed eaters buzzed, kids sold pink lemonade, black Labradors barked.

Outside Wink's front door, I took a deep breath. I wiped my damp palms on my Bermuda shorts, dipped my chin to my armpit to do a last-minute check for BO, shoved my hair back behind my ears, and knocked.

I heard footsteps and a dog barking, and instead of seeing Wink when the door opened, I stared at Coach Sparrow. *Did I have the wrong house?* Wink loped toward the door, elbows flying like live wires, and said, "Honey, you should see your face. The minute I met you and you told me you'd gone to Hilltop, I came home and asked Sharon if she had coached you."

Coach Sparrow grinned at me. "Are you going to stand there, or are you going to come inside?" I couldn't believe they were roommates. The coincidence stunned me. I stepped through the open door.

Inside, sun spilled across the glass-etched coffee table where stacks of *Sports Illustrated* and *Ms. Magazine* collected dust. A prism of light made rainbows across the carpet. I sat on the couch, crossed and uncrossed my feet at the ankles. Wink disappeared into the kitchen. "What'll it be?" she asked me. "Beer? White Russian? Mai tai?"

Since I didn't know what any of the other things were, I said, "Beer, thanks." I wasn't about to turn down free alcohol or the opportunity to be treated like an adult. Wink popped open the top of a Coors and handed it to me before plopping down on the couch. She stretched her legs across me; huge feet, planks with toes, rested in my lap. Sparrow turned on the Moody Blues on the stereo. A photograph on an end table showed Wink with her arms draped around Sparrow's neck, their legs intertwined. In another, they were in a bar, two-stepping with cowboy hats and boots on, close enough to kiss, staring into each other's eyes with an intimacy that made fire dance behind my breastbone. I understood in that moment that Wink and Sparrow were more than roommates. They were a couple.

Wink saw me looking at the photos and said, "I would have told you about us sooner, but I had to make sure Sharon was okay with me outing her to you. No one wants to get fired. That's why we live so far away from everything."

I sat on their country blue upholstered couch and drank the next cocktail Wink offered me in a few large swallows. My brain obsessed: They were gay. Their friends were gay. Their house and dog and cars were gay. *Gay, gay, gay.* I curled the corners of the pages of a magazine while Wink told stories about living with Martina Navratilova and playing basketball for the Dallas Diamonds. I drank one cocktail after another and prayed they'd forget that I was still a teenager with a learner's permit who couldn't vote or buy a pack of cigarettes or get into an R-rated movie. I wanted to stay and I wanted to flee, because up until that moment, I had wanted to be just like Sparrow. I admired everything about her, but I didn't admire this. Two women weren't supposed to live together like husband and wife.

"So you should call me Sharon now," Sparrow said. She led her dog over to me and I let him nuzzle into my hand. I nodded. I had more in common with them than with kids my own age. Plus, they trusted me—something few people had ever done—by telling me a secret that had the power to get them both fired. I wasn't gay, and hanging out with them wouldn't make me gay. I could overlook this one thing about them, especially if they didn't *do* anything around me—like hold hands or make out. It took me a few minutes to make up my mind. Even though Wink and Sparrow were in their thirties and I was fifteen, some part of me understood that they were a refuge. In all the time I knew them, they were never too busy to see me, and they never once asked me to leave.

CHAPTER ELEVEN

Jill and I pull up to the entrance of my parents' subdivision in San Marcos, loaded down and sagging with presents and the residual weight of our argument about Sacred Heart. In the interest of holiday cheer, we table our decision about whether or not to keep Connor at the school until after Christmas. We are weary and sticky, the way only parents of a four-year-old can be after a five-hundred-mile road trip. We idle in front of the closed iron gate. I press the security buzzer, and say, "Michelle Theall to see the Thealls." I hear the shuffling of papers before we are admitted.

My parents' Christmas lights and white reindeer twinkle in the yard, and the artificial tree blinks in the window. My mother scoops up Connor and busies him with a marching Santa and a novelty toy of singing penguins. My father, Jill, and I unload the car. I haul our cooler into the kitchen and put the Silk soy milk and PediaSure in the refrigerator next to their skim milk and leftover meat loaf. My father has set out a second coffeepot on the counter for us because he knows we drink our coffee by the bucket and can't survive on decaf. I slide our fresh-ground Peet's French roast next to their Folgers and tins of Splenda and flour and peek into the dining room. Though Christmas is still two days away, my mother has already set the dinner table with silver, china, and crystal atop a red tablecloth. Matching napkins nest inside their metal rings. A centerpiece of fake poinsettias stretches toward the chandelier. On glass place tags, my mother has neatly printed each of our names—because nothing says "home" quite like assigned seating. The house smells like pecan pie, but also of Lysol, perfume, and lemon Pledge—sweet and sanitized—welcoming us and asking us not to touch anything at the same time.

I follow Jill with a piece of our luggage up the winding staircase to our room on the second floor. In the hall, I pass a collection of crosses, assembled like a small shrine. Inside the guest bedroom above the bed where Jill and I will sleep, I note seven Virgin Mary statues arranged upon a shelf. God forbid we even think about having sex.

I unpack our pillows, the fluffy down ones we have brought with us because my mother's are flat and hard, and also because we feel like we are bringing a part of our world with us that is familiar and brings us comfort, like a child with a security blanket. I look at the double bed. I remember my mom telling me years ago, "I will never be one of those mothers who accepts whoever you're with into my home. I will never think it is okay. And you will absolutely never sleep in the same bed under my roof." I try to recall exactly when she broke that rule and realize it was shortly after I got sick. Before I was diagnosed with MS in 2003, I thought that people who said their illness or disease was a "gift" were just trying to appear brave. But now I get it. Though for me, it has nothing to do with bravery. The only reason I am happy to be sick is because it made my mother accept Jill.

Six years ago, my body started buzzing like the rumble of a subwoofer. I'd leave the house for a run and return bloody from falling, tripped up by something I couldn't see. Stairs and curbs became obstacles for me. Holding a newspaper and drinking a cup of coffee left my arms weak and shaky. The pinkie and ring finger of my right hand lost feeling. Because of the Internet, I already suspected I had multiple sclerosis before the MRI showed nine lesions on my brain.

After years of denying who I was, I shouldn't have been surprised that my immune system attacked me too, waging war against my healthy brain tissue as if it were something foreign. My neurologist explained to me that MS was sort of like lightning hitting the fuse box of a house. Sometimes after getting struck, the television still worked, but the refrigerator shorted out. The lights might come back on, but the microwave could be gone for good. Damage from MS could affect any system of the body that the brain or spinal column controlled: mobility, cognitive function, speech, balance, and sensory assimilation. The loss could be temporary or permanent. It could also be painful, as I'd lately been finding out. The only thing certain about the disease was its uncertainty.

When I got the diagnosis, I didn't want to worry my parents, but it wasn't something I could easily keep from them. After I told them, my mother was angry at first. "Maybe if you went to Mass more, this wouldn't have happened," she yelled at me over the phone, her voice raw with tears. "Or it was all those sports, all that running." I told her it was going to be okay, but she kept at it until I yelled back at her. "You know what? I'm tired of reassuring you. You be the mommy for once. You tell me it's all going to be okay. You tell me you can make it better!"

Over the ensuing months, her rage switched to desperation. She researched every new treatment and therapy, sending me several emails a day, and flew me into San Marcos to meet with a renowned neurologist in nearby San Antonio who specialized in MS. There, I sat on a paper-covered table, sandwiched between my parents, as I'd been when I was a little girl with chronic ear infections, and listened as the doctor said the same thing the other six I'd seen had: You have MS. There is no cure. You need to start treatment to slow the progression.

My parents fretted over me and tried to lift my spirits with phone calls and action plans, but it was Jill who took care of me after a spinal tap left me unable to move for a solid week, and Jill who went with me for an EMG test where needles were inserted into my muscles to test nerve conduction and rule out muscular dystrophies. Jill who learned from the home health nurse how to give me the thrice-weekly interferon injections so she could help me on the days they were in a place I couldn't reach, like my buttocks or the back of my arm. It was Jill who vowed she'd never leave me, even if I was in a wheelchair or blind from a disease that we couldn't understand.

That first Christmas after my diagnosis, Jill and I lugged our bags up to our separate guest rooms only to have my mother say, "I didn't have time to make up two beds this time. You'll just have to share. Hope that's okay." I never had to sleep on the pull-out sofa bed again, and I assumed my mom had accepted Jill as part of the family.

That's what I liked to believe, until Jill mentioned the Christmas newsletter. Now in the bedroom I share with Jill in my parents' house, I glower at her as she gets Connor settled onto the mattress beside our bed, angry with her because I don't want to be suspicious of my mother and because she has made me aware of all the mounting evidence.

Jill reads *Giraffes Can't Dance* to Connor, and I go to the adjacent study, the one my mother has made into her writing room, to search through my father's thrillers and my mother's mysteries to find something to replace the novel I finished somewhere around Amarillo. Because my mom joined a book club, she's broadened her selections. I pick out *The Help*.

Mom's office is covered in photographs of our family. Frames hang from the walls and decorate desks and shelves, along with Rolodexlike, flippable albums. My sister, her husband, Eric, and Madison and Dylan stare back at me from behind a sheet of glass. There are several shots of my sister on her wedding day. On the wall next to a coatrack, I discover the series of four-by-six photos of Connor's baptism that I mailed to my mom months earlier: Connor in his little white suit. My parents standing next to him as they agree to be his godparents. Me with Connor. And though I sent several group shots with Jill, Connor, and me together—my family—those are not displayed here. Jill is missing from all of them. That said, my mom asked Jill and me to bring red and black clothing to wear at Christmas dinner so she could take a color-coordinated family photo while all of us are together. I give her the benefit of the doubt. Maybe she noticed Jill's absence too. Maybe I won't have to bring up the Christmas letter after all.

Down the steps, I walk in on my mom and dad in the kitchen in an embrace. They kiss. Then my father spins her, even though there is no music. I tiptoe into the other room and sit on the couch. I don't always understand how their relationship works, but I know they love each other, and that their commitment to each other is a core value I've emulated with Jill. They fix cocktails in the kitchen. I call out to them, "One for me, please?" to let them know I am there.

Other than a glass of sangria at El Chico's when I was growing up, my parents never really drank. Now that they've retired, though, with the exception of some substitute teaching, they've loosened up a bit. There are other changes too. My mother quit smoking years ago, a feat that took her several tries—complete with hypnosis and meditation tapes—and impulse control that none of us knew she had. My parents have friends now and activities. As far as the drinking goes, I have to admit that I like the liquored-up version of my mother way more than the sober one. Tonight, they are both in a good mood, which allows me to relax.

My dad hands me a Shiner Bock beer. "Got those just for you, sweetie," he says. He lowers himself into his easy chair and sighs.

"Ah, me," and wipes the sweating glass in his hand with a napkin before setting it on a coaster. My mother joins him on the other side of the table in her matching easy chair. We raise our glasses and say, "Salute."

Their cat, Shadow, jumps up on the back of the sofa and licks her front paw. I pet her in long strokes, and she leans into my hand to make sure I get all the important spots.

Mom picks up a copy of *Time* magazine and tears out a page with Obama on it. She crinkles it into her fist. At first, I think she's going to launch into a tirade against Democrats. Instead, Mom grins like a schoolgirl and says, "Watch this." She hurls the wad of paper across the room and Shadow leaps over me and runs toward the wall. She picks up the piece of trash in her mouth like a golden retriever and brings it to my mom.

"You taught her to fetch?"

"Actually, she just started doing it naturally on her own, but isn't it the cutest?" Mom throws the paper a few more times and the cat brings it to her. Unlike Mittens, this cat seems to enjoy performing the trick for us. When Shadow loses interest, we go back to drinking, and Mom notices the book in my lap. I turn the cover toward her.

"Can I borrow this? I haven't read it yet."

"Oh, you will absolutely love it. It reminded me so much of the black ladies who came and helped out at our house when I was little and my mother got sick. I loved those women." She looks wistful. "And they were so funny too."

"When was this? Grandma didn't have Alzheimer's when you were a kid."

My mother takes a sip of her rum and Coke and rubs a fingertip around the rim. "No, she didn't. But you know, she was never well."

I'd heard stories about my grandmother having tuberculosis, but didn't remember this. My mom crosses her legs and shakes the glass in her hand. "Well, she got TB and they put her in the sanatorium for years. They took a lung, and then she never really recovered. Carol was seven years older than me, so she did the best she could with the house and me while Daddy worked at the oil refinery."

Shadow climbs into Mom's lap, nestles in. "Carol was thirteen and all of a sudden expected to be an adult because we needed her to. She didn't get to go to college like I did. I suppose she resented that." Mom smooths Shadow's fur. "We had a few black women come over to cook and do the laundry. After that, I went to St. Agnes's and saw more of the nuns than I did of my own family."

I look at my hands clutched around my beer because it's too sad to look at her. "How old were you when they sent your mom away?" I ask.

My mother turns up the volume on *The Tonight Show*, but I hear her answer just beneath the applause. "Five or six. Just a little older than Connor, I guess."

ON CHRISTMAS MORNING AFTER PRESENTS have been opened, my parents fight in the kitchen while Bing Crosby croons "White Christmas" in the background. "Honestly, Al, top shelf, right-hand side. Straight in front of you. Are you blind?"

"Phyllis, I'm doing the best I can."

"Jesus, Mary, and Joseph. Open this for me. I've got my hands in the giblets."

I hear the lid pop off of something and then my mother screaming, "You got it all over me! You people are just worthless!"

"Well, damnit, I'm sorry. We can't all be as perfect as you." I hear my dad running water and a rag wiping the floor. He's on his hands and knees as I round the corner. He looks like a dog that's been kicked.

"What can I do?" I ask my mother.

"Nothing." Mom waves her fingers in the air, dripping with turkey goo. "It's easier if I do it myself."

Jill has escaped with Connor upstairs and has set him up with a DVD he got from Santa playing at high volume. She isn't used to this type of family bickering and doesn't want Connor exposed to it.

Because my parents sang at midnight Mass, and Jill, Connor, and I attended the 5 P.M. Christmas service last night, I have time for a quick run. I slide under the security gate onto the main road. Running at sea level is infinitely easier than in Boulder at five thousand feet, at least on my lungs. Cars whiz by, horns blast, people try not to kill each other on the way to pray on Christmas morning. I pass the McDonald's and Walgreens and negotiate strip mall entrances and sidewalk curbs. I block out the distractions of the city. *Thank you, Father God, for sending your son to be born on this day, to become a man and endure a physical life with all its complications and difficulties. Thank you for my family, my health, for Jill and Connor. Be with my mother and help her to relax and enjoy this time with the people she loves without worrying herself sick over every last detail. Be with Connor and teach him that you are always there, just as we are, watching over him and keeping him safe. Amen.*

I take a left into my sister's neighborhood. I press in the code she's given me and the gate opens. I run until I get to their empty driveway, knowing they are at Mass this morning, but still using their home to track time and distance. Their cat, Bandit, nudges the glass pane with his nose, wends his way through the carnage of Christmas morning. He chews on the edge of a red bow, like he's not fully committed. The hurricane inside my sister's house reminds me of when Kathy and I were teenagers. My mother left us a typed note taped to the mirror of the bathroom we shared. It started with: "Unfortunately, your rooms are part of this house," and ended with the lines: "We are not animals and we must not live in squalor. Start today and someday you will thank me. Love, The Management (Your Mother)."

I think about those parentheses. Last night, Jill and I opened a card from my parents with a one-hundred-dollar check inside. We were truly grateful, and because my mom is nothing if not fair, the check was identical to the amount that they gave my sister and Eric—except the signature on our card was different. On our card, my mother deliberately placed parentheses: "Love, Mom (Phyllis) and Dad (Al)" lest Jill get confused about her place in this family. Kathy and Eric's card just said, "Mom and Dad." Each step toward my parents' home, I think: *I may not like it, but doesn't my mother have the right to decide the type of relationship she wants to have with my partner?* My mom isn't perfect, but she's come such a long way. How much further should we expect her to go? I turn onto my parents' street; the gate is open. I won't have to crawl under it and get dirt and gravel embedded in my knees.

I open the front door, and the alarm chimes to announce my arrival. My mother is yelling something I can't make out, followed by, "Connor, go ask Jill where she put the extra PediaSures."

Connor says, "Who's Jill?" From upstairs, Jill shouts, "Phyllis, he calls me Mommy." There is frustration in her voice, an unmistakable pointedness to it.

"Oh, Rosa, I mean Jill, I just want to find out where his drinks are." While my mother often calls me Kathy-Eric-Al before she finds Michelle, she has just confused Jill's name with their maid. I wince and tug at my eyelashes. A few come out loose into my hands.

I grab the PediaSures out of the pantry for my mom and try to figure out if these slights are intentional. It is one thing for Mom to deny Jill as my partner, but quite another to dismiss Jill as Connor's mother in front of him. I'm relieved Connor's too young to notice. My mother's heels click across the foyer toward me.

"Get cleaned up, sweetie. Tell Jill she's got thirty minutes. And I need you all to be dressed in red and black for the family photo." She wags a finger at me. "No blue jeans."

HALF AN HOUR LATER, I descend the steps and join my sister and her husband loitering in the kitchen. My mother buzzes by us. She grips my shoulder. "Michelle, put water in that silver goblet and ice in the glasses. Kathy, set the butter dish on the table. Honestly, Madison and Dylan, turn off that TV before I lose my mind." She swoops through the kitchen with a casserole dish of sweet potatoes topped with marsh-mallows and parts us like the Red Sea. "It's Christmas, for Pete's sake."

"Hey, girly," my sister says. She gives me a glancing kiss on the cheek. "Merry Christmas. Where's Jill and little man Connor?"

"On their way down. Connor doesn't want to stop playing to eat."

My brother-in-law grabs a handful of mixed nuts out of a ceramic Frosty the Snowman dish on the countertop. I squeeze him from be-hind, before my mom sneaks up and shakes the nuts out of his hand. "You'll ruin dinner."

Jill slips past me and leans into Eric. "Those are decorative. You should know better."

"Listen, you two," Mom says. "I heard that. Don't give me any flak. And you, mister." She pokes Eric in the ribs. "I made your green beans and took the onions out of the stuffing, so just hush."

It's all good-natured teasing. Sarcasm as blunt weapon.

"Hey, lady," my sister says to Jill. They embrace.

Eric takes a Shiner Bock out of the refrigerator. Before he can get the top off it, my mom hits him with a towel and says, "Put that back. We're having wine with dinner."

Eric turns to my dad, who is carving the turkey. "Pop, why won't she let me have a beer?"

My father shrugs. "Don't blame me," he says. "I just work here."

Throughout dinner, I listen as Eric calls my mother "Mom" and my father "Pop," and wonder what kind of hell would break loose if Jill started doing the same. We all behave—our cloth napkins in our laps, Waterford crystal and china on the table, until Connor takes a bite of stuffing and spits it back out on his plate. He looks up at us and with his brown eyes watering and his face pinched he says, "That was a close one. I almost threw up my intesticles." We laugh until we are crying, relieved and united by the absolute innocence of a four-year-old boy.

A few hours later after dessert and caroling, Kathy and Eric are about to go home, and my mom assembles us in front of their tree. "I want to get several different poses," she says. "Let's do the group shot first, and then I want to get one of Al and me with Kathy and Michelle." Mom arranges Kathy and Eric in the center next to each other, and Madison and Dylan on either side. Grouped together in our red and black outfits we look like a giant hematoma. "Where do you want me?" I ask. Mom leads me to a spot on the end and places Connor in front of me. She rests my hands atop his narrow shoulders. My tall father stands in the back, in his place. My mom turns to Jill, and I think she's going to position her next to Connor and me. Instead, she hands her the camera. "Be a dear and take the photo for us. I don't know how to work the self-timer, and there's nowhere to put it that's the right height." Before Jill can answer, my mom scoots away from her toward my father, who puts his arm around her shoulder. "It's that top button," Mom says and motions. "Make sure you get us all in the frame."

Jill grips the camera and raises her right eyebrow at me. Instead of saying "Smile," or "Cheese," she says, without a hint of sarcasm, "Sure, Phyllis. I wouldn't want to accidentally cut your head off."

• • •

THE DAY BEFORE WE LEAVE to drive back to Colorado, I enjoy a cocktail and watch the late news with my parents. A photo of Pope Benedict XVI appears. Brian Williams reports:

"The Pope made some of his strongest comments against gay marriage today, telling diplomats from nearly one hundred and eighty countries that the education of children needed proper settings and that pride of place goes to the family, based on the marriage of a man and a woman."

Why on earth had I thought we could make it through a family holiday without this coming up? My father picks up a section of the paper he read this morning. My mom brushes lint off the armchair cover. No one turns down the television or says a word. I stretch and yawn. "I guess I'd better get to bed," I say. "We've got to get going early tomorrow." My parents leap from their chairs to hug and kiss me good night. But, there's no escaping the Pope. The sound bite follows me out of the room.

"This is not a simple social convention, but rather the fundamental cell of every society. Consequently, policies which undermine the family threaten human dignity and the future of humanity itself."

I walk up the stairs, but the Pope's words, along with what's been going on with Father Bill and Sacred Heart, weigh me down like cement blocks on my feet. The Pope is using the welfare of the world's children to make his point about gay marriage. Father Bill wants to stop Connor from attending Sacred Heart. Maybe Jill is right. At the very least, we could send Connor to a more progressive school. I hear my mom downstairs, washing their cocktail glasses in the sink. If she knew what Father Bill was trying to do, would she take my side?

MY PARENTS HUDDLE TOGETHER in front of their house in their robes and slippers. They wave to us as we back out of their driveway. Mom wipes at her eyes; Dad pulls her close to him. The gate opens and Jill drives to the gas station to fill up before we get on the highway. I run in for snacks. When I come back, Jill has her hand on the gas pump and I say, "Well, that went more smoothly than I expected. No major yelling or fights." She doesn't respond and her shoulders shake. She breaks down crying.

I take the pump out of her hand and place it back in its cradle. I pull her into my arms. "Hey, hey. Petey, it's okay." She doesn't hug me back or move other than to wipe her nose.

"You have no idea how hard that is. The edge of it. The tension."

"I do," I whisper into her ear. "I'm just used to it."

She leans back and tries to laugh. "God, it's stupid, crying over them."

"It's not stupid. But all things considered for my family, I thought it went pretty well. I had no idea—"

"You never do. You just check out. You go for a run or rationalize it all away. I knew you couldn't tell them about the Christmas letter. And maybe it's for the best. God, can you imagine?"

"I thought about it. A couple of times, I thought I could do it."

"I know you're scared of her. You all are. I just hate feeling so blatantly unwelcome. It's like I didn't make it into the sorority, but I still have to serve drinks at the parties." She drags her sleeve across her eyes. "I'm a good person."

"You're the best person I know."

"No, I'm not, because I'm listening to you about keeping Connor at Sacred Heart. It's wrong to make him go to a school when they don't want him there. It's just like me at your parents' house, except I have a choice and he doesn't."

I can't remember the last time I saw Jill cry. I'd rather pull Connor out of Sacred Heart than have Father Bill tell us to leave. "We'll take him out. Okay? It's done. We'll find a new school for him."

I press my nose into the dimple of her wet cheek. We get back into the car and buckle our seat belts for the long ride. "Safe trip, God," Jill says. "Safe trip, God," Connor and I echo.

Once we are on the highway headed toward home, I ask, "Is it okay if I wait to tell my mom he doesn't go to Sacred Heart anymore? Also, I still want to go to Mass. I don't want Father Bill to think he's scared us away so easily. We can worship wherever we want to."

Jill doesn't answer. She focuses on the road and keeps the wheels moving forward.

CHAPTER TWELVE

IT'S POSSIBLE TO FALL IN LOVE without really knowing it, especially if you don't know what love is. My sophomore year more than two thousand kids attended my high school. We competed for limited spots on athletic teams, student council, choir, and academic honors. From a distance, I imagined our class looked like a test for color blindness, where a clear image was supposed to emerge out of a chaos of dots. I needed to find a group of people with common interests or else I'd become invisible. I wasn't anxious to repeat the loneliness of junior high. I made an effort. I got my ears pierced at the mall, permed my hair, wore Calvin Klein jeans. I liberally applied Love's Baby Soft and Bonne Bell Lip Smacker. I allowed my mom to take me for a makeover at Saks, where she happily bought me some plum-colored eye shadow and blue mascara that I used daily. When a senior boy from the track team asked me out, I said yes immediately.

Even though Jack was an evangelical Christian and I was a Catholic, we messed around on the floor of my room religiously—fully clothed, but still. I let him touch me and rub against me, fantasizing, until it felt unbearably good—at which point I realized he was still in the room with me and would tell him to leave. I made out with him because I was supposed to. It was like putting on deodorant or brushing my teeth or learning to moonwalk—a universal part of growing up. All anyone ever asked me after how old I was and what I was interested in school was, "Do you have a boyfriend?" So even though Wink and Sparrow were gay, it didn't seem to have anything to do with me. I thought of them like roommates. *How did sex between two women even work?* I still didn't know. In my world—the real world—people dated and got married and started families with people of the opposite sex. But every time I listened to songs like "Endless Love" or "Every Breath You Take," I knew I was missing out on something. When I was with Jack, I just kept thinking: *Is this what all the fuss is about?*

In the gym after school one day, a few of the track and basketball coaches held the first meeting of the Fellowship of Christian Athletes. I tagged along with my cross-country teammates, the only kids I knew, to check it out. Fifty kids split into smaller groups called "huddles." I joined the ten girls closest to me and we sat together on the gym floor. Our leader, a senior from the basketball team, read 1 Corinthians 12:12 to us. "'The body is a unit, though it is made up of many parts. So it is with Christ.'" She paused. Held the Bible against her forearm. "When you think about that Scripture, how do you think it applies to what God asks of us as teammates and athletes?" she asked. "Find a partner, learn something new about them, and talk about how this verse might be useful in your sport."

Girls who already knew each other broke off together. I forced a smile. My armpits grew damp. "Looks like you're alone too." A volleyball player I recognized from my English class stood next to me. "We should be alone together."

Ann spoke with a quiet voice, but her words were thoughtful and assured. "I think the verse means that we're all equally important to God and to each other," she said, "because as Christians, we're brothers and sisters in Christ." She bent back her fingers as she spoke, stretching them like she was getting ready to set a volleyball.

I rubbed at a spot of dried ketchup on the gym floor and said, "It's sort of like when one player gets injured, you want to play harder and inspire them to get better, because without them, you can't win?" I had no idea what I was talking about and my voice lilted into a question at the end.

She leaned in with encouragement. "I think as believers, we're part of the most important team. We're all valuable and unconditionally loved, and we're supposed to take care of each other and build each other up."

Ann's limbs were long and graceful. She had alabaster skin—the color of Michelangelo's *David*—straight blond hair pulled back into a ponytail, and a tiny gold cross dangling in the divot where the tips of her collarbones met. She was serious and smart and seemed to know what mattered: Life. Death. Love. God. *With so much suffering going on in our world, who has time to worry about the color of leg warmers or homecoming posters?* Before we left that room, we were on our way to being friends.

I expected my parents to be pleased I'd joined the FCA. Instead, Mom clicked off *Guiding Light* and stood in front of the television with her arms crossed. "Sure, turn your back on the Catholic Church."

I straddled the arm of the sofa, about to spring away. "Catholics belong to the FCA," I said. "It's nondenominational."

"I expect you'll be accepting Christ as your personal Lord and savior?"

"I guess I could start smoking crack and drop out of school," I said.

"Al!"

My father appeared in the doorway to the kitchen where he'd been eavesdropping. "It's probably mostly about athletics." Dad took three steps into the room with us.

"I just can't win," I screamed. "Every single thing I do is wrong. You hate the way I dress. You think I'm stupid for running track—"

"I would never, ever tell you that you're stupid. Honestly, I've told you a million times how smart you are. You just don't have any common sense."

I punched the armrest of the couch. "Why do you hate me so much?"

"I'd die for you girls, you know that." And I believed that she would. After all, she'd been doing it for years.

"We're getting a little off track here," my father said. He sighed at his pun with a nervous chuckle.

"Fine," my mother said. "Just remember, there's one true church and you were baptized in it, my dear."

To which I responded, "Trust me, if there's a purgatory, I'm in it."

LIKE MOST TEENS, ANN and I had parents who embarrassed us, and we realized this was one of many things we had in common. In the beginning, Ann kept me from meeting her mom and dad, told me they weren't normal, blushed when she said it. I told her to join the club. But I wasn't prepared for Mrs. Baker or for the power she might have over the trajectory of my life.

I knocked on the Bakers' door, wincing from a headache. Ann led me through their house to the kitchen. I passed framed needlepoint pictures of kittens and chicks with Scriptures sewn beneath them. A well-worn Bible, its pages marked with colored tabs, graced the coffee table. Jim and Tammy Faye praised Jesus from the television screen. I heard Mrs. Baker singing before I saw her. We rounded the corner; she stopped and smiled. "Oh, you must be Michelle," she said. She wrapped me in a bear hug. I hung there limp, unsure what to do with my hands.

"Mom, Michelle needs some aspirin," Ann said.

Her mom held me at arm's length, assessing me, and I studied her too. Tall, with a shock of thick, short white hair and a prominent nose, Mrs. Baker reminded me of a bald eagle. She held me firmly by the shoulders and maintained eye contact with me until I looked away. Behind my forehead, the pain sharpened. Mrs. Baker placed her hands atop my head. There was a lengthy pause and I wondered if she was going to pet me or had simply forgotten where her hands were. But then she closed her eyes and spoke.

"I just pray you be healed in the name of Jesus," Mrs. Baker said. I stood there, mouth open, wondering if I'd still get aspirin. After an awkward moment with her hand pressed against my scalp, she released me and disappeared into a pantry. She returned with a glass of water and plopped two Tylenols into my hand before wandering away humming. Ann glared after her mom and her face flushed red just below her cheekbones. "Sorry," she mouthed to me.

FCA wasn't charismatic enough for Ann's mother's approval. And my mother viewed it as too radical, almost some type of cult. So in a way, belonging to FCA was a form of teenage rebellion for both of us. That said, there was no substitute for Catholicism in my mom's book, so I continued to go to CCD class and Mass every Sunday, where I watched sad little Jason ring a bell at the altar of All Saints every time his father, Father Kos, consecrated the host. Then I'd go to FCA and lead a Bible study group and try to witness to my classmates to lead them to Christ. All the while, I worshipped God and believed in Ann, though sometimes I got the two confused.

ONE SATURDAY AFTERNOON, I DROVE to see Wink. Sparrow was out of town. Their house smelled like hazelnut and pinesap, and a breeze whispered through a window that was open an inch. Wink welcomed me inside with a hearty embrace. She hugged with her whole body, something straight women never did, as if they had opposing magnets strapped below the sternum. Wink tolerated my fevered evangelism and preaching, and as devout as I was, I still took the beer she offered me.

I plopped onto the couch and caught Wink up on school and Ann and FCA and track. Wink listed to the side until she fell over into a fetal position on the floor. "Stop, girl. You're killing me."

I nudged her back with the toe of my shoe. She rolled over and up to a sitting position. "Michelle, come on. You more than *like* Ann. I think you love her."

"I do love Ann, but not the way you mean it."

Wink took a drink of her beer. "With God's love, I suppose."

"Yes."

She burped and smiled. "Well, God made me too."

I opened my Bible, the one I brought every time I visited Wink and Sparrow to justify my visits with them. I turned to Leviticus 18:22 and read: "'Do not lie with a man as one lies with a woman; that is detestable.'"

"Are you trying to convince me or yourself?" The corners of her mouth turned down. "Sweetie, do you know how old that text is?"

"Jesus is the same yesterday, today, and tomorrow," I said.

"Honey, you may not understand this yet, but sex is a gift. It's a way for us to connect with someone else in a deeper and more meaningful way. If God had meant it just for procreation, He wouldn't have made it so enjoyable, especially for couples who can't conceive." Wink patted the top of my hand. "Let me see that a minute." She took the Bible from me, turned pages before and after the Scripture in Leviticus. She untangled her legs and let the dog out the sliding glass door. But she didn't come back right away. She stared into the yard.

"What are you doing?" I asked.

"Looking for pigeons."

"Why?"

With her back to me she said, "According to the Bible, I'm going to need to sacrifice a few of them after I finish my period." She turned and gave me that goofy grin of hers, her wide braces glittering like a teenager's.

On the drive home from Wink's that day, I considered what she'd said about Ann and me. I'd never had a single sexual thought about Ann, ever. I wanted us to room together in college, and after that, buy houses next door to each other where our Christian husbands would build a tree house in the middle of our adjoining yards for our kids to play in. But that didn't make me gay. Gay people were lost and confused and in need of God's guidance. I wasn't. I was saved.

OVER THE ENSUING MONTHS of high school, Ann and I shared advanced classes, clothes, and before long, a locker where we left notes with inspirational Scriptures scrawled for each other. We ran FCA meetings as copresidents, attended Right to Life concerts where we prayed for the unborn, and ministered to kids at the junior high school chapters. After school we spent most of our time at her house, rather than mine. In her bedroom, I wrote Christian songs on my guitar and we listened to Amy Grant and Russ Taff and prayed about making varsity or getting a scholarship. When we weren't singing and praying, we studied the Bible the way other girls our age analyzed hairstyles in *Seventeen* magazine before prom. One day in Ann's room, we read John 15:13: "Greater love has no one than this, that one lay down his life for his friends." We listed the names of everyone we knew who we'd be willing to die for and then switched pieces of paper. On Ann's list: her volleyball coach, the song leader of FCA, and her family. On mine: Sparrow, Wink, Mittens, and my parents and sister. After we finished sharing our lists, I said to Ann, "I'd die for you too." And when she didn't respond, I added, "You know, because you're my sister in Christ. You don't have to say it back. I just thought you should know." She didn't have to love me as much as I loved her; she just had to love me enough.

Every time I was at Ann's house, I did my best to avoid her mother, who preached to me about the Rapture, quoting Revelations and praising Jesus while unloading the dishwasher. I reminded her that I was already a Christian, but it didn't help. She continued to see something in need of conversion.

CHAPTER THIRTEEN

JILL, CONNOR, AND I SLIDE into a pew at Sacred Heart and try to keep Connor from chewing the button off his sleeve. He is spiffed up and coiffed and so are we. Father Bill steps to the lectern. I'm still angry with him, which makes it all the more important to me that we be here, as a normal family in his parish. Over a month ago, we took Connor out of Sacred Heart. After interviewing five different preschools, we chose Mapleton Montessori because they encourage diversity and independent learning and curiosity—all things Father Bill seems to be trying to exterminate at his school. He gazes out over the pews and smiles.

"Anything goes in Boulder," he says. "Live and let live, right?" He shifts his weight forward, leaning out. "Many people believe that the only acceptable path of love means never speaking the truth about anything that would upset another person.

"So I ask you, would it not be far more loving to confront a loved one than to be silent about his or her pursuing, for instance, a destructive addiction or inappropriate sexual behavior? The parties involved could say that they derive some sense of 'happiness' from their choices. Nonetheless, the wisdom of the Church tells us that wrong sources of this supposed 'happiness' are ultimately harmful."

I steal a look at Jill, who is grinding her teeth. A muscle pulses along her jawbone. Father Bill steps in front of the podium now with the mic attached to his vestments. He makes eye contact with the front row.

"This also extends to the more recent political and cultural debates on how we define marriage and family. Denver Archbishop Chaput has said that the Church teaches that sexual intimacy by anyone outside marriage is wrong; that marriage is a sacramental covenant; and that marriage can only occur between a man and a woman."

A man across the aisle from us clears his throat. When I glance toward him, he nods his head and smiles as if to say, "Well, this is awkward."

"These beliefs are central to a Catholic understanding of human nature, family, happiness, and the organization of society. The Church cannot change these teachings because, in the faith of Catholics, they are the teachings of Jesus Christ." Father Bill's voice is loud. It overtakes the hum of a few parishioners who mumble in dissent or agreement with his homily. I stare straight ahead. Connor squirms next to me. "Mama, I'm hungry."

I whisper, "In a minute, buddy, this will all be over." *This will never be over.*

Father Bill wraps up. "In Boulder, I see a lot of love, but a lack of discipleship. Jesus calls us to take up our cross and follow Him. He does not say it will be easy or that we will be praised for it. But the word of God is the same today, yesterday, and tomorrow, and it cannot bend to the whims of the times."

When Mass is done, Jill and I round our shoulders against the cold, and I carry Connor in my arms to shield him from a biting wind. "I feel like I need a scarlet letter. Please don't make me do this anymore," Jill says. "You go. I support you." I jut my chin toward Connor, in the backseat, and Jill gets the hint. We won't talk about this in front of him.

When we get home, we settle Connor in his room for quiet time, which means he'll play with Legos and Jill and I will get a few minutes to be adults—alone. And, even though it's Sunday, and likely sacrilegious in some way, it's also the only time we get to be two women who love each other instead of Mommy and Mama.

I follow Jill up to our bedroom where we shed our dress clothes with each step toward our closet. "Unreal," she says. "So now he's comparing us to drug addicts."

"I know," I say. "People abuse their own kids, and we're the bad guys." I unbutton my shirt and take my earrings off. "Don't worry, Petey, I can't go back there again either."

The relief between us is palpable like drinking cool water on a hot day.

"The man is on a crusade. He's not going to stop," Jill says. She tosses her bra onto a shelf and looks at me. "Are you going to leave on your socks?"

"My feet get cold." I slip off my bra and underwear. "This is a really odd form of foreplay," I say.

"Yuck. The last thing I want to think about right now is that old man."

Standing naked in front of each other, we start to giggle and say in unison, "We need to find a new church."

AN HOUR LATER, AFTER WE'VE made love and had a Sunday-afternoon nap, I lie in the bed reading our local paper and thumbing through the Faith section. "The Siddha Yoga Center has an evening of chant and meditation," I say. "Or there's an intro to Peruvian shamanism where we can explore earth-honoring practices for personal and planetary healing."

Jill lowers her reading glasses. "Yeah, that's not going to work for me. We weren't even allowed to read our horoscopes. They were Satanic."

"And you think my religion is weird." I press my lips to her bare shoulder. "If God's all-powerful, why put limits on Him? Miracles happen every day." I point out the window to the Flatirons. "Births, metamorphoses, seven billion people on the planet all with different fingerprints. Why couldn't God send us messages through a configuration of stars?"

"You're really cute when you get all weird and fired up over something." She kisses me.

Jill and I are back to our old selves, moving as one. A united front.

THE FIRST CHURCH JILL AND I try in Boulder feels like a leadership and empowerment convention. The spiritual leader talks about positive thinking and the impact our words have on ourselves and others. He cites the experiments of Dr. Masaru Emoto, who attached words like "Adolf Hitler" and "Love and Appreciation" to glasses of water and then viewed the crystalline structure of the water beneath a microscope to note any changes. The "Love and Appreciation" glass showed symmetrical and stunning formations, like delicate snowflakes. The "Hitler" ones looked like something stuck to the bottom of a person's shoe. Because all human beings are 75 percent water, Emoto maintained that our bodies reacted to the labels in our environment in similar ways.

I'm a writer, so of course I believe in the power of words. And Emoto's theory makes sense to me because if God wants to change the composition of water, He will. But the spiritual leader seems to revere Emoto more than God, and Jill doesn't think it's "churchy" enough, so we move on.

At the second service we attend, a congregation chants in a

circle around a pile of pretty rocks, paying homage to goddesses and Mother Earth. The smell of incense mixes with patchouli oil and the pungent scent of unshaven armpits. There is a banjo and a didgeridoo, which I'm used to seeing at music festivals and on the Pearl Street mall in downtown Boulder, but not at my house of worship. Jill and I can't look at each other throughout the service because we have reverted to second-graders in our level of maturity. We press crystals against each other's chests, suppressing giggles until we erupt into loud snorts. We lower our heads and run to the car.

Jill and I want to find a community of believers who accept us—but we also crave the traditions and beauty of our Catholic and Baptist faiths. The prayers and hymns we grew up with brought us comfort and peace and furthered our connection to God. Though those churches ultimately rejected us, they gave us a moral foundation that has served us well throughout our lives. We want these values for our son and to nourish us as a couple on our own spiritual path. So we keep looking.

The third church we attend is filled with sleepy-eyed parishioners repeating rote responses; the sermon is about giving from the heart and is followed by a collection of money. We leave deflated. To us, a church is a living, breathing thing that makes a first impression like a handshake or a wink or a slap on the back. Its arms might be outstretched to hug you or to squeeze out a donation. Like finding a soul mate, Jill and I both think we'll know it when we see it.

"SNOW IS GOD'S SPIT," Connor tells the man who greets us at the entrance to the First Congregational United Church of Christ. It seems like ages ago that he told my mother something similar, and I'm immediately smacked with guilt. Mom has no idea that I'm cheating on the Catholic God with this one. And I can't help but feel as if by being here instead of at Sacred Heart that I'm doing something wrong. The man chuckles. "You're a very smart boy, aren't you?" he says to Connor. Despite my guilt, the space inside feels familiar and comforting. A majestic pipe organ plays inside the old pink-tinted sandstone church beneath its 1908 bell tower and red tile roof. An elderly man with a hearing aid shakes my hand and gives Jill a program for the service. I stomp my feet on the mat by the door, and Connor shakes the late spring snow from his coat. Light filters in through the arched stained glass windows and douses the pews in a kaleidoscope of color. The stone-and-wood-beam building has a sacred, centuries-old feel to it. The choir stands and bell ringers assemble at the front. The female reverend greets members of her church on the way to the altar. Jill nudges me—a woman is leading this church. I read the back page of the program.

"Everyone is welcome here: believers and agnostics, conventional Christians and questioning skeptics, people of all sexual orientations, the despairing and the hopeful, those of all races and cultures, and those of all classes and abilities. Jesus didn't turn anyone away—neither do we."

Around us a few gay men and women mix with old, young, straight, single, and married people—different races, different types of families—all worshipping God together.

The reverend asks us all to stand "in body or spirit," which I take as an inclusive statement to disabled church members, and introduce ourselves to those around us. The choir sings "Eagle's Wings" for the first hymn, one of my favorites from my years at All Saints. Listening to the sweeping harmonies, the cello and violin, is like hearing God sigh. I'm so moved I don't realize I've closed my eyes until I hear Connor say loudly to the choir, "Stop singing! Mama is sleeping."

After the opening prayer, an associate minister asks all the kids to assemble at the front of the altar for the "Children's Moment." Connor ducks his head and Jill reassures him that he doesn't have to go. The minister talks to the group about what it means to forgive others and asks them for examples from their own lives. Then he dismisses them to "Faith Camp."

The format of the service resembles the Catholic Church's in many ways, with a few Scripture readings mixed with music liturgy and responsorial psalms. We hold hands and say the Our Father. There is an offering. Communion. But First Congregational isn't the Catholic Church, and I realize how angry I am with Father Bill, that he has taken away my church. Stripped away all the good I found there and replaced it with all this bitterness.

In the sermon, the minister discusses reconciliation. She reads Ephesians 2:14–22. "'For He himself is our peace, who has made the two one and destroyed the barrier, the dividing wall of hostility.'" She tells us we need to take responsibility for our conflicts with others. "We own a part of every relationship breakdown," she says. "Nothing is completely one-sided." I think about Father Bill, stubborn in the fact that I've done nothing wrong. She asks us, "Is it more important to be close or to be right?" *It is more important to be right,* I think, *because I am.* If I am culpable, perhaps it's because I should have protected Connor better. He should never have been put in that school in the first place. Because of Father Bill, I've walked away from my Catholic faith and taken Connor with me. *If it's the right decision, why can't I make peace with it? Why do I want to go back?* At the root of it all, I know exactly why. A part of me still believes that a church that accepts gay people isn't much of a church at all.

The lector announces a mission trip to Haiti and a new Habitat for Humanity project. He asks for volunteers at a booth the church will have at the upcoming Boulder and Denver GLBT Pride events. After the service, members of the church gather in the community center below the main chapel to serve meals to the homeless.

As Jill, Connor, and I file out into the sunlight, we pass an International Peace Pole, identical to the one I saw in front of the YWCA across from Sacred Heart that day before my first meeting with Father Bill about Connor's baptism. I take it as a sign from God that this is where we belong. Jill and I watch other families leaving, including several gay women who all seem to know each other. Two moms have their children sandwiched between them. A rainbow flag flies just outside the entrance. Jill starts to speak and I put my hand up. "Wait, just wait until we get into the car." Her nose crinkles like she's trying to suppress a sneeze. Once Connor is in the backseat and all the doors are closed I nod to her and she says, "It wasn't *too* gay, was it?"

CHAPTER FOURTEEN

ANN AND I DID NOT handle snakes or heal quadriplegics or stand in front of the 7-Eleven clad in sandwich board signs saying REPENT, JESUS IS COMING! On the evangelical scale, FCA sat palatably in the center. Ann knew that I drank and that I was friends with Wink and Sparrow, and never judged me for either. But my drinking bothered her more than I realized.

One night, Ann picked me up in her parents' Cadillac and started driving toward south Dallas. She kept checking a map and wouldn't tell me where she was going. After a half hour of driving, she pulled into the parking lot of an oblong brick building with the sign JACKSON BAPTIST CHURCH in front of it. I assumed this was her mother's church, that maybe Ann would make me walk to the front where feverish people would shove their palms against my forehead, fill me with the Holy Spirit, and make me faint into their arms. I knew so little about those kinds of events, my greatest fear was that I might lose control of my bodily functions and poop myself in public.

Ann opened the door to a side entrance. Smoke swirled up to greet us, but none of the people did. About thirty adults sat in rows of folding chairs; they glared at us like we were wedding crashers. We grabbed the first two seats in the back, faced forward to the empty

podium without moving. Above it hung a banner: WELCOME TO ALCO-
HOLICS ANONYMOUS. I sank low into my seat. Ann crossed her legs and
pushed her hair back behind her ears. I leaned over and said, "Are
you out of your mind?"

"I didn't realize this was just for adults," she whispered back. She
uncrossed her legs. "We should go," she said. But the meeting started.

One by one, people introduced themselves as follows: "My name
is Jack, and I'm an alcoholic," and the room answered, "Hi, Jack."
When it was Ann's turn, she murmured, "Hi, I'm Olga, and I'm an
alcoholic." "Hi, Olga!" I yelled, in chorus with the others. The adults
in the room looked at us doubtfully. Using a European accent I said,
"I'm Svetlana, and I'm an alcoholic."

Our emcee for the evening, a rotund woman with doughy skin,
introduced our speaker. His name was Billy and he cracked his
knuckles one by one as he approached the podium. For the next
fifteen minutes, his voice rasped like sandpaper rubbed along a rusty
pipe. He talked about robbing a liquor store and the year he spent
in jail. He said the "f-word" seven times in as many minutes. I stole a
look at Ann, who winced. He didn't thank God or his ex-wife for his
single year of sobriety, but he did get weepy when he acknowledged
his parole officer.

Ann and I fled the room the minute the meeting ended. Inside
her car, the seats vibrated with our laughter. I wiped at the corners of
my eyes. "I can't believe you did that for me."

"You mean did that *to* you," she said.

"I was truly frightened. You know this building's right next to the
correctional facility? Couldn't you have picked an AA meeting in
Highland Park?"

"I know, right?" She took a deep breath and let it out with a remaining giggle. "Did you answer the questions on the back of that
brochure you picked up?"

"I took a look at it." Car doors slammed around us. The sky lit up with lightning.

"Are you an alcoholic?"

"No, it classifies me as a problem drinker. I could've told them that. I drink to settle my anxiety."

Ann placed her hands at ten and two on the steering wheel even though the motor was off. "What are you anxious about?"

"You have met my mother, right?"

Ann swigged some Gatorade, gave a half smile.

I said, "Seriously, even the parakeets we used to have as kids didn't want to live with us. They'd escape from their cages and fly straight into the walls. They actually committed suicide."

Ann spewed lemon-lime liquid out her pursed lips, held her palm up like a crossing guard, and tried to swallow.

"We kept replacing them. We didn't even bother to give them new names, we just called them Sesame one. Sesame two. Sesame three."

Ann wrapped an arm around her ribs. "Stop, please."

"Lots of teenagers drink. Catholics drink."

"At parties, maybe. Not with adults twice their age. Not alone."

"I talked to a priest about it once," I said. "Something happened to me."

"This isn't confession." Her voice trembled like an old lady's. "Tell me, Michelle."

"You won't look at me the same way."

"Try me," she said.

It was one secret, but it was a big one, and in my mind, her reaction would cement our friendship or blow it up. The only person I had ever told about Mr. Crandall was Father Kos, and he didn't really count because I hadn't cared what he thought about me. I was invested in Ann. I loved Ann.

"I can't."

"Well, burying it hasn't gotten you anywhere." Raindrops spit onto the windshield. Ann started the car and punched me in the quad. "Stay over tonight. Let me help you."

On the drive back to Ann's, I thought about the early graduation presents we had exchanged. I'd given her a James Avery ring, a silver band with a cross etched into it, matching the one I wore on my left-hand ring finger. She gave me a gold-leaf Bible with a leather cover. In the inscription, she quoted the Christian singer Michael W. Smith: "Friends are friends forever, if the Lord's the Lord of them. And, a friend will not say never, because the welcome never ends." She signed it, "I love you." Maybe I could tell her. When I got to her front door, I lingered on the porch a moment longer and searched for a patch of sky without storm clouds. I found a bright star and pinned my hopes to it. Only when it moved did I realize I'd just wasted my wish on a Boeing 747.

WE BEGGED HER MOM and mine by phone to let me spend the night. After they agreed, we squirreled away in Ann's room. I told Ann about Dale Crandall and Holly. I crossed my arms, dug my fingers into the flesh along my triceps, and tried to stay present.

"So, he raped you?" she asked, her face awash with pity.

"Stop looking at me like that!"

"Like what?"

"Like I'm a deer you found run over on the highway."

I watched the rain falling outside her window. Ten minutes passed. When I looked over at Ann, she had her head leaning against the edge of her dresser.

"Now I really want a drink," I said. I tilted my head, smiled a little. "I just feel like a piece of crap when I think about it. It's beyond humiliating to me, okay? Plus, I left Holly without helping her at all. That's what kind of friend I am."

"Do you know what happened to her?"

I peeled the skin from my thumb. "She ran away."

"And you think that's your fault? You can't control what happened."

"No, not now. But I could have."

We sat with this between us.

Ann pushed a pile of magazines out of the way and faced me with her hands extended. "We could pray for her."

We did. She took my hands inside of her own, and with tears streaming down my cheeks, I asked God to help Holly wherever she was. To keep her alive and safe. I asked God to forgive me because I hadn't helped her when I could.

When it was Ann's turn, she said, "Father God, be with Michelle and let her know that you have a plan for her life. Help her to be strong and fearless and to know how much you love her."

After the prayer, Ann said, "Messing up your own life won't make Holly's any better." She sighed. "God has a plan. There's a reason He brought us together. Maybe this was it," she said. "I'm not going anywhere. You're stuck with me."

Even though Mrs. Baker made up the guest room for me, I curled up in Ann's bed where we talked until 3 A.M. When I could barely keep my eyes open anymore, Ann placed her arm across my back and left it there until morning. As the sun rose across the walls of her room, I noticed that the door we had closed the night before was cracked open a few inches. It was the last time I would ever sleep over at Ann's.

AS THE REMAINING WEEKS OF high school disappeared, Ann behaved strangely, doing things without me and forgetting to tell me about plans she had. For three years, we'd been inseparable; now I felt like a transplanted organ being rejected. I tried to be patient because

I knew I'd be leading FCA camp with her that summer. But when Ann received her huddle leader confirmation, and I didn't get mine, I started to get nervous. I didn't want a clerical error to separate us. Finally, after a few calls trying to follow up on my application, I got a call from Theresa Banks, the head of the Texas branch of the FCA. She asked me to meet her at a diner nearby.

Theresa Banks was in her fifties or sixties with a crinkled face and a neck like a pelican. She wore a knit shirt with a collar and the FCA cross and emblem embroidered over the left breast. I knew she'd been a coach for years, had never married, and lived with a woman. She set my application atop the greasy checkered tablecloth.

"This isn't easy, so I'll just get to the point," Theresa said. "Mrs. Baker is worried about your relationship with Ann. I think maybe she saw or overheard something between the two of you. She mentioned you gave her a ring. She asked me to keep an eye out for anything I thought was unusual."

"Unusual?"

"She thinks you might be a lesbian. She thinks you're in love with her daughter."

The people at other tables kept eating, as if the words hadn't been spoken aloud. "This is crazy! Did you ask Ann?"

"I can't allow you to be a huddle leader." She pushed the application in front of me, a red stamp with the word REJECTED emblazoned on it.

"You can't be serious. I haven't done anything wrong."

"How do you feel about Ann? Do you love her?"

"Yeah, I do. But I don't want to have sex with her."

Theresa tapped the edge of her credit card on the table. "Maybe you're confused about it?"

"I'm not confused. Why are you doing this?"

"We can't have lesbians leading the FCA."

"Really?" I gripped the metal edge of the table with both hands and leaned in toward her. I had ammunition and I used it against her. "And you've lived with another woman for how many years?"

"Sara is my roommate." Theresa folded her hands and rested them calmly on the table in front of her, which only pissed me off more.

"Come on, let's just be honest about this. You're fifty years old and still single."

"We're talking about you."

"I've never even thought about sex with another woman. But I sure bet you have."

Theresa twisted her lips sideways. "I expected you to be angry."

"You are throwing away everything I love. Everything that has meaning to me. The FCA is my family." My eyes filled but my fists shook.

"It gives you something to think about," she said. "I'm not saying this is forever. You can apply again next year. For now, let's give it a break. Okay?"

THAT SUMMER THE WORLD KEPT spinning without me. Ann went to Christian camp for twelve weeks and met a boy. Her mother said the separation would give us time to think about our friendship and the ways it might be becoming unnatural. Ann was nonchalant. "It's no big deal," she told me before she disappeared. When my parents asked me why I wasn't a huddle leader, I told them I'd waited too late to turn in my forms. I was thankful Theresa hadn't told my parents about her suspicions. I was confused enough without having to defend myself to them.

I spent my time at Wink and Sparrow's swimming in sadness and white Russians. I stopped reading the Bible to them. In turn, they forgave me for being a self-righteous jackass. And when I thought my shame couldn't get any worse, the letters came.

The week after I should have been at camp as a counselor, the Theall mailbox filled with envelopes addressed to me from the FCA camp. I opened them as if they held live snakes. Young teens from all over the state of Texas wrote to me, quoting Scriptures condemning my homosexual behavior. In order to explain my absence, the leaders of the FCA had made an announcement to the kids at an assembly, telling them all that I was gay. As if I had a disease, the kids let me know they were all praying for me.

"I don't want to be judgmental, but it's unnatural."

"I miss you. Come back to God so you can come back to us."

"God is crying."

"God made woman from man and for man."

"I looked up to you."

I shredded the letters so my parents wouldn't find them. I sat on my Crayola box bed and clung to the things I thought I still knew: I was an athlete. I was a Christian. I liked chocolate and knew all the words to *Grease*. *But who was I, really?* The letters from the kids all ended the same way: They mourned their loss as if I had died. For the longest time, it felt that way to me too.

CHAPTER FIFTEEN

CONNOR RUNS AROUND THE PERIMETER of the basketball court wearing his Darth Vader costume, a suit complete with mask and light saber. I'm in the middle of a fast break when he shouts from the sidelines, "Mama, I have to go potty!" The other women in my rec league, most of them moms, laugh in the knowing way of women who are just trying to take one single hour for themselves.

"We just went," I yell back to him and pass the ball to my teammate.

"Mama, now!" I jog sideways off the court where Connor dances and holds his crotch.

I lead Darth Vader to the ladies' room. He cannot go into the men's room alone, and I cannot go with him. Because he has two mommies, he likely will be thirty before he ever sees a urinal.

In the stall, I strip off his black jumper and hold his plastic mask and light saber in a futile attempt to improve his aim. When he finishes, I tell him I need to go too and to wait; instead, he opens the lock and wanders out into the locker room, leaving me exposed and grabbing for the door. After I flush, I find him staring at a very butch, very naked African-American woman with short-cropped hair and no makeup.

"Are you a man?" he asks her. I grip his hand and hope she hasn't heard him. I drag him toward the door. But before I can get it open he says to me, "Why does that man have boobies?" I cringe.

"I am not a man," the woman says in a baritone as deep as James Earl Jones's.

I let go of the door handle and turn back toward the woman, who is still very naked and facing me with enormous and pendulous breasts. "I'm really sorry," I say. And for no logical reason, "He's got two mommies, so he gets confused sometimes."

I shake my head at my stupidity and sprint out the door. Once we are back in the gym, on the sidelines, I explain to Connor that we don't say some things out loud because they might hurt people's feelings. "But how do I know which things?" he asks. "Well, if you're not sure, just whisper it to me first, and I'll let you know." He puts on his mask and slices the air with the light saber, slashing—I imagine—the injustices he's suffered for being four years old among adults who make no sense at all.

After the game, a few of the girls want to grab a beer. We head to a brewery nearby. Connor squeezes into the booth and I hand him my iPhone. He already knows how to work it better than I do and he scrolls and clicks until he gets to his favorite game, Pocket God, the one Dylan introduced him to at Christmas. In the game, he controls the entire world for a group of cartoon pygmies. He makes the seagulls poop on them and strikes them with lightning and has them run through hell with the devil chasing them.

Feeling sluggish, anemic, and self-indulgent, I suspend my vegetarianism and order a black-and-blue burger with fries along with a pint of IPA and a chocolate milk for Connor. Mara, a woman in her early twenties with a Mohawk, slides in next to me. She wears men's BMX biking-style shirt. The waistband of her men's underwear rises a good six inches above the oversize jeans she keeps loose and low, barely clinging to her square hips. I know Mara is a gay activist and that she was in the military. Jill and I have never marched in a Pride parade. The most gay thing we've done in our eleven years together is watch *Ellen*. Mara is bold in a way I could never be, which should make me proud of her. Instead, I feel embarrassed—and embarrassed that I'm embarrassed. *Shouldn't I want someone to fight for our cause if I'm not willing to do it myself?* I think about Mara and the woman in the locker room whom Connor mistook for a man. Though I don't hide my sexual orientation, I don't broadcast it either. Based on my appearance now, most strangers wouldn't assume I was gay, though in college, I did get called "sir" a few times by waiters or sales cashiers. I never wanted to be a man, though. If I think about it now, I wore men's jeans and cut my hair short back then because I was afraid to be soft and feminine—it didn't feel safe for me to be a girl in the world. It took decades for me to be comfortable in my own skin. But Mara is perfectly okay with who she is, so much so that she expresses it boldly.

The check comes and Mara pulls out a men's wallet from her back pocket and chips in for beer. I doubt she wants to be a man, though that's something I've never asked a woman who identifies more masculine than I do. It's confusing and disorienting to me, and the two pints of beer I've had don't help.

On the drive home, I realize I am not sober, but I don't think I'm drunk either. I focus on going the speed limit and staying in my lane. It is only a couple of miles to our house. *Why does it bother me when gay women dress and act like men?* I idle at a red light and force myself to think of an honest answer. I come up with this: I want the world to see that gays are more like everyone else than we are different—that there is nothing abnormal about us. In college, I'd gone so far as to give up the person I loved because of what other people thought. It's ingrained in me that the opposite of "passing" for straight is failing—which says nothing about Mara and volumes about me.

When the light turns green, I've gone fifty feet when a Boulder police cruiser turns on his lights. I slow and he moves around me, sirens screaming, off to catch someone else.

"You going to jail, Mama?" Connor asks.

"No, baby, everything's just fine."

"You scared?"

"Nothing scares me, baby boy. Besides, I haven't done anything wrong." It is a lie, one worth telling to make him feel secure. And, if I say it enough, I just might begin to believe it too.

The next morning, my head hurts, and I vow to take it easy on the alcohol next time. Jill has already left for work. I peer down at Connor on Winston's bed where he has slept consistently from seven to seven in our room for over a month now. Helen's advice to treat him like a newborn until he felt safe was proving that sometimes it was best to go back in order to move forward. The next step would be getting him back into his own bed.

I get Connor dressed for preschool, make his lunch, drop one of his gummy vitamins on the floor, watch Daisy gobble it up, and wonder when it will end up on the living room rug. In Connor's backpack, I find a parent folder with an update for the week and a directory of students in Connor's class at his new school. I thumb through it hoping to find a child who lives nearby, someone whom Connor might be friends with. I dream of playdates and birthdays and corner lemonade stands and wonder if Connor does too.

Fifteen minutes later, Connor runs serpentine after a fox and her kits before the animals disappear beneath the white clapboard porch of Mapleton Montessori. He is playing alone, but seems happy. I've worked with him, role-playing, trying to get him to feel confident enough to join in with other groups of kids. "Put it out there," I tell him. "Don't be shy. Tell them your name. Smile." Somewhere along the line, I developed the Mommy gene, the one that makes you instantly feel all the joys and sorrows of your child as if you were one with him. I just need to remember that my dreams and his might not be the same.

The mama fox pokes her nose out from under the lattice and sneezes. Connor drops to his hands and knees, peers through the gap in the thin wood, and says, "Bless you, lil' foxy fox." I snap a picture of him face-to-face with the fox, its red tail poking out beneath Connor's chin like a beard. Connor runs through a sandbox the size of most backyards. I decide I like this loosey-goosey school. I picture Father Bill at Sacred Heart dressed like Elmer Fudd with a tranquilizer gun trying to dart and relocate the mama fox and her babies. "Rabies!" he'd shout. *Bang.* "Can't have our children exposed to something so dangerous!" *Boom.* Even as I think this, I'm struck with the guilt that my mom has no idea we've taken Connor out of Sacred Heart, and worse, put him into a school she would deem experimental, full of Mother-Earth-worshipping, hippie nonsense.

Connor passes a group of girls who sit in a circle along the fence weaving strands of grass into necklaces and bracelets for each other. He picks up a stick and slices it through the air. It whooshes like a light saber. Connor is all boy—with an innate penchant for dirt and swords and superheroes. He gravitates toward toy trucks and action figures on his own, with no sway from Jill and me, no prominent male figure in his life—save a few friends we've named honorary uncles— to introduce him to those things. A woman pulls up in a minivan and her son joins Connor beneath a slide. He has honey-colored loose curls and a sweet smile. He grabs a stick and they start to duel like pirates. The woman slides next to me and we watch our boys stab and swipe at each other.

"Ever worry they'll end up being little serial killers?" I ask.

"All the time," she laughs. "Nah, they're just boys. I'm used to it. I've got three more." She sweeps her hair behind her ears. "Just wait until they start burping the alphabet."

"Four boys, unbelievable. We can barely handle one. I'm Michelle," I say and extend my hand to her. "That's Connor."

She takes my hand. "Jackie," she says and points to the boy with the mop of hair. "Luke. We live on Eighth and Cascade."

I bounce on my tiptoes. "We're around the block from you!" My voice gets high and squeaky.

"We should have you over. My husband, Sam, and I would love it if Luke had someone his age to play with in the neighborhood," she says. She turns into the sun to face me and light glints off the gold cross dangling from a chain around her neck.

Damn, I think, and then just as quickly, *when did being a Christian become a bad thing?* After all, I'm one too.

"You're in the directory, right?" she asks me. Her eyes are kind.

I've been at this crossroads enough to know that this is the time. I have to take the advice I give Connor. Suck it up. Put it out there. You never know. Maybe she won't hate us. I stare at our boys, who are kneeling in the dirt using their sticks to dig up bugs.

"Yes, under Connor Theall. I had no idea a boy Connor's age lived so close. My partner, Jill, and I have been here for ten years and we're surrounded by empty nesters." I steal a look at her, watch her eyes flicker when I say "partner" and "Jill." It's unmistakable. I want to blurt out: "Oh, I see your cross. What church do you go to? We just love First Congregational. I love Jesus, don't you?" But I leave the ball in her court. "Well, just email me a day and time that works. I think they'd get along."

The teacher at Mapleton Montessori rings a tiny bell and the children skip into a wiggly line facing her. Connor and Luke stand side by side. Connor turns his head to find me, and I wave and blow a kiss. I watch him until he is inside the quaint Victorian schoolhouse, removing his shoes and stuffing his fleece jacket into a cubby.

WHEN I GET HOME, I pick up our trash, strewn along our alley, and make a mental note to lock the bins now that the bears have come out of hibernation. Inside, I wash my hands before taking the school's directory of parents and students up to the loft. I scour the roster line by line until I find Luke Randall on Eighth Street. Parents: Jackie and Sam. On Facebook, I type in Jackie's name to see if I can find out more about her and her family—to see if there's a chance she'll accept us. There are photos of her with her husband and four children. I marvel at how she can juggle four kids when I can barely stay sane with one. I click on the "About" tab and the first thing I see is a Scripture: "The grace of our Lord was poured out on me abundantly, along with the faith and love that are in Christ Jesus. 1 Timothy 1:14." *I have a favorite Scripture,* I tell myself. Lots of people do. It doesn't mean she will condemn us.

I scroll furiously through the pages she "Likes" to find a Human Rights campaign emblem or even a pro Obama sticker. Instead, I find: K-Love Radio, the Bible, I Love Jesus, and a photo of her bathroom with a placard reading: WASH YOUR HANDS AND SAY YOUR PRAYERS. JESUS AND GERMS ARE EVERYWHERE. I refuse to give up so easily, though. I'm assuming she will judge me, and that means I'm making judgments of my own. I bounce around through her status posts looking for any evidence that she might be open to our family, until I find a photo of her someone has posted from the 1970s wearing a wig with a T-shirt. The shirt is purple and the graphic stuns me: GONG SHOW REJECT. Holly, the T-shirt she used to wear. The one I had on that day. The memory is such a jolt it's like a train that's jumped the tracks. Disoriented, I stare at the cursor. It blinks at me from the top of the page next to an empty rectangle: "Search for people, places, and things."

I never stopped wondering what happened to her, and now because of technology, I have the chance to find out. I peck in the letters of her name: H-o-l-l-y C-r-a-n-d-a-l-l. I filter my search with Meeker Middle School. One name returns. No photo. The arrow of my mouse hovers over the words "Add Friend." It's what we were, but it's not what we are. I don't want to be presumptuous. Instead, I type a private message to her: "Wondering if this is Holly Crandall who used to live on Oakwood Court. Write back and let me know!" Given our past, the exclamation point might be overkill, but I want her to know I'm enthusiastic about reconnecting. I hit send before I can chicken out.

WHEN I PICK UP CONNOR that afternoon at Mapleton, he asks me if he can have a playdate with Luke. I tell him we'll see. I gather his backpack and jacket and help him put on his shoes. I believe I'll never hear from Jackie again, but I cling to a sliver of hope, as fragile as the links of her gold chain and those between childhood friends.

CHAPTER SIXTEEN

THE ADMINISTRATION BUILDING at Texas Tech University in Lubbock towered over the circular entrance of a campus carved from buff-colored stone and capped with red-tiled roofs. The Victory Bells pealed a welcome to new students from the two ornate bell towers that stood on either side of the round university seal. The Fury had finally broken down for good and I left her back in Dallas, so my parents followed behind me in their Caprice Classic, while I drove a loaded-down Chevy Malibu across campus. We parked at Wall Hall to unload my things.

After I set up my room, my parents sat on the twin bed across from me, my father with sweat stains beneath his arms and my mother with water pooling beneath her eyes. "Well, I guess that's it," my father said. My mother handed me a gift bag with a ribbon tied between the handles. "For later," she said. I hugged and kissed them both, thanking them for their help and for getting me here. I watched them drive away from my third-floor window, feeling sad but also relieved, like the rest of my life might actually begin.

Inside the bag I found a thick photo album. I assumed it would be full of shots of my parents and me and Kathy on various vacations. Instead, I opened it and found a meticulously assembled scrapbook of photos and newspaper clippings from every race I'd ever run. The album began with me at the starting line of a field-day event on a dirt-and-grass track at Meeker Elementary School, when I was ten years old. Our old PE coach held the starter pistol, towering over us in his red mesh shorts and white T-shirt, without a clue he'd be fired by midsemester because of our rather innocent, unsupervised game of tag. It ended with a photo of me at my desk just a few months ago signing the yellow letter of intent forms for a partial scholarship to run track in the NCAA Division I at Texas Tech. Compiling the scrapbook of my running career must have taken my mother years of attention, hours of work. She affixed stickers to the pages, included track banquet programs, cards from teammates and coaches, award certificates, and even locker decorations she must have retrieved from my garbage. While she had hated the fact that I loved running and didn't understand my obsession with it, she had rooted for me anyway. I shook my head and thumbed through each page. Between two of the sleeves of the album, I found an envelope. Inside it, my mother had typed me a letter on pink stationery.

I can hardly believe that you are all grown up and ready to leave home for the first time. I still see the precious little girl who used to wiggle so when I would pull those ponytails too tight or get into some mischief or another when I wasn't looking!

When you have devoted eighteen years to nurturing, caring for, and just plain loving another person—especially your child—it's heart-wrenching to have to let go. We want you to know how proud we are of you, first and foremost as a human being. The greatest accomplishment in life that one can have is to be a good Christian first, and a loving, caring person toward your fellow men, and that is what we see in you. I hope that your love and dedication to the Catholic Church will grow. It is quite a feat in this day and age to raise children who have good moral values and can make a difference in this world, and we feel that is what you have and what you will do.

Don't ever forget how much we love you, Michelle. Unconditional, unqualified love is something only a parent can feel for a child, and you have always had ours. God bless you. Love always, Mom

I lay back on the bed with the weight of the album on my chest. Though my mother wrote that she loved me unconditionally, I was fairly certain there were conditions, and that I'd likely explore one of them soon. The fact that I would fall in love with a woman seemed all but inevitable to me. I had plenty of time to think about the way I'd felt about Ann. I wanted to be closer to her. But because of Mr. Crandall, I couldn't associate sex with connection. The idea that someone who touched me might do so out of love was as foreign to me as that unending West Texas sky. All I knew was that when Ann put her arm around me that night I spent at her house, I felt worth something to someone in a different way than I ever had before. I wanted to feel that way again. But I had no idea what to do about it, and also knew that maybe I wasn't ready. After all, I had come to this school as a runner—so, it was possible I'd leave that way too.

MY FIRST TRAINING RUN WITH the track team started in Buffalo Canyon at three thousand feet above sea level. I sucked red dirt into my lungs and felt them heave and shudder trying to pull something out of the air that wasn't there. Prairie dogs popped out of holes and a north wind blew in the thick reek of stockyards. The terrain was layered and complex and colorful, sixteen shades of green and brown and rust instead of the monotonous gray concrete and steel of Dallas. At the top of the canyon, I could see beyond Lubbock in every direction. West Texas farmland spread out like squares of a quilt. Tumbleweeds rolled in a bouncing trajectory, halted only by tangles of barbed wire, or else they'd end up somewhere in the Atlantic. Oil pumps bobbed their heads like horses trying to drink out of a river I couldn't see. People made fun of Lubbock, singing "Happiness is Lubbock, Texas, in my rearview mirror," words from a Mac Davis country song. But it was beautiful to me, isolated and wild. For the first time I could remember, I felt free. Which was surprising since my new coach sometimes treated us more like prisoners than runners.

Coach Alex Dane dangled an arm out the window of the Texas Tech track van and nudged the backs of our calves with the bumper as we slogged through our warm-up. "I will run over you," she said. With her gold tooth, square jaw, midnight skin, and degree in Criminal Justice, Alex Dane was not beyond putting a few wayward athletes beneath the wheels of the van. "Today, you'll be doing three to five," she said and revved the engine. One of my teammates said between breaths, "You think she's talking about a jail sentence or miles?" We picked up our pace.

Alex sidled the van next to us, speaking out the window, and trying to sideswipe us with the door. "I'm not your mommy or your daddy. But they entrusted me with you, so you are my responsibility. You will run and study. You will not eat junk food or gain the freshman fifteen. No one on my team gets arrested, or pregnant, or expelled. You may not all become champions, but make no mistake, ladies, you will train like them."

After our second loop around the canyon rim, Alex lined us up and sent us downhill in two-hundred-meter repetitions. "Sprint to the bottom as fast as you can and then jog up to recover. If I catch you walking, you can run all the way back to campus on your own." She blew a whistle and I took off. I was wondering why on earth she'd let us run down and jog up when the reverse sounded much more difficult. With my body in fifth gear and gravity helping me, my legs got ahead of my brain, like the Road Runner, a wheel of spinning feet, and I flew chest down and rolling, twisting my right ankle, and landing in a heap with part of my hand in a cactus. I spit gravel off my lips. Stood. Brushed off my shorts and T-shirt and finished the last fifty meters. Alex met me at the bottom. "Let's see it." I pushed down my sock and my ankle pulsed a swelling red. "Get it looked at." She jutted a thumb toward the van. I hobbled away from my teammates.

Inside the van was Cassie Dickens, a sophomore athletic trainer assigned to our track team. She wrapped a packet of ice around my swollen ankle with an ACE bandage and handed me a couple of Tylenols and a cup of water. I watched as she dug through the medical kit before sitting next to me on the empty bench seat. "Keep it elevated," she said. She cupped my bare heel with her hand and put a pillow beneath it. "Give me your hand." With a pair of tweezers, she plucked cactus quills from my outstretched palm. A moment before, the van had reeked of mold and sweat, but Cassie's red curls smelled like lavender. "The good news is, I don't think you tore any tendons or ligaments in that ankle. The bad news is, you'll have to see me every day this week to get it taped before practice and again to ice it for twenty minutes after." Alex yelled at my teammates running past the window. "Is that all you've got? Don't let me catch you!" Alex sprinted after the girls.

"I think I'd rather be in here with you than out there with her," I said and smiled.

"Why do you think I'm hiding in the van?" she said. "That woman scares the heck out of me."

I recognized Cassie from a football game we watched last year, when I was considering where to attend college. She stood about five foot two with shoulder-length nutmeg hair tied back into a loose knot and eyes the color of a swimming pool. I'd noticed her because she was the only woman on the field, dwarfed by the male players, trainers, and coaches at the stadium. During one of the plays a three-hundred-pound lineman separated his shoulder, and she walked him off the field, letting him lean on her until they reached the bench on the sidelines, where she gave him a towel so he could cover his face while she worked on him.

Cassie held the tweezers above my right hand. She brushed my open palm with her fingertips. "I'll try not to hurt you," she said.

COLLEGE ATHLETICS WAS A FAMILY of sorts that forced intimacy between teammates and coaches and trainers. I spent more time with my team, and with Cassie, than I did in class or in lab or with my professors. Our team practiced in the mornings and afternoons, had meals together in the dining hall, and slept on buses and vans en route to cheap hotels where we talked most of the night, two to a bed. On those trips, an electric current surged between Cassie and me. When our shoulders brushed against each other in the middle of the night sharing a double bed at a La Quinta Inn in one of the many towns and cities where we competed—Norman, Oklahoma, or Austin, Texas, or Kansas City, Missouri—neither of us shifted back to our side of the mattress. After a while, without ever discussing it, some nights we even started out that way.

When we weren't at practice or traveling with the team or in class, Cassie and I were together. It wasn't enough. I wanted to see who we might be to each other away from campus and track. I suggested a road trip to Colorado, a place neither of us had been, on a four-day weekend. Without hesitation, she said yes.

We took turns driving. Across New Mexico, thick vegetation covered the tops of mesas like cheap toupees, and hillsides folded into each other. The highway opened up in front of us and cut through granite. With a couple of cup holders and an armrest separating us, Cassie and I talked about our lives before Tech—our families, religion, our affinity for sports. A foot away from me, her skin smelled like the sun.

She had known someone who was gay, a girl at her high school who had committed suicide. I talked about Wink and Sparrow. But we avoided discussing our own sexuality. When we got hungry, we stopped on a dirt county road and walked out to the rim of a deep canyon to eat some sandwiches I'd packed. Atop those steep walls we exchanged our biggest secrets. Growing up, her only sibling, her brother, had repeatedly molested her. "It escalated until he tried to strangle me," she said. Her eyes squinted into the sun. When she told her mother, she hadn't believed her.

I took her hand and nested it inside my own, and she pressed her head into my shoulder. I wanted to kiss her on the forehead, the way a parent might. We took in the silence of the canyon beneath us. We dangled our feet over the edge and watched a hawk swoop between two trees where wounded joints formed knotted spires that twisted into one another. In between bites of my sandwich, I asked Cassie, "How can those things grow in stone like that?" And she said, "Maybe they don't have deep roots. Maybe that's why they're clinging to each other." We packed up our leftovers and brushed the red dirt from our clothes. We drove through the mountains and watched the scrub oak turn to views of the Continental Divide with the unmistakable feeling that we were headed someplace exciting and new beyond the foothills and peaks; and we were speeding there together.

Around dusk, we drove into Eldorado Springs, a sleepy town outside the jaws of a canyon formed by South Boulder Creek, and pulled up to a small yellow house. We walked across a narrow bridge with our luggage and knocked on the front door. A golden retriever bolted out to greet us followed by a friend of mine several years older than me whom I'd met once while playing guitar at her church. Cassie and I were poor college students who needed a place to crash, so my friend had agreed to bunk at a friend's house and let us stay in the meager attic space she rented from an old hippie couple. She walked us into the kitchen, climbed up on the table to reach the end of a dangling rope. She unfurled stairs leading into an attic and we climbed up to see our accommodations for the night. Her bedroom "loft," as she called it, had just three feet of clearance from the ceiling and a double mattress on the floor. Next to it sat a Bible and a headlamp. After she left, Cassie and I lay on the mattress side by side. Without getting up, I turned a crank on the skylight above our heads and opened it. Through that gap aspen leaves sang, accompanied by the bubbling of the creek. The sounds of an owl, crickets, and someone playing a guitar on a deck nearby found their way to us. As dusk fell, we watched the night sky develop like a Polaroid. I told Cassie, "I feel like I'm home, like I belong here."

Six inches. That's all that was between us, though sometimes I could feel the delicate hairs of her arm brush against mine like the thin filament inside a lightbulb. I thought about that for hours, until I was watching the pink clouds of sunrise above our heads. Was she gay? Was I? I didn't know. Even though I was facing out, away from the wall and away from Cassie, I knew she was facing me. The floor creaked as she stretched out, wakening. I inched backward until we touched. She could dismiss it as an accident if she wanted. Instead, her arms wrapped around me, hands holding my own, so that she was helping me to hug myself. She buried her face in the nape of my neck. Because it had been cold in the attic when we went to bed, we had stayed in our clothes. Layers of denim and cotton separated our bodies, but I felt more naked than I'd ever been. If I turned my head, two inches, we would kiss. I convinced myself that we'd done nothing wrong yet, nothing sexual. A hug was something friends did, but my body knew a lie. The kiss was irrelevant. My body was having sex, whether the rest of me was in on it or not. I couldn't stop and I couldn't go back. Couldn't undo what I was doing and didn't want to.

I rotated toward her, three degrees. Our lips touched. And for the first time in my life, I felt something beautiful without feeling preyed upon. My chest rose up to meet hers. My breasts, hips, and every bit of me that was soft or curvy felt protected, not vulnerable—more, not less.

I ached for her in a way I'd never experienced before, and certainly not with any of the boys in my life. I wanted to know what it felt like to hold her and taste the salt of her skin. I wanted to know how many freckles she had and where. I wanted to cup my hand over her breast and feel the softness of her whole body wrapped against my own. It didn't feel wrong or dirty. It felt ordained.

It was weird navigating the world of being in love with a woman. Though neither of us had ever been with a woman, it hadn't taken us long to figure out the particulars. I tried everything I'd learned from Whoopi Goldberg in *The Color Purple* and Mariel Hemingway in *Personal Best* and somehow made it work. I didn't consider myself gay, or even bisexual. I just loved Cassie, and she loved me. But I was also terrified we'd be caught, which made it feel like we were doing something wrong. If I sent Cassie flowers at her dorm, I signed them "Love, Matt" or "Love, M." She left notes on my car with "1-4-3" written on them instead of "I Love You." We dated boys who asked us, because it created the perfect cover. After those dates, we fell into each other's arms. The only person who knew Cassie and I were lovers was Allison, a girl who lived across the hall from me in my dorm. Allison was an advertising major and an Alpha Delta Pi sorority girl with a biting sense of humor and the walk of a jock. Cassie and I envied Allison because her girlfriend had an apartment, which made it easy for them to conceal their relationship. Cassie had a dorm roommate and so did I, random strangers assigned to us that made being alone together impossible. But on track trips, we were required to share a bed without anyone thinking twice about it, which is why Cassie and I started taking risks. No more than a few months into our relationship, in a Hampton Inn outside El Paso, Cassie and I fumbled around beneath the sheets, unable to keep our hands off each other despite the risk of getting caught by my teammates one bed over. A single particleboard nightstand and plastic lamp away, two middle-distance runners snored and twitched in their sleep. Our night meet at UTEP had left all of us exhausted, so I didn't think Charlotte or Deanna could possibly be awake. Cassie kneaded my quads beneath the cheap, squeaky blanket. After we'd gotten away with it once or twice, it just became a habit.

"HERE SHE COMES." They were the first words I heard as I boarded the team van for an early morning workout at Buffalo Lake. My duffel bag bounced against my knees. I looked for Cassie as I moved down the aisle, and when I found her, she wouldn't meet my eyes. My teammates whispered. Deanna and Charlotte shared a seat in the back and placed their hands over their mouths and rubbed their faces together making smooching noises behind their palms. I tossed my bag into an empty seat. Cassie, who was a few rows behind me, looked as if my fingerprints were pressed into her skin. The girls continued their noises, complete with fake orgasms, until I couldn't stand it anymore. I twisted around and said, "What the fuck, are you twelve?" To which Deanna, a half-miler with skin like an orange peel and square hips like a boy, said, "What the fuck, are you gay?"

I faced forward. I closed my eyes. They knew. The rest of the ride to the lake my stomach cramped and I fought off panic. If I didn't admit anything, they could never really know for sure.

At the bottom of the canyon, Alex told us to start stretching and she disappeared back into the van. Wisely, Cassie stayed inside too. I bent over to touch my toes, and without warning, Deanna shoved me from behind. I hurtled off my feet. The rest of the girls crowded us. I held up my hands. "What the fuck's your problem?" I said. Alex trotted across the road toward us, and the girls dispersed like ripples in a pond. She approached Deanna and me and we took a step back. What little I knew about Alex was this: She had grown up among the gangs in South Central Los Angeles. She fought poverty, sexism, and racism, and by the time she was my age, she was an Olympian. So I shouldn't have been surprised when she dragged her Nikes in the dirt. "Don't let me stop you." She made a circle around us with the toe of her shoe. "By all means, go at it until it's done."

For a split second, I thought Deanna and I would fight, and wondered what it would feel like to take a punch and give one. But Deanna snickered and took off across the trail with another girl to warm up. I stood in the circle, my hands still clenched into fists.

Cassie and I denied we were together. But it didn't matter. On the next road trip in the hotel lobby, Alex handed out room assignments, and murmurs grew loud enough to be understood. "I'm not rooming with a lesbian. Fuck that shit."

Alex said, "If there's a problem, work it out. I don't care if you sleep in this lobby." I took my key and because we had the same room, Cassie followed behind me to the elevator. Two other runners came in after us, found their empty bed, and decided there was enough distance between us and them that they wouldn't catch whatever it was that made us gay. But nothing was the same again. The carefree days we'd spent together were over and a toxic haze settled over us like a pesticide. We pretended, denied, hid, lied. We kept pressing on.

Late one night after ten hours in a van coming back from Austin, I staggered to my dorm. I dug through my duffel bag at my feet for my keys. A low keening came from the room across the hall. Allison's door was ajar. The resident's assistant bent over a woman who looked like a middle-aged, more feminine version of Allison. I dropped my keys and the RA heard me. She motioned to me to come into Allison's room.

I stood in the doorway, watched Allison's answering machine light blink with unanswered messages. Allison's mother wrung her hands, chafing with worry. Allison hadn't been to class in two weeks. No one at her sorority had seen her. Allison's mom crumpled Kleenex into each fist and sat on the dusty comforter of her daughter's bed. "We talk almost every day," she told me. "This isn't like her. We should call the police." The RA looked at me. "You guys are friends, right? Any idea at all where she might be?"

They agreed to give me an hour to make some calls. Instead, I hopped in my car and drove to her girlfriend's apartment and banged on the door. Allison opened it, looking for the very last time like she hadn't a care in the world.

Two hours later, I helped Allison and her mother pack up Allison's things and load them into their separate cars. Her sorority sisters whispered and pointed at us as we moved about the narrow hallway. Though Allison was on her way to a degree in advertising and had been making good grades despite her two weeks of skipping class, her mother withdrew her from school. Allison would go home to Houston where she would live with her mother and receive psychiatric care. She didn't get to tell her girlfriend good-bye. Her mother thought she was mentally ill. She would never graduate from college.

That night, I met up with Cassie at a duck pond close to our dorms. We sat on a barren patch of ground, huddled together and shivering. Shame and fear pounded on me like a persistent knock on a door. I loved Cassie, but I couldn't do this anymore. She leaned over and kissed me softly on the lips.

"I can't," I said. "I want to, but I can't."

"I know." Cassie pushed my hair back from my eyes, her hands fluttering along my brow bone. I thought about all the things I'd miss: The way her breath warmed my neck. The rightness of her skin against mine. Our bodies fitting together like puzzle pieces. We let our tears fall onto each other, until we were wrung out from grief. "This is so stupid and sad," she said.

Under the cover of night, we held each other one long last time.

It didn't take long for my track career to derail from the weight of all my shame. I didn't want to be gay, to be a joke or a cliché. I loved sports and hated wearing dresses. I wore sensible shoes and listened to Melissa Etheridge. I was a stereotype, and I was furious about it. I wanted a normal life just like everyone else. I couldn't bear being around Cassie, and it was painful for her too. Coach must have caught on to our breakup. She put us in separate rooms and sent me to a different trainer when I needed to get my ankle wrapped. But it didn't matter. I started losing races. My running fell apart.

Coach Dane called me into her office one afternoon after practice to find out why I'd gone from promising athlete to train wreck in a matter of months. She sat behind her desk, a fortress of a woman with both feet planted on the floor. I slumped in the metal chair in front of her, and she said, "You haven't learned to use the downhill."

"Excuse me?"

"You know why I make you all sprint downhill? Momentum. The downhill creates the momentum you need to climb out of the valleys. But instead of working with gravity, you brace for it." She stood and shook her head at me. "I can tell by that hangdog look on your face that I'm not getting through. So I'll be clear. Prejudice is blind. Rich, poor. Black, white. Woman, man. Old, young. Christian, atheist. There will always be someone who says you aren't welcome at the table." Her forearms flexed in between words. "Stop apologizing for who you are and using all your energy to change their minds. Yes, you will lose friends, maybe even family, but you will gain your self-respect. You will know your worth. Once you have that, nothing can stop you."

I wanted to believe her, to be brave and go back to Cassie. But as strong as Alex was, I suspected she was gay and hiding too. She had a two-year-old son without any father I had ever seen. And a woman we only knew as Aunt Cathy joined us on most of our track trips. If someone like Alex couldn't live her life openly, there was no way in hell I could pull it off.

ON THE NEXT VISIT TO my parents in Dallas, I walked across our backyard to All Saints. I kept the screen closed, even though I knew Father Kos would know it was me on the other side. I needed to unburden myself. I needed to start over again, and this was the only way I knew how.

"Bless me, Father, for I have sinned. My last confession was Easter. I lied to my parents. I skipped Mass while I was away at college. I took the Lord's name in vain. I slept with a woman. Had impure thoughts. Cursed." I took a deep breath. "That's it."

"Let's go back to that fourth one."

"I took the Lord's name in vain?"

"Nope. The one after that."

"I slept with a woman."

"That's the one."

Silence. Uncomfortable silence. This room was tiny. It should have a height and weight limit like rides at Disneyland. And it was hot. My eyebrows started to sweat.

Father Kos cleared his throat. "Is this a one-time thing?"

"Yes, Father. I fell in love with her, but I broke it off." Perspiration trickled down my nose. I bowed my head to my folded hands. It was obvious this was way worse than the drinking I'd done in eighth grade. He might condemn me, tell me that I'd done something unforgivable. The wait was excruciating, like being blindfolded while an executioner loaded his rifle.

Father Kos coughed and sighed and said, "Your penance is ten Hail Marys and one Our Father."

"That's it?"

"Please say the Act of Contrition."

Father Kos finished with the prayer of absolution, "I absolve you in the name of the Father, the Son, and the Holy Ghost. Amen. Go and sin no more."

I left the tiny room in a daze. *Had Father Kos gone easy on me because what I had done with Cassie was nothing to be concerned about or was so bad that he had given up on any chance for my rehabilitation?* I settled somewhere in between. I told myself that being with Cassie was a momentary lapse in judgment, and God would forgive me for it. My real penance would be to get used to the idea of being alone. I walked home to my parents' house. My slate was clean, except that I could not unkiss a girl. My body remembered it, even as I tried to forget.

CHAPTER SEVENTEEN

FATHER BILL FILLS THE SCREEN of my television. He stands in front of Sacred Heart with a reporter from Channel 7 News next to him, refusing to answer questions. I sit on the edge of the bed and listen to the anchorman while Biscuit plays with a chew toy at my feet.

"A preschool student at a Catholic school in Boulder will not be allowed to return to school next year because of what is going on at home. The student's parents are two women and the Denver archdiocese says their homosexual relationship violates the school's beliefs and policy."

Immediately, I know it's Reese. The girl with gold French-braided hair running across our yard chasing after Connor on his birthday. She was the only other preschool student besides Connor with two moms. According to the reporter, Father Bill called the school staff together to announce the new policy and told them not to speak to the media about it. Anonymous staff members said they were disgusted by the decision. One employee said she could not believe that a student will have to suffer because of her parents' sexual orientation. The news story, apparently leaked by one of the teachers at Sacred Heart, includes a statement from the archdiocese. "Homosexual couples living together as a couple are in disaccord with Catholic teaching."

For a second, I forget that Connor doesn't attend Sacred Heart anymore. My stomach cramps with nausea. It wasn't Connor who got expelled, but it could have been. Did I cause this? Did my confrontation with Father Bill set these wheels in motion? Even if I couldn't have prevented Reese from getting expelled, I could have at least given her parents a heads-up. Maybe she'll be better off at a new school, but it's awful she's in the middle of this. I picture my parents' old mailbox in Dallas stuffed with letters to me from junior high kids after I'd been kicked out of the FCA.

I text Jill who is at Home Depot with Connor buying caulk, pansies for the yard, and a couple of parts for the refrigerator, which has stopped making crushed ice for us. I would have waited until something major broke before going to the trouble to fix it, or else I'd let it die and then buy a new one. I text Jill: "Father Bill pulled the trigger."

She responds, "Just heard."

"Going for a run now."

"Of course you are. Make it a good one."

I RUN UP THE CANYON beneath the Flatirons with mud clumping in the treads of my shoes, trying with every step to forget about Father Bill and the archbishop. I concentrate on the spring pasqueflowers as they poke their heads through dead grass and pine needles, but the thoughts of Reese and Sacred Heart stick with me just like those clods of mud. I can't shake them off. I push myself harder, turn up my music.

I pass a pile of bear scat on the trail. Mist hovers over it, fresh. I stop and sing a few bars of "Home on the Range" and clap my hands. I remember the overturned trash cans in our driveway. The bears are back, some with new cubs, all of them hungry. I inspect the mud and the patches of snow beneath the trees for paw prints; I see evidence of dogs, but not bears. I run with my headphones off and my iPhone in my hand. I wield it as if I have downloaded some magical bear repellant app that will protect me. The trail narrows down the back side of the hill, dense with bushes and trees and my own unease. A hiker passes me. Her black Lab runs off the leash. No self-respecting bear would stick around for that. If bears were in the area, they'd be long gone by now.

Relieved, I put my headphones back on and crank up the music. After fifty yards, I round a bend in the trail and see the black bottom of a bear cub disappear into the brush. I freeze. Sweat trickles down my cheek. *Where's Mom?*

I've been in bear country long enough to know that the most dangerous thing I can do is get between a mom and her cubs. I whistle random notes, unable to assemble a tune. I listen. *Maybe she was in front of the cub, leading it across the trail. But what if I'm wrong?* The voices of people hiking on a trail parallel to mine carry on the breeze. A dog barks. I feel silly. It's not as if I'm in Alaska. I can almost see my front yard from here. I shiver and wait.

"Yo, bear!" I yell. "Yo, bear!" *Clap. Clap.* The brush gives way, cracking and parting. Mama bear crashes through the junipers following the path of the cub I saw, but not before turning to notice me. We stare at each other until I remember that looking a bear in the eyes is a threat. I lower my gaze to my shoes and watch her out of the corner of my eye. She is beautifully dangerous, massive, with three hundred pounds or so of muscle, loose black rolling fur. "Go on," I whisper. "I'm not here to hurt you or your cub. Nothing to see." She raises her chin. Makes a low chuffing sound. I take a step backward. I will move slowly and give her wide berth to follow her cub.

Something squeaks behind me. I turn my head to see the branches bend without breaking, popping like whips, as a second cub emerges from the woods and stands at my back. I am between them.

Mama bear rises up on her hind legs, stretched out to five feet, making noises like an engine revving. She drops to all fours, digs at the ground with her front paws, sends up dirt as she shakes her massive head at me. I make myself small. I drop to my knees, ready for her to charge me. I tuck my body into a ball and cover the back of my head with my hands.

Fur brushes against my legs. The cub moves around me. He goes to his mother. I wait. When I look up again, they are gone.

I stay on the ground a few more minutes, shaking, but awed by something wild and close. On my way back to the house, I pass several more runners and hikers and tell them about the bear. They choose alternate routes. As scary as the whole thing was, I feel sorry for the people I see, as if I have been granted special powers to walk among bears without getting hurt—as if I am one of them.

Across from where I run, our sweet house stands with its front door and windows open, as if it is breathing in fresh air and enjoying the view. Jill and Connor are back from the store and out in the yard. Jill prunes back the roses and throws out the old growth. Connor follows her. He wears chaps and gun holsters, boots with plastic spurs, handcuffs and a cowboy hat. Though I expect him to be the outlaw, he has been surprising me lately by choosing to be the sheriff. The star-shaped silver badge pinned to his shirt catches the sun, gleams in a burst of light. Something is shifting for all of us—just like the seasons.

I don't tell Jill and Connor about the bear because I'm still processing it, and also it feels like something that is mine alone. In the shower, I think about the bears. Their smell: Like dirt, musty and thick. The cub's fur against the back of my legs: Soft rather than bristly. The smooth surface area of their paws: the sound they made slapping against the ground. The powerful chest of the mama bear: expanding and bending as she churned up the path. This much I know: she would have done whatever it took to protect those cubs, and I would have understood it. I write about bears and mountain lions, and my views have always been clear. We moved into their backyard, into their territory. We have no right to tell them to find someplace else to live or to be anything different from what they are or always have been.

I towel off and go into the closet. I believe things like this happen for a reason—that I'm supposed to learn something from this. *Maybe I'm the mother bear.* I'm living in the only place I've ever considered home, and Father Bill is the outsider, the one threatening my cub. *Is God trying to tell me I'm a bad mother?* I don't think so. I mean, I didn't exactly cower when I met with Father Bill. I spoke up for Connor—not once but twice. I presented my case. And then I protected our son by walking away.

It sounds good to me, altruistic even. I could almost believe it except for the hollow place in my gut where the truth should be. I pull on a pair of jeans, get caught up in them, hop on one leg, and fall over. Somewhere God is laughing. We both know I'm not that brave. It's one thing for me to have a private dispute with Father Bill, and quite another to end up exposed to the world on the morning news. I didn't walk away from Sacred Heart because things would get difficult for Connor or because Jill wanted me to. I did it because I am a lesbian and still seem to choke on the word rather than say it out loud. I did it because it was the easy road to take, even if it doesn't feel that way now.

THE NEXT MORNING I WAKE after a fitful sleep. Jill is already downstairs and she has poured me a cup of coffee. "The news is quite gay this morning," she says. "And I don't mean happy." Still in her white T-shirt and rainbow-trout-printed boxers, she sprawls across the brown leather couch in her office. "Can we please go snowboarding today, just to get away from all of this Father Bill crap?"

"Let me guess, there's a lot about Sacred Heart."

"Yeah, in the local section of the paper, but there's some good stuff too. Mara's in here."

"From my basketball team? I didn't think she was Catholic."

"No, not for that. Here." Jill hands me the national section of the paper. The headline of the Associated Press article reads: "CU-Boulder Alumna Mara Boyd Among Those Arrested at Don't Ask, Don't Tell Protest." In the color photo, Mara stands in her camouflage uniform with five other gay members of the military, each of them handcuffed to the black wrought-iron gate in front of the White House. I read the entire article. Essentially, I learn this:

Mara didn't know she was gay when she entered the military. When she figured it out, she tried to keep it a secret, but found herself having to make up lies. It didn't matter if no one directly asked if she was gay. It was such an undeniable part of her life that the question was implicit in every conversation. Even the simplest questions— "Are you seeing anyone." or "What did you do this weekend?"—had to be answered cryptically. She believed in the Air Force honor code, but how could she live up to it when she was lying all the time? So she told her commanding officer she was a lesbian. They kicked her out of the military. They sent her a bill for her college tuition, which had been paid during her Air Force ROTC. Still, she says she'd reenlist if the law were repealed—that she welcomes the chance to serve her country. The piece ends with a quote from Mara where she says, "We've been talking about 'don't ask, don't tell' for the last seventeen years. It's time for some direct action, for some pressure."

Mara's stand is heroic. But what will it change, except that now she'll have an arrest record? Will her efforts get "don't ask, don't tell" repealed? Probably not. And that's when I realize God is nudging me again. Because every time I think about Sacred Heart, I can't shake the feeling of responsibility—that I should be doing something. But what—chain myself to the altar of Sacred Heart?

JILL AND I DECIDE TO skip organized religion altogether and head to a different kind of church—the mountains. At the slopes, we snowboard while Connor is in ski school. We weave in and out of trees and take jumps like twelve-year-old boys, trying to grab the ends of our boards and whooping at each other's attempts. We kiss in the snow, disguised by helmets, goggles, and scarves. We take time for lunch off to the side of a run the locals call Chapel Glades where we share a PB&J sandwich beneath a wooden sign reading: SUNDAY WORSHIP HERE 1PM. When we get going again, the powder spreads beneath my board like cake icing, and a sky the kind of blue I've only seen in Colorado reflects onto the snow. By 3 P.M., Jill is whipped. She stays at the lodge while I take a few more runs.

I am coming down a green trail when I see Connor's class. He makes turns using his whole body, the way children do, like little robots fused from the neck and shoulders down to the wedge of their skis. He holds his arms out in front of him like Frankenstein. He sees me and smiles with pride, the upward curve of his mouth visible in the two-inch space between his neck gaiter and jacket and goggles. I am so in love with this kid.

Once he sees me, he doesn't want to keep skiing with his class. So I take him with me up the mountain. I have never skied with him before because he has always been in lessons and has only recently graduated to the chair lift. We ride up. He points to rabbit prints in the snow and tells me that the Easter bunny made them. As we near the unloading zone, I wave to the lift operator and point to my son. He slows the chair. I help Connor slide off, and it's me who almost falls.

I follow Connor down a green run, yelling at him to turn when he picks up too much speed and acting like a defensive lineman trying to protect him from other skiers. There is a short blue run ahead of us and Connor stands at the edge of it. It is steep, in a gully, and full of moguls. But he wants to do it. He slides his skis down the hill, turning around some of the bumps and bobbing over the crests of the others. He starts to go too fast, and I tell him to slow down. He doesn't. He teeters on one ski and the other rises straight up in front of him in the air. Arms and legs go in four different directions and his face plows through the snow until he is still. My throat closes and I am at his side in seconds filing through all the first-aid things I've ever learned. He moves, and his little red, raw lips move in a shudder. I wipe the snow from his goggles, fetch his skis, and ask him if he is hurt. He says, "Let's just go, Mama." I think that he means that we should go home, but I follow him to the lift line where he says, "I want to go again. But I don't want to do the gully." I tell him okay.

Thirty minutes later when Connor and I get to the same spot on the hill, he stops at the edge again. I look at him and say, "I thought you didn't want to do this run." His dark brown eyes peer from behind the plastic lenses, a few wild strands of hair from under his helmet pointing to the ground like arrows. "Just because it was hard and scary doesn't mean it wasn't worth it." So we go down again, and this time he makes it.

ON OUR WAY HOME FROM spring skiing, we pass Sacred Heart and Jill slows the car. A crowd of parents, along with their children, Connor's former classmates, hold signs and march in the rain in front of the church. A woman hands out coffee and doughnuts to the protesters huddled in the cold drizzle. A little girl holds a rainbow umbrella. Her father's sign reads: WHAT WOULD JESUS DO? An elderly woman and man stretch a banner between them: BRING ALL THE CHILDREN TO ME AND DO NOT FORBID THEM—JESUS.

An NBC affiliate and a CNN-marked news truck idle in front of Sacred Heart. Reporters interview the parents. Jill turns the corner until our car is out of sight. We park for a minute.

"I didn't expect that," I say. I wipe the fog off the inside of the passenger window.

"I didn't see Reese's moms. The newspaper said the family doesn't want to be identified, but that they plan on making an anonymous statement of some sort."

"I can't blame them. I think it's the kind of battle where even if you're right, you're still going to get hurt by putting yourself out there."

The rest of the drive home, I think about the bears, Mara, and my son's bravery on the slopes. I was supposed to be at that protest, even if I might have ended up on CNN. I thought that all the controversy would go away, but it's only getting bigger. I know that it's time for me to step up—to be brave. But before I do, I want to reach out to Father Bill one last time.

At the house, I scan the Internet looking for everything Father Bill has said or written about the new policy in the last seventy-two hours. I want to make sure I am fully informed of his position if I am going to challenge him. I start with the Sacred Heart of Jesus Web site and stumble upon a short bio.

Father Bill Breslin was born and raised in Red Bank, New Jersey, the 4th of 4 sons. He was educated in the parish Catholic grammar school and high school. His mother died when he was 13 and his father finished raising him and his next older brother alone. The principal at his Catholic school took an interest in him, and Bill started to work as a janitor at the school in order to spend more time there.

I read it twice. Now I know why he gave me such a funny look when I said the word "orphan" in our first meeting. Maybe the fact that Connor had been abandoned gave him pause, softened him. The Church raised Father Bill, just as it did my own mother. But at the end of the day, it couldn't hug Father Bill after a nightmare or brush the tangles from my mom's hair until it ran like silk. *How could they give to others what they never had themselves?* It's not an excuse, but it's worth considering. *What becomes of our motherless children?*

I leave his bio and find his blog. My empathy evaporates. Father Breslin says, "It is not about punishing the child for the sins of his or her parents. It is simply that the lesbian couple is saying that their relationship is a good one that should be accepted by everyone, and the Church cannot agree to that. People who are divorced do not say divorce is good. There are no pro-divorce parades. Divorce is a tragedy for everybody. So there's no comparing other issues to the issue of gay marriage." He goes on to say: "We need to fight for our Catholic values because here in Boulder, it seems no one else is."

I continue my online research until I find an article saying that Denver's Archbishop Charles Chaput supported Father Bill Breslin on the new policy, reiterating that the archdiocese of Denver's admission policy states that "Parents living in open discord with Catholic teaching in areas of faith and morals unfortunately choose by their actions to disqualify their children from enrollment." My ears heat up at the tips. *They accept atheists into their schools. How can an atheist be supporting the Catholic mission?*

I DO NOT WAIT TO calm down. I am livid, and I act. I send Father Bill my version of a furiously angry email.

Father Bill,
    You run a private school. So you can teach whatever you want and decide who can attend. I agree with that. And I can

decide that I don't want my child taught those things and can send him elsewhere. But as a Catholic, I find tremendous hypocrisy in the way you've conveniently defined who is following the teachings of the Catholic Church and who is not. You've explained away divorce as a one-time deal, and not a continual lifestyle choice. Fine. Let's use another argument. Are you willing to turn away the kids at Sacred Heart of Jesus School whose parents practice birth control? What about those who do not regularly attend Mass? Or are in the middle of fertility treatments? Are you willing to turn away those families? I await your reply.

Father Bill's response is quick, and it is also a brush-off. Within an hour, he sends me this:

Dear Michelle,

Thank you for taking the time to write. I don't want to simply jot off an answer to you that isn't as thoughtful as your question. So, please give me time on a less busy day to get back to you. And will you remind me if a week goes by and you haven't heard from me? Thanks, Michelle. God bless you always.

My next emails aren't emails at all, but letters to the editors of the *Boulder Weekly* and *Daily Camera* newspapers. My fingers fly over the keys. I tell them that I am an insider at Sacred Heart and that Father Bill baptized our son in secret. I mention the admissions director and her promise that Connor would not be penalized in any way because of who his parents were. I lay it all out on the table. In the space where my name is required, I put: Withheld. But I enter my email and phone number for them to use for verification. Thirty minutes later, my cell phone rings.

The man on the other end of the line tells me his name is Jefferson Dodge. He's a reporter at the *Boulder Weekly*. He's been following the Sacred Heart story carefully and, rather than print my letter, he'd like to interview me for an article he's working on that will appear in the next edition. "I would need to quote you, though. You couldn't remain anonymous."

I hold the cell phone to my ear and a paper towel to my thumb, which bleeds onto the papers on my desk because I've been gnawing on it for the last hour without realizing it. This is just a local paper. I need to do the right thing. I am smart enough to know that I will never win Father Bill's approval or the Catholic Church's, even though I still feel Catholic. If I move forward with this, I'm betraying the Catholic Church—my church, my mom's church. If I don't, I'm betraying myself. I press the edge of my thumb to my lips. The reporter is waiting for my answer. I start talking.

CHAPTER EIGHTEEN

WE WERE NOT IN CHURCH, but my mother whispered the rosary from her chair in the corner of the hospital room. The divider was open a few inches so my father, mother, and I could watch my sister's first child, my niece, come into the world. My sister, Kathy, screamed from behind the accordion-folded plastic door, her contractions coming in regular waves. The nurses hurried around her. Eric fed her ice chips. As Kathy wailed and strained, in more pain than I had ever seen her, I wanted to cheer and throw up all at the same time. Though I rarely saw my sister unless I was the one making the effort, I was glad I lived in the same city with her so I could be here for this. Eric wiped Kathy's brow and tried to make her laugh, his face a mixture of worry and wonder. Everything fell away except the present moment.

For one of the few times in the last four years, I was still too, paying attention, without anywhere else I had to be. After I graduated from Tech, I landed a position as marketing manager for Kaepa athletic shoes in San Marcos, where my sister had married Eric and bought a house across town. My parents still lived in Dallas, hours away from me. But, it didn't matter how close or far I was from anyone or anything, because I was never around. I took a job where I traveled 80 percent of the time, trying to get college and high school volleyball teams to wear our product. As long as I kept moving, I didn't have time to fall in love or be lonely. But watching Kathy and Eric, my decision felt hollow. I was devoting my life to a career that didn't change the world or make a difference: I sold shoes. I had three hundred thousand frequent-flier miles but no one to ask on vacation with me, so I never used them. For the previous four years, the only serious relationship I had was with my box of Kaepa shoe samples. A body in motion stayed in motion, until something forced it to stop. When my sister went into labor, I canceled my trips and cleared my schedule. I raced across town with a teddy bear in the passenger seat.

Hours passed in our sequestered section of my sister's room, and my mom put down her rosary beads and took out a deck of cards. We played gin and blackjack and hearts. My dad brought us food. When it was time for Kathy to start pushing, we stood behind the divider like teammates watching from the sidelines.

A monitor began to beep like a smoke detector and we heard a nurse explain to my sister that the fetal heart rate had slowed. It became clear that my sister wasn't making the kind of progress the doctor had hoped. He turned to Eric and said, "We're going to speed things up a bit." The nurse handed him a pair of forceps. Mom grabbed my hand and my father held her other. In a human chain, we panted and prayed and held on.

Eric took turns running to the foot of the bed and to Kathy's side with status reports until he said, "I can see her head." Kathy scrunched her face and grimaced and bore down. My mom gripped my hand, and my pulse beat into my fingertips. A few seconds later, the little squirming red-faced miracle, my niece Madison, came into the world. The doctor placed her into Eric's arms.

· · ·

THAT NIGHT, I CAME HOME to my rental house exhausted. I opened the refrigerator. No beer. Expired milk and withered broccoli spears mocked me. Since I'd canceled my trips, I had no place to go, which forced me to keep company with my own thoughts. Seeing my niece born shifted something inside me. It slowed time down to a single breath instead of the treadmill I'd been running on. Now that I'd stopped, I saw that my days were stacking up like unread newspapers on my porch. I didn't know when it had happened, but I was definitely living someone else's life.

I flopped onto the couch. I had been more than happy to let Kathy give my parents the fairy-tale wedding because it took the pressure off me to do it. My parents liked to say that I was married to my job and, in a way, I was. The job kept me company. It kept me from empty moments like this.

Finding a partner wasn't an option for me, because being gay meant more than just the bullying and ridicule I'd been subjected to in high school and college. If I settled for being gay, I'd never have kids or dance with my father at my wedding, or have many other milestones in my life celebrated. It meant hiding my whole life and worrying about getting fired for who I loved. That wasn't living. But this wasn't either. After seeing my sister and Eric and their new baby, I didn't want to be alone anymore. *But what other option did I have?*

Unless—a thought rocked me back on my heels—*what if I wasn't gay? After all, what real shot had I given heterosexuality? Maybe if I could somehow get closure on what happened with Holly's dad, on being sexually abused, my feelings toward men would change. There were books on this sort of thing, right? Workshops or support groups I could join?* If I could pile up all my secrets and shame, maybe I'd finally be able to stand on top of them. I would get some therapy, confront Dale Crandall, find out what had happened to Holly. I'd have sex with a man I trusted. That was my plan, and I believed in it.

TWO DAYS LATER, I CREPT into a Barnes & Noble. I wore Ray-Bans and pulled the hood of my Texas Tech sweatshirt over most of my face. I felt like a shoplifter. Because I generally avoided human contact, I decided that I would buy a book and deal with my sexual abuse issues in the privacy of my own home. I hurried to the self-help aisle, looking every bit like I was in need of it. I didn't linger. I grabbed the biggest book I saw dealing with abuse, entitled *The Courage to Heal: A Guide for Women Survivors of Child Sexual Abuse*. It had a workbook to accompany it. *I graduated from college summa cum laude. If the authors can't cure me in 608 pages, I'm beyond hope.*

When I got home, I tossed the book onto the coffee table, poured myself some Wild Turkey, and settled into the couch to read. The book told me to write a letter to my child self, to tell my story and identify the reasons I never told my parents or other people who might have helped me. My mouth felt dry and gritty. I read all of chapter one and drank half the bottle of whiskey before I admitted that this wasn't something I could face alone. There was no syllabus for this—I couldn't "learn" my way out of it.

After scouring the Yellow Pages, I found a support group for survivors of childhood sexual abuse and started going to meetings weekly. In group, about ten women sat in a circle with a therapist asking questions and directing the conversation. She asked us to share some of the specific ways being abused manifested itself in our daily lives. I crossed my arms in front of my chest and told her that I flinched if someone put a hand on my shoulder. I never sat with my back to a door. If a man whispered, even in a commercial, I saw the weathered lines of Mr. Crandall's face. A man adjusting the belt of his pants shot panic through me like a bullet. Left alone with men in a business meeting or warehouse full of shoes, I had to grip the edge of a shelf or stair rail to keep myself from running. Many of the women there had some of the same stories.

In the weeks that followed we delved in deeper. I was shocked when one of the women brought up rape fantasies, admitting that it was the only way she could climax with her husband. She started crying and asked the therapist, "Does it mean I wanted to be abused?" Our therapist's answer was simple and profound: "Not at all. In fact, it's the opposite. Many women who've been sexually assaulted are aroused by thoughts of having sex against their will. It's because you can't give yourself permission to agree with an act that was connected to shame and violence, or heaven forbid, allow yourself to enjoy it. You can't be complicit without feeling guilty for it." I was relieved to know that there was something normal about the feelings I'd experienced, a rational explanation, even though I hadn't had sex in so long I hadn't even thought about it. I wasn't defective or broken. I was safe among a group of brave women who provided support to one another.

Our therapist posed the question about whether or not we had told our parents, our family of origin, about the abuse as children. When it was my turn, I said that my parents didn't know—that I hadn't wanted to tell my mother.

"Why do you think you keep things from your mother? What would happen if you told her the truth?" our leader asked me.

"Ha!" I blurted out. She smiled and waited. She wanted a real answer. "I guess it's because she can't take it. Everything is a big deal. She's unpredictable and unstable. She'd likely tell me the whole thing was my fault. She'd take to her bed for a week or be unable to stop crying or end up being hospitalized." I rubbed the tops of my legs. "She falls apart."

"How do the other members of your family deal with her?"

"We tiptoe around her. My dad's like Silly Putty. He becomes whatever she needs him to be."

My therapist looked at her watch. "We're out of time for today."

As I stood to leave, our therapist stopped me. She said, "Michelle, there's one thing I'd like you to think about before next week." The other women shuffled by us, straightening their clothing and pulling themselves together after the hard work of healing. I faced our therapist and she asked, "You said your mom's moods dictate how everyone in the family acts and reacts, am I right? And yet you say she's fragile, and you have all spent your energy trying to protect her from anything upsetting."

I nodded.

She held the door for me to walk through it and said, "I guess maybe I'm missing something. She sounds pretty powerful to me."

Over the next six months, I dedicated myself to my recovery. I attended group. I completed the *Courage to Heal* book and workbook. I sang at a "Moving to End Sexual Assault" rally in downtown San Marcos, and in a courageous move that surprised myself, I invited my coworkers, including a man I'd grown close to—our photographer, Ray—to attend. I checked off "recover from sexual assault" on my list of things I needed to do to assess my heterosexuality. Then I drove to see Dale Crandall.

AFTER HALF A DAY'S drive through the state of Texas, I crossed the six lanes of traffic at the intersection along the East Tex Freeway in Meeker. Strip malls, gun shops, and water towers painted in Bobcat purple and white welcomed me back to town. I passed the old Rexall drugstore, which used to serve root-beer floats and now had boards for windows. I turned into my old neighborhood with a dull thrumming inside my chest. The dense forest of pine that had provided a haven for my childhood no longer existed. Instead, a Hampton Inn, a McDonald's, and a parking lot claimed the playground of trees. *They should have razed the houses instead.*

I idled my candy apple red Eagle Talon in front of our old house, the same beige two-story with the same brown slatted shutters. I pictured Mittens coming out to greet me. She had finally died a year ago in Dallas at my parents' house at the age of twenty. It took me months to get over it. She did those dog tricks because she loved me, but I shouldn't have asked her to in the first place. I hoped in her final years, she had gotten to be a cat.

I parked the car along the curve just behind our mailbox and stared out my window across the street. There, picking up a wrench in the open mouth of his garage, was Mr. Crandall. The sight of him stole my breath. I hadn't thought this through. I couldn't possibly open the door and step out of this car. I inhaled and tried to hold it, but the panic came on with the force of a Texas storm. I bent my head forward, rested it on the steering wheel, tried to stop rasping. *God, please help me. I can't leave here without doing this.* I cranked up the air-conditioning, let the cold air push into my throat and lungs. I was an adult now, a grown woman. He couldn't hurt me anymore, especially in broad daylight. But as I opened the door and strode across the asphalt, I was eleven years old again.

He saw me before I reached the edge of his driveway, his stony face searching my own for recognition. *Don't run. Just get information, maybe Holly's phone number or something, anything. If you can't confront him, at least don't leave here empty-handed.* When he stood within four feet of me, he wiped the back of his neck with his hand.

"Well, I'll be damned," he said. "I don't believe it. How are you doing?" Before I could stop him, he leaned in and gave me a half hug. I still hadn't spoken. I couldn't find my voice. He took the opportunity to look me over, pausing his gaze at my legs and crotch and breasts before saying, "You sure do look good. All—grown—up." I pulled my oversize gray sweatshirt down past my hips and folded my arms across my chest. If I could have moved, I might have walked away or thrown up or punched him. But I was paralyzed, waiting for something to break this spell. Then he said, "You're not as mean-looking anymore."

"What?" I cocked my head at him and narrowed my eyes.

"You were a mean little brat, just mean." He inhaled and his nostrils flared like barrels of a shotgun.

"I was just a kid. You were an adult. What did I do, kick you in the shins or something?" *Don't cry. You are not eleven.*

"I guess not." He rubbed his hand across the strip of sun-bleached gray still left on top of his head. "So Holly's all grown up too. Got married, but it didn't work out. She came back here for a spell to get back on her feet after that. I'll give you her number before you leave. She's out in Arizona, but I'm sure she'd like to hear from you. Danny's got a little baby girl. She visits all the time. Beautiful little girl." His grin showed tobacco stained teeth, tiny and crooked, a rusted saw blade. I needed to leave. I couldn't stand there one more second.

He wrote down Holly's number and address and touched my fingertips as he passed the piece of paper to me. As I walked away I heard him say, "Yep, you really do look good."

Out on the East Tex Freeway, I drove without stopping, peeling off the layers of clothes he had touched, using cruise control and swerving. I changed lanes with one hand and punched the steering wheel and dashboard with the other until my knuckles swelled up and blended into one another. The second I was in my hotel room, I opened the phone book and found the number for the child abuse hot line—1-800-4-A-CHILD. I explained my situation. "I want to have him arrested," I told the woman on the other end. My fingers trembled against the receiver. She rustled papers and seemed to be taking notes. "Okay, honey. How old are you and when did the sexual assault occur?" I answered, "I'm twenty-five. It happened when I was eleven." The silence on the other end spoke for her. "I'm too late, aren't I?" I asked.

"There's a ten-year statute of limitations in Texas," she said. "Unless you have a current victim ready to come forward, I'm afraid there's nothing anyone can do."

He was still a pedophile. I just couldn't prove it. He talked about his granddaughter—how beautiful she was, that she visited all the time. *How could I know such a thing and not intervene in some way?* Holly could have stepped in, but she hadn't. In fact, she ran straight toward her dad when her marriage failed. She wouldn't turn on her parents. They were awful people, but they were all she had. I looked at Holly's number, and I threw it away. But I wasn't done yet. I hadn't saved Holly, but I could save this little girl.

I took out a pen. I wrote an anonymous letter and addressed it to Danny's wife.

"This is a very difficult letter for me to write," I began, "but I realize I can't live with myself if I don't speak out. If I were a mother, I would want to know if my children were in any kind of danger so I could protect them . . ."

It took me four pages, but I told her everything that had happened to me, and that I believed Dale Crandall was still a predator. Her daughter was in danger. I asked her to protect her child. I told her she would never hear from me again.

On my next business trip, I mailed Danny's wife my letter from Atlanta so it couldn't be traced back to me or anywhere I had ever lived. When that letter hit the bottom of the mailbox and I closed the lid, I felt, finally, free.

• • •

AFTER THERAPY AND CONFRONTING Dale Crandall, I felt ready to go to the final step of my plan to fully test out my heterosexuality—but first, I had to find an accomplice.

Ray worked with me at Kaepa and I traveled with him often to photo shoots at college campuses. After a few years of relacing pair after pair of Kaepas, we had grown close. Six-packs of beer led to intense discussions about everything from God to girlfriends. In his darkroom, surrounded by chemicals, our faces glowed in the red light, and he told me about his father's explosive temper, the nights he'd upend the table in the middle of dinner in a rage. In turn, I told him about my relationship with Cassie, about Mr. Crandall, and the sexual abuse I'd suffered as a kid. I told him the things I'd learned in therapy. Ray was a kind man, with a golden retriever, who loved a good cigar and hiking in the mountains of New Mexico. The few times I had seen him angry, his voice shook like it was scared of itself. I spent more time with him than with anyone else I knew, and considered him my closest friend. One night, we worked late at a rented studio. I hauled blocks of dry ice and chipped away sharp pieces to create billowing smoke behind some rather average pairs of athletic shoes. Ray complained that he needed a real vacation. I watched his hands set the aperture and shutter speed of his camera. His movements were attentive and precise. I invited him to Vegas using my frequent-flier miles, and he said yes. He seemed the most logical choice for my experiment in Vegas.

Ray met me in the lobby of Caesars Palace. He wore a pressed short-sleeved cotton button-down with khakis and loafers, and wheeled his monogrammed luggage behind him. His whole face smiled when he spotted me. A cocktail waitress passed us wearing nothing more than half of a bedsheet, wrapped and secured with a gold belt. Her cleavage reached out to offer us a drink before the rest of her did. Ray locked his eyes on hers, a gesture that impressed me, because even I looked at the woman's breasts. "Did you know there are seven different kinds of togas?" he asked her. The waitress shook her head and walked away. Ray's face bloomed red like a tulip. We ditched his luggage in the room and moved through a haze of smoke to the craps table. I pressed the six and eight, placed the nine and five, and covered the hard ways. Ray stayed conservative. Moments before, he had mirrored my bets, eager to learn the game from me. But once he knew what he was doing, he shifted his strategy. He was either smart or lucky or maybe both, but he seemed to sense when the shooter was about to crap out, and he pulled his bets off the table. I let mine ride.

The stickman pushed the dice across the felt toward me, and I doubled my pass line bet. The dealer yelled, "Coming out!" I rolled craps out of the gate and watched the dealer to my left sweep away my chips. When it was Ray's turn, he picked up the dice and shook them in both hands. The boxman warned him to use one. "Wow. Okay. Sorry," he said, truly apologetic. He threw the dice with one hand and they ambled toward the back wall without touching it. "Hit the end of the table, shooter," the boxman said. Ray nodded and leaned over to me. "Did you know dice were first used in Asia over five thousand years ago?" I did not. The stickman waited for him to pick up the dice. I nudged Ray. Ray made his point. "Pay the line!" I clapped Ray on the back and let my winnings ride on the pass line. His next roll flew off the table. The stickman collected the dice, examined them, and then allowed Ray to select from the six cubes he offered. He threw them in an arcing lob and they bounced to a stop. "Three craps." Damn. The dealer took my bet, then paid Ray. Ray had bet against himself, and won.

I allotted myself one thousand dollars of gambling money. I never figured I'd spend it, especially when I only cleared around $25,000 a year at my job. Ray and I circled the tables on the casino floor. We played craps, blackjack, slots. I lost and kept losing. The further behind I got, the more long shots I took, bets of desperation.

Then I found the machine. A woman smoking a cigarette and trailing an oxygen tank behind her played a slot that paid out almost every time she pulled the handle. I waited for her to leave, certain her machine was primed to hit the big jackpot. A Porsche 911 rotated over the bank of machines. I sat down on the stool, held my bucket of quarters, fed the coins one by one. Ray wandered close by. Within thirty minutes I held an empty plastic container in my hands. Ray asked if he could try the machine. He inserted three quarters, hit three red sevens, and won three hundred dollars. He filled my empty bucket with handfuls of coins, apologizing profusely.

Drunk and teetering, I followed Ray around to watch him win over and over again, until I'd had enough. I dragged him down the Vegas Strip to Circus Circus and then to the Midway. I spent my last twenty dollars trying to win a stuffed animal. "It's the principle of the thing," I said. "I refuse to leave here with nothing." When the carnie handed me a small teddy bear with blue matted fur, I turned to Ray. "This bear," I looked at the tag on the toy, "made in China for probably fifty cents, just cost me one thousand dollars." He put his arm on my shoulder and I held on to his hand. As tired as I was of losing, I was determined to lose one more thing in Vegas.

Back at Caesars, I pulled Ray through a maze of carved Greek gods, statues of debauched deities: Bacchus, Venus, Neptune, and Apollo. I explained my intentions. I needed to find out for sure if I was gay. He was my friend. He had a penis. He could help me. Standing next to Greek gods in a casino that made night look like day, Ray swayed.

"I think you're drunk," he said. "I know I am. It's probably not a good idea."

"It's kind of the only way it's going to happen," I said.

"But what about our friendship? This could really screw things up."

"You're just helping me, that's all. That's what friends do, right?"

When we got to the room, I took Ray by the shoulders and brought him toward me. We kissed. I undressed myself. He slipped out of his clothes. We dove into the sheets to cover ourselves. Ray was a sweet, passive man—a clean-cut, smart Forrest Gump. He spoke in an articulate and measured, pocket-protector sort of way. I had never pictured him without pants, and never really wanted to.

"I've thought about this," he said. "About what you'd look like naked."

I put my fingertips against his lips to stop words from coming out. *Let's just do this*, I thought. *Before I change my mind.* "Do you have protection?" I asked.

He strode across the room, tore the edge of a square packet, and rolled on a condom. Back in the bed, Ray warmed up his hands like a thoughtful gynecologist. He got on top of me, his lips in a straight, serious line. "You might feel this," he told me. "I'm putting it in now." *Good God, stop explaining. It's not a speculum.* "Now just relax and let me do all the work." *You've got to be kidding me.* "I'm on the small side, so if you do this again with someone else, you might want to be careful." *Oh, my, God. Shut up, please.*

With Ray on top of me moving in robotic rhythm, I realized what a mistake I'd made. A person could have sex with anything or anyone and their body could respond to the act. Penetration felt good. But that didn't mean I wanted a man. I stared at a stain on the ceiling and children squealed down the hall past our door. "Almost there?" Ray asked. I willed myself to have an orgasm, and he followed suit, in a reserved fashion, as if he were trying not to disturb me with any unnecessary grunting or contorted facial expressions. When it was all over, I dragged a sheet off the bed to cover myself and went to the bathroom and closed the door. I heard his footsteps outside. "Everything okay in there?"

"Yep."

"Well? What did you think?"

I opened the door, the sheet like a toga around me. His face looked expectant. Hopeful. I had to give him bonus points for being the only man on earth who would admit to a woman during intercourse that he had a tiny penis. I leaned over and kissed him on the cheek. "You are a very sweet man. A good man," I said. "And that was just"—I tried to find the right word—"lovely. Really. Any woman would be lucky to have you."

"But . . ." He leaned against the door frame.

"I'm gay."

He nodded. "I don't blame you. I like sleeping with girls too."

OVER THE COURSE OF THE next six months, I slept with two more guys—handsome, muscular, sexy men with normal-size penises—just to be absolutely sure. The results of my experiments were all the same. I knew that I was gay, and also that I didn't want to be. I understood why people decided to cash in their chips—just end it. In a last-ditch effort to find meaning in my life, I decided to volunteer at Big Brothers, Big Sisters. I researched enough to know that it wasn't a Christian organization per se, and I liked the idea of working with kids.

I filled out the forms to be a "Big" and after three weeks, took the "personality and psychological profile" assessment test. Specific questions asked things like: "Are you more attracted to people of the same sex or opposite sex?" "Have you ever had romantic feelings for someone of the same sex?" "Do you fantasize about sex with someone of the same gender?" When I asked them why these questions were on the form, I was told that it wasn't a judgment on morality. They were screening for pedophiles and felt that homosexuals posed a greater risk for that than the rest of the population. On top of all the other reasons I couldn't allow myself to be gay, this was the final straw. It was one thing for people to think I was going to hell and quite another for someone to think I might hurt a child—especially when it had become clear to me, I wasn't a danger to anyone but myself.

THERE WERE THINGS ABOUT LIFE I would miss. Trips I hadn't taken to other parts of the world, getting a dog, watching a sunrise. But I had more reasons to go than to stay. God had made a mistake. I could only hope He'd forgive me for fixing it for both of us.

CHAPTER NINETEEN

I GET THE MAIL. There's an envelope for Connor with handwriting I don't recognize. It looks like a kid's party invitation, but there's no stamp, so someone must have dropped it by. I also find the newest edition of the paper—the one with my interview in it. I set the mail on the counter in the kitchen and sit down on a bar stool to start reading:

The lesbian couple whose child was recently denied reenrollment at the Sacred Heart of Jesus School in Boulder is apparently not the first lesbian couple that had a child enrolled at the Catholic school.

But it may be the last. Boulder resident Michelle Theall told *Boulder Weekly* that she and her partner had their son enrolled in preschool there until late last summer, when they withdrew the child after the church arranged a "closet baptism."

Theall says the refusal to admit the children of a homosexual couple is a recent policy change, because church and school officials previously had no problem with it.

According to Theall, before enrolling her son at Sacred Heart, she asked school officials whether a child having "two mommies" would be a problem. They said no.

And when she and her partner decided to have their child baptized, they asked the same question of the person running the baptism classes. That person checked on it, she says, and came back with the same reply.

But last July, as the date of the baptism approached, and after Theall's Catholic parents and sister from out of state had already made plans to attend the baptism, Theall says she was contacted by Bill Breslin, pastor at Sacred Heart, who wanted to speak with her in person about his concerns about the baptism.

Theall says she and her partner wanted to get their son baptized at Sacred Heart, primarily for the sake of her parents, who have been understanding about their daughter's sexual orientation despite being devout Catholics. "It's what I can give to them," she says of her parents. "They've come a long way in accepting us, with this grandchild."

But since the events of last summer, Theall says she no longer considers herself Catholic. She and her partner now attend another church in Boulder, and their son is at a different school. Still, Theall says she appreciates Breslin being upfront about his concerns, and that the school itself is great. "The teachers there were wonderful," she says. "I just can't stand the hypocrisy. Don't say this is for those who are in 'open discord' with the Catholic Church, because guess what? You're going to lose your whole enrollment."

Theall says she decided to speak out because she is tired of the dishonesty.

"People have a right to believe what they want to believe, but they don't have a right to hurt my child," she says. "Stop the lying about it."

The article is fairly accurate. It recounts my conversations with Father Bill and even publishes some of our emails back and forth.

But as soon as I see the quote about not being Catholic anymore, I regret it. It doesn't resonate with me. I still feel Catholic. I was baptized Catholic. Just because I go to another church doesn't make me any less Catholic. I don't know what it will take to make me feel otherwise.

I let Jill read it. "Wow," she says. "Good thing your mom doesn't live in Boulder."

"It's just a little article. I doubt anyone I know will even see it."

THE PHONE STARTS RINGING and it doesn't stop for most of the day. I pace the house until Jill tells me I should go for a drive. I'm in my car for two minutes with the top down when my phone vibrates and I see my mom's number.

"Your father is about to have a heart attack," my mom says on the other end of the line. *God, did she see it? There's no way she saw it.* I zip through downtown Boulder in my Mini Cooper convertible with the top down, hunting for a parking space.

"Jesus, Mary, and Joseph," my mother says. "Your father's email got hacked into, and it sent messages to everyone he knows saying he's been mugged in France and needs money wired to him in order to get home. Don't send him any when you get it. He's not in France. He's right here."

"Wow, so sorry," I say, relieved that my parents are victims of computer hackers instead of me. "I've seen that email before. It's a fairly common hoax."

"He's about to throw his computer out the window. He's called those Geek Squad people to see if they can restore all his contacts. It's just mean spirited, that's all. We're old. We don't need this kind of nonsense." She pauses. "What do they even get out of it? There's no place listed to send the money."

"I honestly don't know."

"Hey, I just want to make sure you're bringing a dress to the reunion. Maybe a little jacket too because the hotel gets cold. We'll grab you from the airport and then start the drive down to Louisiana. Your father is so excited about this, you'd think he's giving the inaugural address instead of the history of the Theall clan. He has an entire presentation. Thank God it didn't get messed up by those hijackers."

"Hackers," I correct her. "Tell him I can't wait to hear it." I round the corner and almost run over a police barricade. "God hates fags!" someone yells, and I cup my hand around the phone and start fumbling for the button to raise the top on my convertible.

"What's that, sweetie?"

"I said, 'I need gas.' I'll call you later. Love you."

A police officer motions for me to move my car, so I back up and park along the curb. A helicopter thumps overhead like a heartbeat. When a SWAT team jumps out of an armored truck with their riot gear—shields, gas masks, and guns—I realize I have entered some kind of war zone.

A woman sings: "God bless America, the pervert home." She is red-faced with anger and dragging a child Connor's age behind her. His sign reads: GOD HATES FAG ENABLERS. A man approaches my window and yells, "Dyke lover! Die!" I flinch inside my car, his words flung at me like spit. I know these protesters are from Westboro Baptist Church. I've seen them on television, usually picketing at the funerals of American soldiers. Now they walk down our streets.

What does it say when a notorious hate group agrees with Sacred Heart's policy? I sit and watch them for a moment, terrified because I used my name in the interview that came out today. I think about those boys who used to run by my house screaming, "Michelle Theall has a dick." They are the kind of people who would be happy Matthew Shepard was left to die tied to a fence post in Wyoming.

A stabbing sensation pricks at my fingertips and toes, making my arms and legs jump as a reflex. It feels like someone is jabbing me with sewing needles. I remind myself that even if they know my name, they do not know what I look like. An officer motions to me and removes a barricade so I can inch through, back up, and turn around to go in the other direction.

I drive to a favorite coffee shop of mine, the Laughing Goat, and order a soy mocha. The barista works on my order and I wait by the back wall next to Styrofoam cup sculptures flattened and framed and selling for $200. My cell phone rings with the number of an editor I know named Geoff, who works at a magazine in Denver called 5280. I pick up because I want to tell someone about the craziness that's been unleashed here.

When I describe the protest I just drove through he says, "I know. I just saw coverage of it on the news. It must be absolutely nuts over there. And I saw the interview you gave to the *Boulder Weekly*."

I nod and know he can't hear it.

"I've been thinking a lot about what's been going on and I wondered if you would be willing to tell your story. Not an interview and not just about this incident. But the story of growing up gay and Catholic and the challenges associated with that."

"I—um." The espresso machine exhales a blast of steam.

"You could really speak to a lot of people in a very personal way. You might even save some kids from giving up."

The barista yells, "Order up!" I pick up my drink and drop it as my hands touch the paper cup. I expect my palms to be blistered from the unbearable scalding heat of the coffee. It's not the barista's fault. The coffee was the right temperature, but my sensory problems have been growing. My MS is acting up like an angry child. I kneel on the ground with napkins and sop up the puddles. The man next to me in line bends to the floor and takes my empty, sticky cup to the trash.

I pick up my phone, which I have left on the counter. "Geoff?" He's no longer there. The barista offers me a new soy mocha, and I thank him.

On my way back to the house, I take a route that I hope will avoid Westboro. But the protest has spilled out onto the streets and I get stuck again. As the crowds build around my car, I try to make myself small. But then I notice that most of the people around me are counterprotesters. They wear tie-dyed T-shirts and hold peace signs, and they are predominantly high school and middle school students. A boy in a green hoodie and a baseball cap holds a sign saying: GOD ACCEPTS YOU. Next to him, a girl who looks like she might be this year's homecoming queen, shouts, "Spread the love!"

The student presence grows until I cannot move my car. The kids sing and put their arms around one another. They ignore a protester yelling at them, "You are going to hell, Boulder," and another screaming, "You hate God." I notice that the SWAT team that I thought was assembled to protect Boulder citizens from Westboro is actually escorting Westboro through the crowds to ensure their safety in a town where they are not welcome.

Before the protest dies down, almost 1,800 kids march. They live in a post-Columbine world with an African-American president in a country where hate took down the World Trade Center. They believe in a future of inclusion and they are willing to stand up for it. They aren't afraid, and I feel like I will be less afraid because I have them on my side. I honk in solidarity. Kids pump their fists in the air, and I give them the peace sign and a thumbs-up.

I pick up the phone, and I call Geoff at *5280 Magazine*. I tell him I am considering the article, but I need to do one thing first.

CHAPTER TWENTY

THE DALLAS/FORT WORTH AIRPORT HUMMED with people oblivious to the fact that the woman running past them in the terminal might be wasting her last precious day on earth just trying to get out of the state of Texas. At the gate, my connection to Albuquerque had been delayed. I dragged myself to the newsstand and bought a cup of coffee and a copy of the *Dallas Morning News*. I fell into a chair and sipped my mocha while arriving passengers trundled down the Jetway. Women my age were flanked by husbands and strollers and embraced by graying dads and soggy-eyed moms. I knew I was just feeling sorry for myself, which only made me feel more pathetic. By the time my plane boarded, I'd exhausted myself with self-pity.

An hour later, I settled into my exit row thinking about the irony of my seating assignment. I had two bottles of Vicodin, pills left over from a recent series of ear surgeries, stuffed inside my suitcase along with shoe samples and brochures for the volleyball tournament I was supposed to attend. As the 747 lifted off, I looked out the window at the houses and tennis courts and country clubs below. My parents were down there somewhere, growing more distant every minute. I owed them a note, some explanation or at the very least a few words telling them that they weren't to blame. *If I killed myself, how long would it take for anyone to realize I was dead?* My coworkers didn't keep track of my travel schedule. My sister was busy with the new baby. I guessed a couple of weeks at most. *This is silly. You're not going to kill yourself.* I kicked my bag beneath my seat.

I ordered a Coke from the stewardess and used the tray table from the empty middle seat. I took my *Dallas Morning News* out of my carry-on and unfolded it to see the entire front page. It was odd to me now that I had lived in this city once. The headline, in tall letters like skyscrapers, read: "Siblings Say Father Kos Abused Boys." I stared at the photo of Kos in his black short-sleeved shirt and white priest's collar.

"Five former parishioners have sued Father Rudy Kos and the Catholic Diocese of Dallas, accusing him of pedophilia and asserting that church officials should have known about his problem. The family of a sixth boy who committed suicide will also be pursuing litigation. Under oath, Kos has repeatedly refused to answer questions about alleged sexual misconduct, citing clergy confidentiality and the Fifth Amendment."

The article went on to talk about Kos being raised by his father and brothers after his mother abandoned the family when Kos was six years old. His two brothers described acts of sexual abuse dating back more than three decades and gave various quotes:

"To me, the guy's a piece of (expletive). He doesn't belong on the earth."

"The Church was the perfect place for him. Who doesn't trust a priest?"

"Rudy knew exactly what he was doing. He'd win the praise and trust of the adults, and from there he'd have his own little world."

The Dallas diocese said that they first learned of the abuse in September. The plaintiffs' attorney contended there was written evidence that Church officials were alerted to the problem several years earlier. In the mid-1980s, an assistant pastor at All Saints expressed concern to diocesan officials about Kos's habit of having young boys stay with him at the rectory. The diocese moved Kos to another parish. It seemed that, in the end, the Catholic Church cared more about its reputation than it did its children.

The plane bumped against things I couldn't see. It bounced and dropped and my stomach lurched. I set down the paper and took a sip of my Coke to see if the carbonation might settle my nausea. I remembered being jealous of my male classmates because Kos spent more time with them than me. Until that moment, I had only thought of men and boys as predators and never as the prey. The article didn't mention names, only dates and ages. I pictured the faces of the kids who followed after Kos and slept at the rectory. Kos was the first person I had told about being sexually abused. He had *absolved* me for being gay. *What was his forgiveness worth? Did it even count?* If I'd had any reservations left about killing myself, they were gone by the time the plane landed.

I got my rental car in Albuquerque and started the two-hour drive toward the town of Truth or Consequences and my hotel for the night. In the trunk, between Kaepa posters and cheerleading and volleyball shoes, the bottles of Vicodin waited for me. I found my way to the feeder road leading to I-25 and stopped at a red light. A man approached my rental car. Then he pointed a gun at my head. At first, I thought the gun was a toy, the plastic dime-store sort that might explode with a bouquet of flowers instead of real bullets. But this man wasn't joking. He rapped the gun on the glass alongside my temple and reached toward the door handle. I fluttered my fingertips along the driver's armrest, searching for something that felt like a lock button. Another man, this one with a semiautomatic, ran in front of my car and lowered his weapon from his shoulder toward my windshield. I stared at these angry men—men who could not possibly know that until this very moment, I had thought that I wanted to die.

The door handle clicked, once, twice. It was locked. He raised the butt of his gun and slammed it into my window. I flinched and ducked, expecting shattered glass, a hand reaching in, and my door opening. He would drag me into the street and shoot me. I covered my head and when the window held, I looked up and saw that the traffic light in front of me had turned from red to green. Green. Green meant go. It occurred to me that I might move the tons of metal and steel around me. I stomped on the accelerator. I swerved to miss the man inches from my bumper—and apologized out loud for almost hitting him. Then I cursed myself—*Why was I still saying I was sorry to people who wanted to hurt me?* I didn't know if my life was worth living, but one thing was crystal clear: I refused to die in the armpit of New Mexico over a piece-of-crap rental sedan.

I raced out onto I-25, passed two exits, and pulled off at a Shell station to call the police. The sheriff was already on the scene. Before the men tried to steal my car, they had wrecked their truck while fleeing from the sheriff for some other crime. I asked the dispatcher if they wanted me to provide a statement or press charges or pick the men out of a lineup. She told me nothing more was needed, not even my name. I hung up the phone. It was as if it had never happened. Except I believed God was giving me a choice: I could end my life, or I could use this moment as a wake-up call. God wasn't always burning bushes or having manna rain from heaven. Sometimes He was a short, scruffy man with a pistol in his hand—and He had my full attention.

Inside my hotel room, I sat on the bed and stared at the black television screen. I tried to steady my hands. I took two steps to the minibar and grabbed a doll-size whiskey. I opened my prescription of Vicodin and gulped a single pill, not the whole bottle, as I'd planned, and chased it with Johnnie Walker. I shuffled my way to the bathroom and shoved aside the tiny bottles of shampoo and conditioner and body lotion and ripped away the paper toilet strip reading, SANITIZED

FOR YOUR PROTECTION. I closed the lid and fell onto the seat, staring at the floor tiles.

I could have let those men blow my brains out, but I didn't. I was alive. And that meant I wanted to be. A whole life could fit into this hotel room, everything neatly packaged, single-serving-size, bleached and laundered. If I was going to live, I wanted a big life, an uncontained life, a life that would count. If that was going to happen, I needed to be honest. I needed to tell my parents I was gay, even if it meant I might lose them. I wasn't going to hide anymore.

I spent the night reading the Gideon Bible I found in the drawer of the side table. I memorized Isaiah 41:10 because it brought me comfort. "Fear not, for I am with you. Be not dismayed, I am your God. I will strengthen you, and help you, and uphold you with my right hand of justice." I spent the night talking to God and, finally, really listening. I knew what I needed to do.

MY PARENTS SAT SIDE BY SIDE on their floral upholstered sofa in Dallas. My mother held her hand close to her mouth, as if she had a cigarette, even though she had quit smoking several months ago. My father casually rubbed his chin, but crossed and recrossed his legs like he was readying himself to spring away at the first sign from my mother. On the mantel above the fake fireplace, a miniature grandfather clock ticked the minutes.

I sat in an uncomfortable white wicker chair. The underside of my upper lip stuck to my teeth, as if my body was attempting to silence me. I would tell them everything I'd ever kept from them, all at once, so that we'd never have to go through this again.

I began my carefully rehearsed speech. "Over the last few years or so, I know I've been distant. I kept a lot of things from you, and sometimes that was because I was keeping them from myself too.

Mostly though, I was afraid that if you knew me, you wouldn't love me anymore."

My father cleared his throat, started to speak. I put up my hand and continued. "Do you really want to know who I am?"

My mother tightened her mouth into a straight line and reached to scratch her scalp. My father jumped in, "Well, sweetheart, we've known for some time that you were awfully close to that friend of yours—"

"Dad, stop. Mom, do you want to know your daughter?"

My mother's voice came out soft, almost a whisper. "If you think it will help you." My father nodded.

I closed my eyes, took a deep, slow breath, and exhaled words I knew would change us all. I told them about Dale Crandall and Holly—that I had been sexually abused at the age of eleven, and had been afraid to tell them because I thought they'd blame me. I also didn't see how they could change it or help me after the fact, and I thought I could handle it. Their faces remained ashen, like mimes. I explained that I was gay—that I was sure—and that if I was ever in a relationship again, it would be with a woman. While I spoke, I wondered if perhaps they thought I was gay because I'd been abused—and I secretly hoped that they did—because it would give them an explanation, and I knew they needed one.

When I finished firing off my disclosures, I waited for them to speak. I shifted my gaze from Mom to Dad and back again, trying to read their frozen faces.

My mother stared at me, dark circles like bruises beneath her carefully made-up eyes. "I know you think I must have had an inkling about this, but I had no idea. None."

It was the abuse that shocked my father. He smoothed the strands of hair across his balding head. "Dale Crandall? The guy who lived across the street? Well, I just can't believe it. For cripes' sake, I used to watch football with him."

"Al, that's ridiculous. What the hell's wrong with you? You've never set foot in his house before."

"I'm sorry, but I'm just trying to make sense of it." He gestured toward me. "I mean, you must have done something to cause the abuse, you know, invited it in some way. Remember that time in grade school when you got caught playing doctor and that PE coach got fired over it?"

I shook my head at him, my insides knotted as if he was twisting them with his bare hands.

"Dad, if an eleven-year-old girl stood naked in your living room and begged you to have sex with her, would you even consider it for a second?"

"No. Of course not. Never."

"Well, that's what I'm saying. It wasn't my fault."

My mom shifted her weight toward me and spoke clearly. "Of course it wasn't. I'm so absolutely sorry that happened to you. I wish you felt you could have told me." She rubbed her hands along her collarbone as if she was going to choke herself. "I would have done anything to spare you pain like that." A flash—a split second of empathy in her eyes—told me she knew well the demons I fought, and she would have fought them with me if only I had let her.

The moment was a wisp of smoke. I had waited more than fifteen years to hear her say those words, for the possibility that she might wrap her arms around me and tell me I was going to be okay. But I was gay. She stayed on the couch, wounded, unable to move. She clenched her hands to her stomach, stood from the couch, held on to the armrest, and said, "You'll have to excuse me." And she was gone.

My father followed her, and I listened to the clock tick. When my dad appeared again, his tall frame bent in the hall doorway. "You need to leave now, sweetie," he said. "For good."

My parents did not hug me or wish me a safe drive back to San Marcos. They did not explain whether "for good" meant forever or a week or a year or explain how we should act around one another. It was as if they had assigned an asterisk to my name, negating every good thing I had done or might do. And because they felt they were responsible for who I had turned out to be, they put one by their names too.

After I left their home in Dallas, I returned to San Marcos and focused on my work. I laced up shoes and checked tear sheets from *Seventeen* and *YM* magazines and argued for better positioning and rates for our ads. I tried to give my parents some time and believed that they would call me once they had digested the news. I knew better than anyone else that unwanted enlightenment could feel as brutal as any assault. They needed space to recover.

I'd had an entire lifetime to deal with my issues and couldn't expect them to adjust on my timetable. After three weeks, though, I couldn't stand it any longer, and I called home. My father answered. When he heard my voice, he whispered from his end of the line. "You've no idea what we've been going through over here. I've about lost my wife, she's so sick over this. Damn near hospitalized."

"I'm sorry, Dad. Really, I am."

"It's a death. That's what it is. You're dead to her. And she can't get over it. It's like you've taken our religion and beliefs and just—excuse my language—pissed all over them."

"If there was anything I could do to fix this, I—"

"You know what you can do."

"If you're asking me not to be gay, then you're asking me not to exist. I can't be any other way. Don't you think I would have made certain before putting you through this?" I thought about the months of therapy, Vegas, and my disastrous attempts at heterosexuality.

"Your mother's coming. I've got to go. Don't call again." The phone clicked dead. Silence was the only thing left between my father and me.

That night, I poured cereal for dinner, and because I had no milk, I sat on the arm of my couch eating dry Alpha-Bits out of the bowl and looking for messages from God among the clusters of letters. I had hoped things would turn out differently, and now that hope was like a hammer. I was free to do what I wanted, but it didn't feel that way. Untethered to my parents' expectations, maybe, but not free. Still, I had no one to answer to anymore. It was time to start living my own life.

CHAPTER TWENTY-ONE

I FOLD MY LITTLE BLACK prAna dress and set it on top of my orange sandals in the suitcase. With its built-in shelf bra and stretchy fabric, I can almost trick myself into believing that I'm going to a yoga retreat instead of to a Theall family reunion. I grab an extra jacket in case the casinos or hotels are chilly, as my mother has warned, and go to the loft to print off a copy of the article I found in the *National Catholic Reporter*, the one I want to show to my mother before I make my decision about the 5280 assignment.

I fly to San Marcos to meet my parents, and in the backseat of my father's Lincoln Navigator, my sister and I ride together like we did when we were kids with our mom and dad in the front seat. We say our Our Fathers and Hail Marys and finish with "St. Christopher, pray for us." We make the sign of the cross. Before we left the house to drive as a family to the reunion in Lake Charles, Louisiana, I gave my mom my old iPhone to replace the flip phone she'd been carrying for years, and we set it up and put a few free apps on it. Most of the ride I helped her figure out how to work it—how to get email, text, use the GPS—interrupted only by her squeals of delight. I invited her to a game of Words with Friends, and we played each other as my father's SUV traveled through the intestine of highways across Houston.

"Darn you. You have to let me win or I'm not playing anymore."

"You sound like Connor."

"Seriously, it's not fair since I'm new to this."

"Okay."

"But don't tell me you're letting me win, even if I ask you."

"Okay."

Every time my mother sends a word over to me, she giggles.

"Will you show me how to download movies onto it? I could get a little holder or something and watch my shows while your father drives."

"I don't think the older ones have enough memory."

"Oh sure, give me all the crummy seconds." My mother jabs Dad in the shoulder with the edge of her phone. "Al, exit here and let's take a tour through the old neighborhood."

It's been twenty years since I confronted Dale Crandall, but my body gets cold with adrenaline. We turn into our old cul-de-sac and I brace for the cracked, red face of him bending over his car, metal in hand. In front of the Crandalls' house, a Hispanic man plants roses next to a Nissan Sentra. I breathe again. He is finally gone.

Our old house has a new patio and some fake columns painted on the front, as if someone were trying to make it look stately. Two little girls ride their bikes across the lawn through muddy ruts and down the drive.

Hours later we park at a casino and are met in the lobby by various members of the Theall clan. My parents had asked that I not bring Connor because there wouldn't be any children for him to play with, yet children are everywhere. One woman even brought her two silky terriers in a stroller. I wear my ring, the diamond band that matches Jill's. No one asks about it. If they do, I won't lie.

My father has put together an hour-long presentation on the Theall genealogy, complete with slides and family-tree charts. We assemble in a meeting room lined with rows of chairs. I take pictures of my dad as he practices the art of elocution, clearly in his element, smiling like he's giving a lesson to a group of incoming freshmen. I'm from winemakers, farmers, oilmen, casino owners. One of my great-cousins slept with a Mafia boss's mistress and they caught him and castrated him. That section of the family tree doesn't branch. I look for anyone who looks gay on the slides and the closest I get is my great-grandmother—a woman who smoked cigars in a rocking chair on her front porch. For a portion of his lecture, my dad leaves up an image of the English Theall family crest, which has a birdlike dragon on it with sharp talons, and a beak, and ears, and webbed wings like a bat's. It's either a bird-bat-platypus creature or an Easy Bake Oven accident. It's possible the artist was trying for a bird because evidently, Theall was a name given to a person who resembled a teal: a waterbird or duck. Yet more than a few of the photos show various members of the Theall clan, fresh from a hunt, gripping dead ducks by their necks. Despite the fact that we apparently kill and eat our own, the scroll above our family crest bears the word "Fideliter"—the credo of our clan—Faithfully.

Looking at that crest, I think about how Connor came to us and about our decision to make his last name Theall. In 2006, when Jill and I finally could talk about losing Jeremy, she told me she still wanted to adopt, but that she had been wrong about wanting an infant instead of a toddler.

"One to three years old," she said.

"You're sure, babe? You still want to be a parent?"

"Yeah, but first, I need to sleep. And then maybe we should take a vacation together. Regroup before we go again."

Like many people dealing with grief, we decided we needed to get lost somewhere in order to regain our bearings. So we chose a place one hundred miles from any road and that could only be reached by plane. The Ultima Thule, a lodge in the middle of Wrangell-St. Elias facing three miles of the glacier-fed Chitina River in Alaska, possessed the resilience we needed, having been destroyed and rebuilt three times by fire and flood. The name "Ultima Thule" meant a land remote beyond reckoning, beyond the borders of the known world.

One afternoon while Jill fished for sockeye salmon, I flew overhead in a bush plane the size of a confessional. Sitting in the lap of a guide named Too Tall, I asked the names of the peaks, anxious to make sense of them. "Those are orphaned peaks," Too Tall told me. "Can't land on them or climb them. No one's ever set foot on them." We banked right and ascended higher. Three serrated peaks spread out across the horizon, cutting holes through a gauze of white clouds, obscuring their beginnings from me. I snapped away with my Nikon and leaned over Too Tall's shoulder to ask him if those mountains had names. He nodded and pointed at each one in succession. He spoke three words and I repeated after him: "Connor. Bona. Jackson."

Shortly after we returned from Alaska, Jill and I got the call for a thirteen-month-old little boy. We met the social workers for a presentation on the child who would be ours. They told us about the boy's mom, Tara, and his father, Brian, the homeless kids who had given birth to him. They gave us his well-worn history. And when they were finished they showed us his photo and told us his given name: Connor Bona Jackson.

I told my sister and parents right away. I knew this was our son and that God meant for him to be a part of our family. My sister flew out almost immediately to meet him and help me celebrate my fortieth birthday. My parents, though lukewarm in their initial reaction, booked a trip to come out for Connor's first Christmas with us. They showered him with presents. We all went to Christmas Mass together, where my mother insisted on holding him when he got too wiggly. He fell asleep in her arms. She stayed seated, ignoring the kneeling and sitting and standing of the other parishioners, with a look of content-ment I'd rarely seen on her face. At Communion, she rose with him sleeping on her shoulder and had the priest bless him.

When the time came to adopt Connor, Jill and I decided he would take my last name because her father had already passed away. We went to court. We signed the papers. We made him a Theall. I made him belong to my family. I created permanent acceptance where I wasn't assured of any.

At the end of the slide show, there are photos of each family branch of the tree, including my grandpa and grandma Theall, then my dad and mom, then my sister and me as kids, then Kathy's fam-ily—all of them. I watch for the next image—for my family. My parents have known for months now that Connor and Jill wouldn't be here with me. I expect the shot that Jill took at Christmas of my parents, sister, and me without spouses or children in it—as if I am still not a grown-up like my sister is, with a family of my own. Instead, Connor and I appear on screen. I am walking him to Sacred Heart, holding his hand. We smile at the camera—at Jill who is taking the picture rather than being in it. It's more than I expected, and I should be happy. But Connor is getting older. And if he was here, he'd won-der why Mommy was missing from our family photo. In order to be a good mother, I may have to be a bad daughter, and it makes me sad that I must choose between the two.

On the drive back to San Marcos where I will catch my plane to Denver, I give my mother the article I printed out from the *National Catholic Reporter*.

"I don't know if you heard about this," I say. I give her three sheets of paper, and keep a copy for myself to read again so I am pre-pared. "This happened at Sacred Heart. We knew it was coming, so

we pulled Connor out of school ahead of time." It is a simple explanation, except that it leads her to believe we've done this recently, not
three months ago.

"You pulled him out of Sacred Heart?"

"Just read," I say.

The article is about Reese's moms, an anonymous and exclusive
interview they agreed to give only to the *NCR*. In the article, their
names have been changed to Mary and Martha.

Two Boulder women have been at the center of a firestorm of
media attention here for the past ten days since news broke that
their daughters would no longer be welcome at the Sacred Heart
of Jesus parish school because their mothers are lesbians.

Local media have been covering the story seemingly around
the clock. Television crews have come to the school. Articles, letters to the editors, and opinion pieces, including one by Denver
Archbishop Charles Chaput in support of the expulsion, have
appeared. Protesters have shown up outside the church with ban-
ners calling shame on parishioners. Police have been called in to
patrol the school grounds for the safety of the children. Division
has emerged within the parish though many Catholics—and others—here ask themselves how this could possibly have occurred in
their progressive, welcoming community.

The women, members of the Sacred Heart parish, describe
themselves as practicing Catholics eager to raise their children in
the faith of their parents and grandparents. From the time they
first enrolled at Sacred Heart three years back they never hid the
fact that they are a lesbian couple, they said. "We decided for a
number of reasons to send our children to Sacred Heart School,"
Mary said. "We have loved it there. Our children were thriving
there."

All seemed quite natural until it came time for next year's enrollment a couple weeks back, when Martha went in to turn in her daughter's kindergarten application and was called into the principal's office. That's when the women were told that their daughters could stay one more year in school and after that they would be out.

The women said there have been surprises along the way. One of the biggest was the amount of support they quickly received from parents at Sacred Heart School. "We have been around for years but just didn't think much about it and didn't think that it would be such an issue for so many," Mary said.

"We want our kids to learn about religion. They love God. They love their school. They love their friends. They love their teachers," Mary said. "We are trying to live up to the promises we make to raise our kids as Catholics and now the church we made the promise to is sort of undermining our attempts to do so.

"We will continue to raise our children with strong Catholic values and hold faith that through our actions, we are doing our part to create a more loving, inclusive world."

When my mother finishes reading, she tells me she saw something about it on CNN. "'Suffer not the children to come unto me, and do not hinder them,'" my mom says, quoting the Bible. "Children should never be made to suffer, because Jesus loved them most of all." We pass the exit to our old neighborhood. "And you notice, this was in a Catholic newspaper, presenting their side of the story?"

Of course I did, I picked it on purpose. I would never have shown her my Boulder Weekly *interview.* "What do you think about Father Bill and the archbishop?"

"It's a shame they've taken this stance. Maybe some good will come out of it."

Maybe some good will come out of it. I want to believe this, but I wonder if her view would change if she knew I was thinking about writing an article on it. *Would she back me over the Church?* "Maybe I should get involved, you know, become more proactive about it."

"Well, I don't know that that's necessary. Since Connor doesn't go there anymore, you really don't have a dog in the fight, if you know what I mean."

"Isn't being gay and Catholic having a dog in the fight?"

"Oh, Michelle, honestly. It's like with the blacks, prejudice against gays and lesbians will probably never be entirely erased." She waves her hand like an offensive odor has invaded the car. "Jesus suffered persecution because He was different. I think you just need to seek out branches of the Catholic Church that are more accepting of this lifestyle. I mean, if the Church thinks you're wrong for being gay, they should want you in there praying every time the doors are open, just like I do."

Her response surprises me. It's softer than I imagined and huge for her to admit that our priest and archdiocese might be wrong. I decide to write the essay for *5280.* I suspect my mother would still not want me publicly speaking out against the Church, especially as a gay woman, but this is important to me—to my family. Still, I convince myself that she will never have to know about the article. My mother sends over the word "crash" on Words with Friends, and for the moment, we are tied.

CHAPTER TWENTY-TWO

BACK IN SAN MARCOS, I gave my two weeks' notice to Kaepa. I traded in my Eagle Talon for a Nissan Pathfinder, adopted a Siberian husky and a malamute-wolf hybrid, and wrote my parents a letter telling them that I was moving and would send my new address when I got there. I added that I loved them, and missed them, and hoped they'd come back to me whenever they were ready. I would always be waiting.

On a bright, late fall afternoon, with the temperature hovering around eighty, I loaded my truck with the last of my possessions and said good-bye to the life I'd been renting. I settled Bear and Chance, all two hundred pounds of sled dog and muscle, into the back and closed the tailgate. I backed out of the drive and pointed the Pathfinder toward Colorado.

Out on I-10, bugs splattered against the windshield. The hill country dipped and rolled in front of me with its roadside peach stands and grazing longhorns. Though Texas contained pockets of liberalism, it was largely a place where men and women hunted, and bought Fords and Chevys, and revered God, football, and country music in that order. It was also the place I was born and raised, where the rhythm of cicadas and dancing fireflies had lulled me at dusk and where bluebonnets and red paintbrush rippled like the colors of the state flag across wild open meadows. But it had never been home.

Just outside the county line, the terrain flattened out before getting lumpy again. The temperature went down as the elevation went up. I sang to 10,000 Maniacs, *These are days that you'll remember*, guitar and mandolin and piano an anthem for my drive. Natalie Merchant told me I'd see miracles in every hour. I had changed. I felt it like the changing altitude.

Back in college when Cassie and I had visited Colorado, we passed warnings about icy roads and tire chains being required, and because it was my first time anyplace cold, I hadn't realized that those were permanent signs, there even in summer. I had stopped my car every few miles or so to get out and touch the pavement to see if the roads were slick. Now I felt comfortable in this environment. It made sense. As I approached the first set of peaks, I enjoyed the heft of my truck. I slowed on the corners and made peace with the curves.

A FEW MONTHS AFTER MY ARRIVAL, I bought a house on ten feral acres of an elk-migration route, dwarfed by the 12,000- and 13,000-foot peaks of the Continental Divide. Out a bank of windows three stories high, snow-capped mountains flared into descending ridges of gold aspens like pleats of a skirt. A waterfall and two trout ponds trickled through the middle of the property. Game trails headed north and west, as if they might lead all the way to Canada. That first night I struggled to hear a single noise and at 2 A.M. woke to the repetitive whoosh of the blood rushing inside my ears. I walked out onto the deck cocooned in a wool blanket and found a sky so layered with stars that I couldn't identify a single constellation.

The next morning, four feet of snow landed atop my house like vanilla frosting. The weight of nature broke telephone poles and electric lines, taking power and transportation with it. Without a plow, my truck would be stuck for days at the bottom of my steeply pitched, one-hundred-foot driveway. But even if I could somehow dig it out, this was the place I wanted to be. I cooked off my woodstove and used it for heat. The deck became my refrigerator. I pumped the backup cistern for water. Bear and Chance buried themselves in snow, diving through it, tossing it, and chasing each other to the point of exhaustion. At 8,500 feet off miles of rutted dirt roads, I felt nestled and safe. In this man-made world stripped bare, all that was left was God. And though I could not see Him, in the same way I could not see the wind, His presence made me weep.

A few months later, I had run through my savings. I landed a job in ad sales at *Women's Sports* magazine, a publication I had loved in my teen years whose name had changed to include fitness now. Sparrow had introduced me to the title back then. I was proud of the magazine and the ability to work for it, but didn't like going into the office. In good weather, my commute to the headquarters in Boulder was forty-five minutes. I used the difficult drive as my excuse to leverage occasional days to work from home. Eventually, after I was bringing in too much revenue for them to argue, I convinced them to let me telecommute permanently. In that peaceful place, four years passed as quickly as the seasons.

DURING MY TIME ON THE mountain, I navigated the wilderness adjacent to my land like a cougar, reading aspens, rock outcroppings, and scat the way I used to read road signs. I trusted wild animals more than people and could go weeks at a time without seeing or speaking to another human soul. For the first time in my life, I left the doors to my house unlocked. I didn't even own a key. In that refuge, I allowed myself to realize several different things: First, living alone and being celibate did not make me any less gay. Second, I wasn't gay because I was abused. Many women are victims of abuse, and they aren't all gay. Third, it wasn't my fault. Any of it. Fourth, there were good men, men like Ray, and my brother-in-law, Eric, who held his newborn daughter like a baby bird. Dale Crandall may have made me into the kind of person who kept her hackles up—one who would rather bump into a mountain lion than a human being—but he didn't make me gay. God made me gay. And He hadn't made a mistake.

I prayed several times a day beneath a sky as big as the apse of a cathedral. As much as I was at ease with my isolation, extraordinarily and blissfully happy, one thing was becoming clear to me: If I lost the ability to love other people, I would become something less than human. So I made a bargain with God. *Teach me to trust and love again, send me my soul mate, and I will leave this mountain.*

The summer of 1998 painted my land with locoweed, larkspur, columbine, and wild iris. Hummingbirds whizzed through the air like green mopeds, dive-bombing the feeders on my deck. Chance and Bear kicked up wild sage and tracked it into the house. For months now, their fur smelled of clover and sap, which I preferred to the occasional stench of skunk or dead marmot. I walked to the barn, turned out my horse, an eleven-year-old red roan named Sundance, and herded him into a small area to graze while I got my wire cutters. Throughout the spring, the elk had jumped the fence like Olympic high jumpers, and when they missed, their back legs caught the smooth wire and took out whole sections for me to repair.

I grabbed the fence-post driver by its ears, hurled it down over the steel T-bar stake, and drove it into the ground a few inches. I did it again and again until I was steeped in sweat and vibrating from the body shock of hard physical labor. I decided to leave the back two acres alone since a pair of mountain bluebirds had built a nest in the wooden house along that fence line.

After an afternoon working on fence repair, my energy flagged, but I took a hike through the adjacent national forest with the dogs so they could explore. I cut wildflowers to put in my kitchen and living room. When I got back, I cleaned up and drove to the mailbox to collect a few days' worth of catalogs and bills—and also a large box.

Most of the communications I had received from my mother since I left Texas had come in the form of anonymous prayer cards and dating-service membership flyers. At one point, she sent me what looked suspiciously like a vibrator, with a quick note saying it was for my sore muscles. I envisioned a priest telling her that as long as I remained single, my being gay wasn't a sin—and the vibrator was her attempt to encourage that effort.

The box my mother sent rode next to me like a hitchhiker. When I opened it at the house, I found a letter taped to the interior packing materials. There were more words on the piece of paper than I'd heard from her in years. In it she wrote:

> *The path you are continuing to follow is against everything I believe in, and I simply cannot get past that . . . I believe in the long run, you will suffer the consequences of your lifestyle. The most troubling thing about this is that I am devastated you have turned your back on the Church. As your mother, I beg you to try and visit a priest in Colorado . . . Perhaps he will not sanction your actions, but we are taught to love the sinner and hate the sin . . . Some congregations are openly trying to find a place for everyone . . . Temporal happiness is short-lived, but the salvation of your immortal soul is for eternity. And please don't make excuses about how you can pray anywhere. I know that, but I do know that Christ established the Church of which you are fortunate to be a member by your baptism. I will love you and pray for you no matter what. I am not your judge,*

*my dear, only your mother who has tried her best to do what
is right for her children. I love you, and God bless you. Mom.*

I unwrapped items from inside the box one by one. Report cards,
finger paintings, spelling-bee awards, and stacks of her photos of me,
some even still in their frames that I recognized from the hallways
of our house and the top of my mother's dresser. I held up my first
Christmas ornament, a tarnished brass star with a cat dangling from
the top. I could still see my name engraved across its chest. I read
in my baby book that my mother's first words at my birth were, "Is
she all right?" And that on my first day of kindergarten, I had "joined
right in with the little boys playing with blocks." My first words were
"Bye-bye" and my first sentence "I want to go." By the time I was four
years old, my mother noted: "Stubborn. Will risk punishment to do
what she wants." I thumbed through Polaroids and prints. In them,
I was playing with Tinkertoys, and race cars, and electronic football
games. I was Fonzie in several. Mittens sat and rolled over, frozen
in perpetual compliance in those snapshots, in such a way I wished
I could release her. There was even one of me at an ice skating rink
with Holly. In it I wore my hair in two ponytails, jutting from the sides
of my head like a donkey's ears. Holly hovered behind my shoulder
with her rainbow crocheted shawl around her and a grin taking up
half of her face.

Some people might have assumed that in sending me my childhood paid in full, my mother was letting me go. All I saw was that she
had reached out to me. I couldn't expect her to give up her religious
beliefs and agree with me, but making contact meant that a relationship between us was again possible. My mother wanted me to join a
parish here. She indicated that a congregation in Colorado might be
more open-minded and accepting. *And wasn't that what I wanted,
to be part of a community that loved God but would love me too*? I

decided I would consider going back to church. I made my final decision a few weeks later after reading an article in the *New York Times*. The article said that a Dallas jury had awarded $120 million in damages after finding that the local Roman Catholic diocese had ignored evidence that Father Rudy Kos was sexually abusing boys and that it had then tried to cover up the abuse.

It was the largest judgment in Catholic Church history, awarded to eleven of my classmates, including Jason, Father Kos's "son" and the family of Jay Lermberger, the boy who committed suicide because of the abuse. In response to the verdict, the Dallas bishop Charles V. Grahmann issued a written apology. Father Kos had fled and hidden under an assumed name in California. He was captured and convicted and sentenced to the maximum of life in prison.

Justice was possible. There were good people in the Church, like the priests who tried to tell the authorities, those brave altar boys, their parents, and my own. That Sunday, I drove an hour into Boulder and made my way to the back pews of a church called Sacred Heart. I was gay and Catholic and would refuse to hide either. And maybe here in the liberal utopia of Boulder, that would finally be okay.

I emailed my mother and let her know that I had started attending Sacred Heart in Boulder. She responded back, and before long, we were calling each other almost every week to talk about the dogs or my horse and the move my parents were making from Dallas to San Marcos to be closer to my sister. In one phone conversation we had, she opened up to me and told me how my coming out had affected her.

"I know you thought that I knew. And maybe I didn't want to see it. But it was as if the daughter I loved and raised had died. I grieved like that." She hesitated before admitting, "I finally went to see a therapist and I told her that your whole life had been a lie, that

I didn't know you at all. She said, 'Name off everything you thought was true about your daughter.' So I did. I said, 'She's kind and generous. Athletic, smart, creative. Headstrong. Passionate. Artistic, vocal, independent. She loves animals and nature. She's a good person.'" I breathed in every word she said and held it. Mom's voice weakened, as if she'd moved away from the phone for a moment. "After I finished my list, the therapist asked me, 'Aren't all those things still there—still true about your daughter?' And I said yes. She said, 'Then you just know the truth about one thing more.'"

Even though my mother had come back to me, it didn't mean she approved of the fact that I was gay. I knew that while my mother was at Mass, she prayed that I would stay single or stop being gay. When I prayed, I asked God to help her understand that there was nothing wrong with me being gay. And I prayed to find my soul mate. *Would our prayers cancel each other out? How could God answer us both?*

CHAPTER TWENTY-THREE

CONNOR SLEEPS AMONG PILES OF stuffed animals, camouflaged beneath them like E.T. It takes me a minute to find his head. I watch him, sacked out in his race-car bed. After months of allowing him to adopt our bedroom as his own, we asked him if he was ready to be back in his own bed, and he said yes. Last night, I hadn't slept. I was sure he would scream for me and I'd need to be ready. But he didn't. Somehow, by giving him what he never had—trust in the adults around him—we were able to reboot his brain into feeling safe at bedtime, even without us there. Plus, it's possible he has a new friend. The envelope he received the same day the article in the *Boulder Weekly* was published about us was from Luke, the little boy who lives one block away whose mother is a devout Christian. He was having a birthday party, and Connor was invited. Perhaps I had Jackie pegged wrong.

In the loft, I shuffle through decades of photos and letters to pull together the narrative of my life as a gay woman in six thousand words or less for *5280 Magazine*. The past and present collide as I type. It is impossible for me to tell my story without explaining my relationship with my family, and every word I type is like a bullet fired into my mother's chest. When I lived in San Marcos, I had groused to my sister about Mom and Dad. At the time, she had agreed with me, but ultimately finished every conversation by saying, "Well, they were good parents, and loved you, and they did the best they could." I know this is true. Like all good mothers, my mom wanted what was best for me, even if we never agreed on what that was.

But it shouldn't change the story. Except that it does, because I keep deleting sentences. I read the opening paragraph of my essay and wonder if I should have agreed to do the article. I hit the backspace key until the letters disappear.

I WAKE IN THE MIDDLE of the night. Something isn't right. My brain won't connect to my hands and feet. I get up to go to the bathroom. I am trying to sprint through waves in the ocean. My body vibrates, weak and uncoordinated. It's like I've lost a bet with gravity. Electric shocks zap at my feet, toes, fingers, and palms; my body jumps in reflex. My knees buckle.

I try to take my mind off my body. My muscles flip and twist like fish on the deck of a boat. My right eye blurs things in the distance and my left can't make sense of things up close. They are at war with each other. Fog rolls into my thoughts—thick, dense, impenetrable. What if this attack doesn't end? What if it's the one that lands me in a wheelchair, leaves me blind? There must be something I can do, some pill I can take, exercise, rest. Turmeric, B-12, or a cold bath. I crawl back into bed, too afraid to close my eyes. I pick up a magazine from my side table along with a book light so I don't wake Jill, but my fingers are dumb, fumbling nubs. Minutes pass as I concentrate on turning a page. I stare at the ceiling. I wait.

THE MRI SCANNER REVERBERATES LIKE a machine gun. A little mirror a few inches above my nose angles in such a way that I can see the technicians in the glass booth in front of me. They laugh about some-

thing, maybe the basketball game last night or the lame auditions on
American Idol. I try to hold still, but my MS makes me twitchy.

"This one's two minutes," the tech says through the intercom.

Inside the luge tunnel, the chamber clicks three times and then
echoes with what sounds exactly like jackhammers and chisels whack-
ing stone. It's hard to tell if I'm under construction or being demol-
ished, but something is under way.

When I was first diagnosed, I panicked. All I could think about
were all the things I hadn't done or seen yet. I wanted to photograph
grizzlies in Alaska, follow polar bears across the arctic ice, and track
lions in the Serengeti. A wheelchair wasn't part of my plan.

Without questioning my neurologist, I got on the medications she
prescribed, even though the injections of interferon, a cancer-fighting
medication, made me feel fluish and created toxic liver levels in my
body. After one month on the drug, my eyes started hemorrhaging, a
completely new and undocumented side effect. After four months on
the drugs, I stopped the injections altogether. I took matters into my
own hands. My doctor said I was playing "Russian roulette" with my
health. I lost fifteen pounds, became a vegetarian, started delegating
more at work. I had my mercury dental fillings removed, tried giving
up gluten, had myofacial-release massage. And then I did what every
sane person who has been diagnosed with a progressive neurological
disease would do: I booked a trip to Africa to climb Kilimanjaro.

Mount Kilimanjaro rose 19,341 feet above sea level and was the
tallest free-standing mountain in the world. Only 33 percent of the
people who tried to climb it made the summit. On the day Jill and I
arrived in Tanzania, I thanked God and the baggage handlers in Am-
sterdam for losing our luggage so that we gained one day of rest at
a hotel before starting our forty-two-mile trek. In Colorado, we had
trained, climbing fourteen-thousand-foot peaks outside Boulder. Still,
I had no idea what effect the exertion and the altitude would have on

my scarred brain, and on top of that, I had picked up a cold and sore throat somewhere en route.

We woke to the smell of wood smoke and the eager brooms of our hotel staff sweeping dirt from the floors, ate breakfast beneath a thatched roof and stared at Kilimanjaro in the distance. We piled into Land Rovers and bumped along washboards that rocked the truck and worked my muscles just to balance. I coughed from the dirt, my chest still congested, mucuslike rubber cement inside my sinuses. When we arrived at the trailhead, I read a large wooden sign: IF YOU HAVE A SORE THROAT OR COLD OR BREATHING PROBLEMS DO NOT GO BEYOND THIS POINT. I lived among fourteen-thousand-foot peaks. Those warnings didn't apply to me.

The first day we trekked for hours through slick, muddy rainforests with monkeys swinging over our heads through candelabra trees. The porters carried our bags on their heads, some in crude sandals, many without warm coats or rain gear. They passed us on the trail, moving forward to set up camp tents and cook for us. Our guide, Jamaica, told us, "Pole. Pole." Slowly. Slowly. "You must acclimate to the altitude. Already we lose one day we needed. We will rise too soon." My muscles refused to cooperate. It took more effort for me to go slowly, to hold a step, than to release it quickly. The fatigue showed up in tremors and spasms.

The second day, less than an hour into our route, I shook uncontrollably. I asked the group to stop so I could recover. *Was I having a seizure?* I downed chocolate and peanut butter granola bars. I didn't want to be treated any differently from anyone else. But shaking on that rock with my coclimbers staring at me with concern, I fessed up to my disease. I still maintained that I didn't want help—didn't need it. Even so, a man took my day pack and clipped it onto his own. He wouldn't take no for an answer. I felt embarrassed, guilty, and, finally, relieved.

By day four, we reached the lava towers, a series of projectiles bursting to the sky from their base of fifteen thousand feet—higher than I had ever been. A woman in our group, fit and in her late thirties, fell ill due to altitude sickness, weaving, vomiting, her skin and lips blue with hypothermia. Jamaica dragged her down two thousand feet to our base camp. Shortly after, a twenty-year-old man crumpled into tears. I wasn't alone in my struggle with the mountain. Still, I was glad I'd told the group about having MS. The secret was one less thing I had to carry.

Inside my tent, my head filled with a dull ache that made me close my eyes. The pressure reminded me of the spinal tap I'd taken to diagnose my MS—the test I swore I'd never take again. I stumbled out of the tent, nauseated and weak, and asked Jamaica about alternative routes and what would happen if I needed to quit and go back down. "Only in an emergency," he said. He adjusted his wool cap. "Even so, we must get to the next camp before we can get on the route where we descend. There is no way down except to go up."

Jamaica gave me Diamox and Advil and some other white pills without names on them. I took them all. I hadn't trusted my neurologist, but I held out my open hands to Jamaica. I just wanted relief. By morning, I felt able to ascend again. I thought about Alex always urging me to use the momentum of going down to get back up a hill. I soldiered on with the group to the Barranco Wall, a nontechnical rock climb. My fingers held to the porous yet inexplicably solid formations, and my body instinctively knew what to do. One hundred feet later, our team perched above a bank of clouds. We watched waterfalls below us through the gaps.

It didn't get easier. Two days later, I was using my hiking poles like canes, unable to bear my own weight without assistance. I staggered into the base camp where we would start our summit bid at midnight. Jill still felt well enough to go on the training hike before dinner, the one that would lead the group up to seventeen thousand feet and back down again. I stayed behind. I sat with a woman named Stacy, a marathon runner who groaned in a fitful sleep and after waking started talking gibberish. She keened with coughing, retching in the breaks in between. I called out to Jamaica and he evaluated her. "The start of pulmonary edema," he said. "Fluid is building in her lungs." He ordered two of the porters to take her down to a lower camp. Another woman volunteered to go with them so she wouldn't be alone.

Inside my tent, I thought about the summit. I tried to lift my water bottle and zip the tent, simple tasks I could not accomplish. There were battles worth risking my health for, and this wasn't one of them. We had prettier mountains in Colorado. Between the terrible food, lack of sleep, filthy conditions, and a trail littered with people and toilet paper, I knew there was only one reason to attempt the summit: to prove I wasn't sick. I didn't want to accept my disease, but it was as much a part of me as my eyes or skin. Climbing this mountain wouldn't cure my MS. Continuing to deny it would be far more devastating than making peace with it.

At midnight, Jill and I joined the others for dinner in the food tent. We sent our climbing friends off on their summit quest and wished them good luck. I watched the light from their headlights zigzag above us like cars on a highway. After they disappeared behind a ridge, I stood alone outside the tent and stared at the sky. It was the only place I'd ever been where I didn't hear or see planes flying overhead. The stars blinked at me from a thick Milky Way. I planted my feet—curled my toes to the soil—and thought about how silly I'd been. Wherever I stood at any given moment, here in Africa or back home, I had the earth beneath me. I didn't need to climb a mountain to stand on top of the world.

THE TECH COMES INTO THE ROOM, tells me to hold still. He pushes a button and the slab slides out of the tube with my head still sandwiched between two pieces of foam. "A little stick," he says. "You might feel warm or taste metal." He injects me with "contrast," the dye that shows if any of the lesions in my brain are currently active. I slide back into the tube and imagine myself inside a NASA space shuttle.

Forty-five minutes later, I drive myself home with a CD-ROM of my brain and spinal scans in my pocket. In my office, I review all the image slices and compare them with previous MRIs over the years. I see the same white spots on the black background, representing the nine scars on my brain that have been there seemingly forever— except for one that looks different to me, larger, and glowing like a planet. And I have to wonder: *Are we headed up or down the mountain this time?*

THREE DAYS LATER, I MEET with my neurologist. "The good news," she says, flipping through my scans from last year and comparing them with the recent ones, "is that you have no new lesions."

"Great. So great." I take the thumb I'm gnawing out of my mouth.

"However, according to the radiologist's report, two of the lesions have doubled in size since your last scan."

I blink at her.

She points to two white spots on the images. "One borders the parietal lobe. The other is in the frontal lobe." She nods at my blank face and says, "The parietal lobe helps you interpret sensory experiences like sight, touch, and sound. The frontal lobe involves voluntary muscle control, concentration, planning, and problem solving."

My hands shake and I tuck them under my thighs. "I haven't noticed anything different." The cheap desk in front of me looks like it's made of particleboard. My neurologist is frumpy, with mousy brown, out-of-style hair, terrible shoes—even by my standards—and she wears her pants high above her hips and gathered at the waist like she is ninety instead of fifty. *Why should I believe her?*

"You've been stable for so long that an aggressive progression can't be ignored. I'd like to get you on one of the disease-modifying drugs before your immune system attacks something that does permanent damage. We could try Copaxone since you had such a bad reaction to the interferon drugs."

I shake my head no. "I haven't been running regularly or watching what I eat. Connor just started at a new school, so my schedule's been off. And then there's this article I've been writing. It's been stressful."

"Life is stressful. Not much you can do about that. Why don't you take some time to think about it?"

I tell her I will, but I have no intention of seeing her again. I know that my exacerbations come from stress. And I'm not stressed about the article. I'm stressed about the nuclear fallout of the article. I made peace on Kilimanjaro with this stupid, ugly disease, and yet every time I censor my story— to try to make it less embarrassing or to protect someone else's feelings—I know that I value other people's opinions more than my own. *How can I ask Connor to be proud of his family if I'm not?* Shame is what's eating away at me. I don't need an MRI machine to tell me that.

I spend the rest of the day working on the article, taking small steps of courage. I pretend no one else will ever see it so I can stop censoring every single word. I remind myself that this is just a small regional magazine for the Denver area, and that there is no way my mother would ever get hold of it. It shouldn't matter, but it does.

For the next few days I work on the essay, researching through old letters and emails and on Facebook, when I see a response from Holly Crandall. After more than three decades, I confirm her friend request. She gives me her email, and in each letter, we open up more to each other, as if we are building back to something we once had. In most of her messages, she uses emoticons and abbreviations like LOL or LMAO as if we are still classmates passing notes to each other between desks. But the content in our posts is anything but trivial. Holly has had a hard life. I check the latest post from her and find this:

After running away and quitting school, I shared an apartment with some friends and tried to become an adult overnight. I worked my childhood away and on my days off, I drank every liquor and did every drug I could get my hands on.

Of her marriage, she says that she met a "jackass" who gave her two beautiful boys, but they were grown now and no longer needed her. Apparently, the marriage lasted a couple of violent, and emotionally devastating, years.

I finally got the guts to walk out, but I had to sacrifice everything to do it. I left with nothing but the shirt on my back. My ex-husband kept my kids away from me, as a way of getting back at me.

She goes on to write that she had also been with a woman and that the relationship had been violent as well, but not one that she regretted. "I can't claim to be a victim of circumstance," she writes. "What has happened to me could have been prevented by my own decisions." After that, she worked four jobs and, at almost thirty, joined the military to "see what she was made of."

That was when she started to repair her relationship with her parents. Her father landed in intensive care and almost didn't make it. During that time, her parents seemed to reassess their relationship with her. "They were proud of what I was doing and who I was becoming, so they came to visit me just to apologize for, and I quote, 'being such awful parents.' That was all I needed. It's all water under the bridge and we are pretty close."

Now she's working at a coffee shop, taking night classes at a local university, determined at forty-three to get her college degree. Toward the end, she closes with this:

I missed you when you left and I'm tickled pink to be talking to you again. It's nice to be able to share some of all this with such an old friend. I don't have that many. I move around too much to make any real lasting relationships, but it would be great if you and I could keep in touch.

P.S. Remember riding bikes around the cul-de-sac? I was a Pink Lady and you were the Fonz . . . HEEEY!!! (with your thumbs up). Getting a visual yet? BIG HUGS. Your friend always, Holly

I'm always telling Connor that our words have power and meaning. Holly's letter is a gut punch and a psalm. I open my folded hands, and before I realize it, I'm weeping into them.

CHAPTER TWENTY-FOUR

MY PARENTS' FIFTY-YEAR LOVE AFFAIR began with a lie. When my father, a graduate of St. John's University, asked out my mother, a graduate of St. Agnes, she fibbed and told him she couldn't because she was heading out of town, back to League City, Texas, to visit her parents for the weekend. "God punishes," she told him years later, because she almost got caught in that lie. That Sunday at St. Anne's in Houston, my father marched to the front of the cathedral for his induction into the Knights of Columbus. He faced the pews and scanned the parishioners. But he didn't see my mother, ducked beneath the missalettes in the fourth row. My mother escaped before he could spot her, skipping Communion and letting her roommate, my future godmother, drive them away with my mother stuffed beneath the dashboard in the passenger seat. None the wiser, my father asked her out one more time. And because she felt she owed God a type of penance, my mother said yes. My father took her to the movies, and afterward, he made her think about a different kind of sinning when he swept her off her feet at the Rendezvous Lounge dancing to "Moon River." Ten weeks later, my father asked her to marry him. She said yes to that too.

Though I don't care to emulate their relationship, I know how much my parents love each other. I believe in forever and commitment and monogamy because of them. Unlike my parents' courtship, my relationship with Jill started with the truth: laser precise, and laden with humor. A book editor I worked with gave my number to a friend of hers who had recently moved to Denver, thinking maybe I could help her get situated in a new place. I had no intention of meeting anyone new and was in the middle of moving a heavy armoire by myself by using a bath towel and my feet when the phone rang. Jill invited me to join her on Friday night for a dinner party with some friends she had already made: I said no. I couldn't think of anything worse than leaving my little piece of paradise to drive two hours in rush-hour traffic to spend time with complete strangers who had chosen to live in the city. And because I lacked appropriate social skills, I told her so. "But next time you're in Boulder, I could meet you there," I said as a consolation.

Never having met me, Jill said, "Oh, come on, who are you, Nell? Even the Unabomber left his cabin to send out a little mail."

So much captivated me about those two sentences and her brashness and wit in saying them that I changed my mind. I said yes.

Two nights later, I drove down the mountain, shifting into my lowest gear, and steering around the hairpin turns leading toward civilization. As soon as I got onto Highway 36, I hit Friday five o'clock traffic, and a bottleneck brought my Pathfinder to a standstill. *This is ridiculous. Not worth it. If it doesn't start moving, I'll take the next exit, make an excuse, and go back home.* The cars inched forward. I put the truck into first. At least the shower I'd taken wouldn't be wasted.

I pulled up in front of a small bungalow on Race Street. In the front yard, a woman with straight blond hair that touched her shoulders was pointing and talking to a man who appeared to be working on her sprinkler system. She was cute—no, she was beautiful. She moved across the lawn in long capable strides. She wore small gold hoop earrings, a simple white T-shirt and jeans, and had her sunglasses pushed back on her head. I stepped out of the truck. She shielded her eyes from the sun with her hand and smiled at me. After briefly saying hello, she asked, "Hey, do you mind running down into my basement to turn off the water? There's a spigot at the bottom of the stairs."

I found my way inside. *Maybe this isn't a date. The woman has her irrigation guys here and is working on her yard. If it were a date, wouldn't she be inviting me inside for a glass of wine or at the very least offering me a bottled water?* But I liked her confidence. If she had been overeager, I would have fled.

After she finished with the landscapers, we went to a house nearby for drinks and hors d' oeuvres. Her friends, five funny, charming, and well-groomed men, delighted me. I had spent time around gay women, but I had never known any gay men. On the back porch, with the scent of cilantro and rosemary wafting toward us from the ceramic pots on the windowsill, I took a delicate cracker topped with seared ahi and a swirl of wasabi mousse, and let it melt on my tongue.

Jill had been in Colorado for just a few months and already she had a close-knit group of friends. Watching her with these guys and the irrigation crew earlier, I could see her complete comfort with men. How naturally it came for her to engage and be engaged with them.

From there, we left for a place called the Grand—a gay bar. The bar was packed, even on the outside porch, elbow to elbow with gay men and women our age, having wine while piano music drifted around us. After being sequestered on my mountain, all the noise and chaos startled me awake like an alarm clock. Plus, there was Jill, who made me nervous and expectant in a way I couldn't explain. She was sassy and bold, sexy, with clear blue eyes, a gleaming smile, and a slight Southern drawl, familiar like family and home, in the best way. A hostess led us to a table, and I realized that I couldn't see the mountains. The skyscrapers were in the way, and I felt dizzy. I couldn't get my bearings until Jill put her hand on the small of my back and the warmth of it moved me forward.

Around midnight, Jill and I broke off from the group, and she suggested we go to a place called the Campus Lounge, over by her house. I was hopeful that her invitation meant that she didn't want the night to end yet, because that was how I felt. *Still, maybe she did this every night? People in cities stay out late on the weekends, don't they?* We ordered beers and slid into a booth. We were alone together, just the two of us for the first time that evening. I panicked, started rambling.

"So, I believe in monogamy," I blurted out. "I think if you're going to be with someone and you've made a commitment to them, that you can never cheat on them. Seriously, a person should have enough willpower to be able to say they're breaking up with someone before they have sex with someone else. It should be a courtesy if nothing else."

"Okay," Jill said.

"I mean, what do you really have with someone if you can't trust them to be with you completely? I'm just saying."

I peeled the soggy label off my beer bottle and rolled it between my fingers.

"Easy, lightning," Jill said. "You're scaring yourself."

And I was. I was trying to scare myself away from Jill because she wasn't giving me any reason to run away yet.

"Sorry. I just haven't dated very much. I haven't found anyone yet who compares to a good book and a hike through the mountains." *Dear God, why can't I stop talking?* "Also, I have trust issues."

She looked at her watch. "It's three A.M. and you're still here in Denver with me. I must be doing something right." Her dimples deepened to tiny caves. I shut up and tried to save myself from myself.

For our second date, Jill agreed to come up to my house and let me surprise her with a Colorado fall rite of passage. "That road is like *Pee-wee's Big Adventure.*" Jill got out of her Camry and I met her on my dirt driveway. "My cell phone doesn't even work here."

"You use a cell phone?"

"Yes, I like talking to people." She waved the phone at me. "I bet they don't deliver pizza up here."

"No, but listen to how quiet it is."

She turned in a slow circle with her head tilted back. After a moment, she said, "I see why you like it here. I've got some heavy competition. But just so you know, I'm not trying to steal you away from any of this."

After I gave her a tour of the property and introduced her to Bear and Chance and Sundance, we climbed into my truck. I played Patty Griffin most of the way out on Peak to Peak Highway. The aspens streaked gold in front of our path. I pointed to the trees. "You know those are all one organism. They share the same root system." *God, don't bore her.*

Alongside the car, the river braided and unbraided itself like a wild child's hair. We pulled over so Jill could look for trout. "Wish I'd brought my waders," she said. "Do you fly-fish?"

"No, but I'd love to learn." A rainbow rose like an oil slick and disappeared beneath a rill. "Tell me the truth," I asked. "What did you think about when you drove up that road to my house?"

"I thought, 'This better be worth it.' And then I thought about what it would be like to be with you all day, and I kept driving."

Over the next hour, we agreed on a few important things. Among them: You could tell a lot about a rancher by his fence. Bird feathers, butterfly wings, and zebras were proof of God's existence. It was hard to trust someone who didn't love dogs or chocolate pecan pie. And we both hoped God graded on a bell curve.

IN ROCKY MOUNTAIN NATIONAL PARK, I took her to my favorite spot, a meadow called Moraine Valley surrounded by peaks with a swath of river rolling through it. We drank hot chocolate from a thermos and shared a blanket when the air got crisp. No more than fifty yards from us a herd of elk led by a bull bedded down. He circled his harem, strutted about with a massive chest, clearing a path with antlers like tree branches. He opened his mouth and tilted his chin toward the peaks and let out a single note. With a resonant screech like a child practicing the violin, the bull bugled to announce his territory. Yellow aspens shimmied behind him. I pointed across the scrub-brush-strewn valley; we had company. Ragged one-horned males crept toward the main herd eager to steal a mate from the bull. Night lowered like a curtain. Antlers cracked as they sparred in the dimming light. Eerie high-pitched calls from the valley serenaded us. *It was the most romantic evening I had ever spent with anyone, but what if it wasn't Jill's?*

Beneath the blanket, Jill rested her hand on top of my own, and began to knead the soft places between my thumb and forefinger. I didn't think it was possible, but she touched every part of me just by caressing my hand. She put her head on my shoulder and softly sang an Alison Krauss song into my ear. "'Baby, now that I've found you I won't let you go, I'll build my world around you.'" No one had ever sung to me. Her notes were pure and sweet. A bull interrupted her with a reverberating squeal, and Jill deadpanned, "Backup singers— always trying to steal the spotlight."

We let the dark envelop us. There were no fences here, unless I decided to build them.

WHEN I WASN'T WITH JILL, I wrote in my journal about Jill. It seemed that what was going on between us was important, something I should record and remember. I thought about her hands rubbing mine, and her warm mouth next to my ear singing. I told her how good she smelled and she told me it was from the Bounce dryer sheets she used, and I liked her all the more for it. She was graceful and elegant and every time I thought about her, something just beneath my solar plexus ached. I rode my horse and hiked the ridge above my house. All of those things became just ways to pass the time until I could see her again.

I sped to Denver, eager to get to the city because she was in it. Over the couple of weeks since I'd been to her house, the remodel had moved into full swing. Her bungalow smelled like sawdust and paint. The bathroom was done, but the kitchen had a hole in the floor and boards across it to get to the basement stairs. On her couch with a glass of wine, we looked through a photo album of hers. She was close to her family, and had grown up with sisters involved in beauty pageants. One was a Miss Lexington, the other a Miss Kentucky who finished in the top ten in the Miss America pageant the year Vanessa Williams won. I imagined that being a lesbian in a family with beauty queens would be traumatic. "My sisters don't care that I'm gay," she said. "They actually get mad if they start to like someone I'm dating and I break up with them." When she mentioned that her mom and dad were devout, born-again Christians, I asked her what it was like coming out to them.

"I was a mess, crying. I couldn't get the words out, and my mom finally said, 'Honey, are you trying to tell me you're a lesbian?' I nodded and she wrapped me up in her arms. I was still sobbing against her chest when she patted my back and said, 'It's okay. Let's go tell your father.'"

"Amazing. I've got to meet these people."

The next page of the album showed a retail store with maroon awnings and a logo reading DESIGNS UNLIMITED. "That was my store. It was right across from the UK campus," Jill said.

"I know this place! I've been in this store." I bring the photo closer to get a better look at it. "I was trying to get the Kentucky volleyball team to wear our shoes, and I went in there looking to buy a simple UK T-shirt—"

"And all I carried were custom orders for frat and sorority parties."

"Yes, and a woman came out of the back and I asked her about it."

"That was me. Was I a bitch?"

"No." I hesitate. "You were—um—rushed."

It was an odd coincidence to have met her in passing so long before being formally introduced.

"I've been to T-shirt shops on college campuses all over this country and I couldn't tell one from the other. I remembered yours because I couldn't figure out why in the hell you'd have such great retail-store frontage when you only did special orders."

"I'm glad we didn't know each other then. I wasn't cooked yet."

"Cooked?"

"Yeah, I wasn't done yet. Grown up. Ready to have a relationship without messing it up."

She set down the photo album, pressed her cheek against mine. She brushed her lips against my skin, like a nibble, and we kissed. It was like cresting a ridgeline for the first time—surprising, limitless.

I stayed over that night, though we never slept. I thought I would be the one to cry first, but she broke down in tears and said, "When I met you, I honestly just wanted to sleep with you. I didn't want a relationship. And now, I just want to be so careful. I don't want to do anything to screw this up. I'm scared." With our arms around each other, and our faces inches apart, skin on skin, we trembled and laughed. "I'm a mess," she said. I told her I was too. "If we're going to jump off this cliff, let's do it together," I said. And I kissed her forehead and eyes and chin and nose. We counted to three and let go.

Around 2 A.M. I walked through the living room and into the kitchen to get some water for us both. Lightheaded from lack of sleep, the ground dropped from beneath me and I was falling—into the basement below the kitchen—saved only by my left hip, which caught me as I plummeted through the hole in Jill's floor. I tried to push myself up, but couldn't get leverage with one leg out in the splits and the other dangling below. Helpless and realizing it, I screamed. Jill sprinted into the room, saw the upper half of me sticking up from the splintered wood, and yanked me by the armpits onto the sheets of plywood like she was pulling me from a frozen lake.

My hip bled from a four-inch gash and we wrapped it. And it happened just like that. Among bloody washcloths and gauze, with splinters and raw spots on my skin, I fell in love and kept falling.

FOR THE NEXT TWO YEARS, Jill and I commuted back and forth in all conditions—snow, sleet, hail, rock slides—in the utter wreck of the happiness of being in love. Jill didn't want to live in the mountains and I refused to live in Denver. We talked often about what a compromise might look like, but every time I thought about leaving the place that had healed me, I folded in on myself. I didn't know if I could do it. And because we respected each other, neither one of us wanted to crush the soul of the person we had fallen in love with. As Jill put it, "Taking you out of the mountains would be like chopping the wings off a hummingbird." So we waited. We might have stayed like that forever if God hadn't intervened.

As the end of a blistering summer sparked wildfires across the state, I woke one morning at my house and breathed smoke, thick and acrid in my lungs. Outside, a haze enveloped the decks and barn and Sundance tossed his head and trotted back and forth, pacing against the fence line. Across the ridge, ash blew in from the north as charcoal-colored snowflakes. I climbed up to the highest part of my property. Miles away, flames devoured trees in spectacular orange bursts like fireworks. The reservoir, the place where Jill and I had first said we loved each other, provided a natural firebreak, but with fickle winds that sometimes blew at hurricane force and unending fuel from drought-dry trees, I feared losing everything.

Slurry bombers roared overhead, dropping retardant over the blaze. Fire marshalls closed the road to incoming traffic. I kept Jill updated by phone and boxed up photos, computers, and important documents and loaded them into my truck. I made sure to grab the package my mom had sent, knowing that my entire childhood was inside it. I faced the Pathfinder toward the road for a quick escape. A neighbor who knew I had a horse barreled down my drive, swirls of dust and the hum of a diesel pickup announcing her arrival. Three horses, their eyes bulging white against the windows, stamped their feet inside the metal trailer. She had room for one more. I found eighty dollars in my wallet and pressed it into her hand even though she didn't want to take it. She assured me she'd give a portion of it to the rancher who was taking care of them. Sundance waved his tail good-bye to me down the drive.

Every hour or so, I climbed up the ridge to watch the mountains be consumed. For three nights, I refused to leave. I slept in fits and starts, imagining myself burning to death inside the house, alone with my dogs. The police assured me that a reverse 911 would notify me in time to evacuate if the fire changed direction. I picked up the receiver in the middle of the night just to hear the dial tone.

By the fourth night, the fire had been largely contained, and residents around my area were taken off pre-evacuation. I unpacked the boxes of photos and keepsakes, and reloaded my truck with my dogs and some clothes. I drove down the mountain to see Jill and breathe some fresh air. I spent the evening sneezing and coughing black gunk from my sinuses, throat, and lungs, knowing with each snort and gasp that staying up there as long as I had hadn't been healthy. Late that night, my cell phone, the one Jill had given me for my birthday just three months after we met, buzzed on the side table next to me and I turned on the lamp. I recognized the number. My neighbor, the woman with the horse trailer. On the other end, she spoke in a panic of words. "The wind's shifted. It's gone around the edge of the reservoir. They're evacuating us. I can see the flames now, and they're roaring right toward us." Her voice sounded raw. "They're giving us one hour to get our belongings. I just thought you should know in case you weren't up there when they did the reverse call."

I thanked her and sat up in bed. Jill put her hand on my back. I pictured blackened trees like dead skeletons where my aspens used to be. Trout boiled, eyes popping, in the shallow ponds. The barn and house reduced to ash. A wasteland. Chance licked the top of my hand as I dangled it over the edge of Jill's comforter.

"I'll do whatever you want," Jill said. "Let's go up there and get some more of your things."

"An hour's not enough." I thought about the box with everything from my childhood in it. My horse was safe and the dogs and Jill were all with me. My house was a building made of cedar and glass and impermanence. And the mountains—I never owned those. God loaned them to me. And He was everywhere.

I kissed Jill, soft and long and with commitment. "I have everything. It's all good." I laughed. I nudged the dimple in her cheek with the tip of my nose. "Besides, you knew God would have to light a fire under my ass to get me to move from that house."

. . .

I SLEPT IN A MARMOT sleeping bag on the hardwood floor inside my empty house, still standing untouched after the fire lines held and the mountain was spared. The sun dipped below the Divide; the curved silhouette of a stand of pines bent permanently, like old ladies, from the wind. They never broke, but you could appreciate what they'd been through. For six years, I had measured time by the ending of seasons. Now as the late-summer flowers lost their color with the first frost, I would move on too. I sold my horse to a rancher on the Western Slope, and with the moving truck loaded and gone, I spent my last night alone to say good-bye. The peaks around me flashed white against a full moon, like trout bellies in a river. I thanked God for every second in this place, and prayed for a send-off, a final blessing from this land that made me whole again. I didn't expect or demand it; instead, I called it to me.

At 3 A.M. I heard knocking. I slid from my sleeping bag and tiptoed to the doors and windows. Elk, a herd of eighty or so, formed a ring around my home, antlers tapping the wood siding. They remained like that until sunrise, hugging my house, so close that their breath fogged the windows.

The next morning, I whirled down the spiral of the canyon and called Jill once I had cell service. "Do you promise to love, honor, cherish, and make me pee in my pants laughing as long as we both shall live?"

"I do," Jill said. "I love you, babe. It's going to be great."

MIRRORING US, OUR NEW HOME in Boulder splits the line of mountain and city, half wild and half tame, with wilderness out the front door, and civilization out the back. The minute we close on the property, we start adding on to it to make it our own. We take a 1941 bungalow on a spectacular, oversize lot and turn it into a Craftsman, popping the top, moving the front door, and opening up the floor plan. Because I want to see the mountains from every area of the house, without having to squat down or stretch out on tiptoe, we add multiple transoms and glass French doors. Jill selects cherry floors, granite countertops, and high-end stainless steel appliances. We get moss rock for the fireplaces and stone tiles for the floors. We help the builders frame and put in the insulation, and paint. Finally, amid the construction of our new life, we write our initials in a patch of wet cement by the back door, and encircle the letters with a heart.

CHAPTER TWENTY-FIVE

Is it possible to become an orphan at forty?

The magazine in my hands feels substantial and weighty. My life on glossy paper in *5280* is eleven pages long, and I am proud and scared and freaked out by all of it. There's an illustration of me, a full page, looking quite a lot like the Virgin Mary, which is not only embarrassing, but also highly inaccurate. I stare out at myself from paragraphs of text as an eight-year-old having her First Communion and as a scrawny ten-year-old running. At thirteen, I am wearing the dress I puked on at my grandparents' fiftieth wedding anniversary, except that this photo was taken prior to that at my Catholic Confirmation. My saint's name, Catherine, is spelled out and glued letter by letter across a white felt sash. The article is broken up into sections, one- or two-paragraph vignettes. I read the part of the article recounting the day I told my parents I was gay. "A single drop is nothing, but my mother cries and doesn't stop. Water like this will carve a canyon between us." I hope not. *She will never see this magazine*, I tell myself again and again. After all, it has a circulation of only a few hundred thousand, and all of that is concentrated around the Denver area.

I ask my editor to forward me any and all letters that come to the magazine regarding my article. One of the most interesting ones I receive is this:

> *Michelle, I don't know if you remember us, but our daughter Reese was in preschool at Sacred Heart of Jesus School with your son (Connor, right?). I wanted to write after reading your article. I found it to be extremely well done. Sacred Heart and Father Bill must be squirming again. As you probably know, it was our family that was given the boot. It was a traumatic few months for us, but we managed to keep the kids oblivious to the drama surrounding them. We've moved them to Boulder Jasper School, and they're doing great. We were wondering if you and your partner (Jill?) would like to go to dinner sometime or come over. It seems like we have a lot in common, and our kids want to know other kids with two moms.*

She includes their phone numbers at the end, and I email back to say how great it is to hear from them and throw out a date that will work for us to get the families together.

PEOPLE WRITE PASSIONATE AND LENGTHY EMAILS, many full of painful and moving personal disclosures and gratitude for the article. I answer all of them. Meanwhile, I continue to talk to my mom on the phone. We exchange emails and play games on our iPhones. Two weeks after the article has been in print, I start to relax, until my mother resigns from Words with Friends right in the middle of the game. I text her: *Why did u quit? I wasn't even winning. Did u hit the wrong button?* She does not respond. I know she has seen it. I wait to hear from her, but she doesn't email or call. The editors do not receive one single piece of hate mail. But I do. It is from my father.

I have had it with you and your writing. Your mom loves you and loves her religion. You despise your religion because it does not allow your lifestyle. And so you do everything you can to hurt your mom and me. In your article you did a lousy job of keeping any anonymity for us—naming the years and what towns we lived in. Your mom is in tears right now. We have done everything to give you a good life. Most of what you have done was based on your life choices. If I lose your mom . . .

If you want to complicate your life—fine. But leave us alone. We have a pleasant life here and you have no right to screw it up as we near our last years. If you continue to write about these issues, use a goddamned pseudonym. Your dad, I repeat, your father!

My father has rarely spoken or written to me in this way, and though there are plenty of things I might be upset with in his email, the line that hurts the most is, "If I lose your mom . . ."

He is not afraid of losing me.

It takes me two days to respond, and though I still can't bear to talk to them, I put my thoughts in an email. I tell them I love them and realize all the wonderful things they have done for me. I tell them that I'm grateful I was raised believing in God and that I want that for Connor as well. I write for five pages about honesty and forgiveness, but I also remind them that there is a fine line between silence and shame. As far as Sacred Heart is concerned, I say:

The church in Boulder was wrong. Straight parents at Sacred Heart stood up against their decision to ban children of gay parents. But my own family wouldn't have picketed like they did or gone on talk shows or taken a stand. Apparently, they don't even want me to write about it. If someone is going to hurt me or Jill or Connor because I am gay, I would expect the people who love me (my family) to side with me rather than the people trying to hurt or discriminate against me. Even strangers do as much.

In the last few sentences, I make it clear that I am a writer, and I will continue writing the truth about my childhood, being gay, and my experience with the Church. I add that they have the choice to have nothing to do with me or Connor or Jill. It's not what I want, but I would accept it.

THREE WEEKS PASS, AND AFTER our war on paper, I begin to believe that my parents are gone for good. When my mother finally calls me, this is the conversation we have:

My mother screams at me on the other end of the line. "Why do you have to broadcast that you're gay? Your sister doesn't run around telling everyone she's a heterosexual."

"I'm not broadcasting it. I'm telling my story."

"Well, no one wants to hear your story. You're not a celebrity. Who cares? Who's even going to read this?"

"Maybe no one. But it's my story to tell." I try to stay calm, but my voice starts to get louder in volume. "And it's supposed to be inspiring, you know, about how you learned to love your gay daughter without giving up your Catholic faith."

"I'd never give up my faith."

"Well, then, I don't know why you're so upset about this article, except that you are afraid your friends will find out that I'm gay—which means you are ashamed of me."

"We're not ashamed of you, damnit. I don't believe in what you're doing, so I don't want to be included in it. I am a very private person."

I think about the scenes my mother has caused in hundreds of public places and want to reach through the phone and shake her by the shoulders. "Fine. Why isn't Jill mentioned in any of your annual Christmas letters, and why aren't there any photos of the two of us together in your house?"

"There *are* photos of Jill in our house. And from now on, I just won't put any of you in the Christmas letter anymore. Not you and Jill, not Kathy and Eric. How's that?"

Great, my sister will love being punished because of me.

"If you're not ashamed of me, what do you tell people when they find out I have a child or when they ask if I ever got married?"

My mother pauses, her voice weakens. "We tell them you're a single mom."

I close my eyes. I'm sad more than anything. "That is shame. It's a lie, and when I write about my life, you are caught in that lie."

"Well, you're not married. You can't legally marry. So it's true."

"It's lying. It's shame. If someone judges you for having a gay daughter, maybe they're not your real friends."

"We live in a different generation than you do, and it's none of anyone's business."

"Maybe you could talk to someone about this, like Jill's mom. I mean, she's a born-again Christian, and she loves and accepts us."

"I'm not talking to anyone. I saw a therapist. I got on medication. That's what you did to me when you came out."

"What I did to you." I hold the phone away from my ear for a moment and breathe.

"And, my dear, don't be so surprised if Jill's family isn't as accepting as you think."

"No, they are. Her sisters call me their sister. Her mom calls me her daughter."

"Well, that's just terrific. Good for them."

I tell her, "You're free to tell people whatever you want, but you have no right to silence me."

"Really, you don't have our permission to write about us. I'll sue you for libel."

"That's terrific. You know what? Go for it. How exactly have I misrepresented you? Clearly, you are a devout Catholic and you aren't happy your daughter is gay."

I stare at the mountains and wait.

"You're selfish. You do what you want to do without thinking about how it affects anyone else."

"I'm selfish?" I am yelling at my mother. "The Church kicked out your own grandson. Our fucking parish growing up hid a pedophile priest. I can see why you'd support them over your own daughter."

"I didn't know about Sacred Heart right away because just like everything else, you didn't tell me. You're always hiding something."

I hang my head. She's right, I know. "I'm trying to be truthful now."

"Sure, at our expense."

"So, now that you know, you could still do something. You could write a letter or call Father Bill." She doesn't respond, so I say, "But you're not going to do that."

"You are trashing the Church over what a few people have done. The abuse problem is terrible, but they're rooting out those priests and prosecuting them. There's still good in the Church, and you could still find a parish that accepts you."

I pause to choose my next words. "I'm not Catholic anymore. I'm done." I finally said it. I feel relief. "I'm also not going to write under a pseudonym," I say. "It defeats the purpose. The whole idea is that I'm proud of who I am. If you're ashamed to be associated with me, you change your name."

"What is wrong with you? How can you be so disrespectful to us?

We've done the best we could for you and you're absolutely killing us."

"Fine. But I won't hide behind a pseudonym. I'll take Jill's name legally and change Connor's too. He'll become Connor Thomas."

I can hear my mother considering this. "Do what you want to do," she says.

But I will not let her off that easy. "No, I'll do it if you ask me to. I don't want to change my name. I'm proud of who I am and what I've done in my life. You decide."

I hang up, feeling like I've just come out of a warm bath, cleansed. I wipe my face and join Jill in the kitchen. She pours two shots of fine rum that one of our friends brought to our last party.

"Sweet Pete, I'd be more than happy for you to take my name. I promise it's a good one." She pulls me toward her and we kiss.

"We'll see what they say, I suppose." I hold up my shot glass and we clink.

"You know, you have a choice in this too," she said. "Who you are and who you become have never been up to them. It's always been up to you."

CHAPTER TWENTY-SIX

THOUGH I LOOK MORE LIKE my father, I have my mother's Italian nose, olive skin, petite build, and hands—a fact my mother once pointed out to me during a piano lesson when I was five. "Poor thing, you got my hands," she said. "They're so ugly." In that moment, I had wanted to give them back to her but couldn't figure out how. Now my hands are knotted and crooked and as different from hers as my life has been. I snapped a tendon in my pinkie while snowboarding and it bends at a right angle. A horse kicked a rope out of my right hand and sent me to the emergency room. I mangled it more trying to drive my stick-shift truck down the twisting road out of the mountains to get to the nearest hospital. The fingers of my left hand have been broken, jammed, and sliced open from years of playing basketball and wrestling with barbed-wire fences. My hands are ugly. But they are also evidence of a life well lived.

There's a story that's passed down through my family that says when my mother was two years old and visiting her grandparents' farm, she begged them to let her hold a baby chick. She was careful at first, but when they asked her to put it down, she couldn't fathom giving it up, so she crushed it in her hands.

Seven decades ago, my mother had no idea what she'd done to

that chicken except love it, but she knew emphatically what it had done to her. As her grip closed on the little ball of feathers, it defecated in her palm, at which point she screamed and dropped it.

I know that at times my mother has felt that I have left a mess inside her open palms, and I alternately accuse her of holding on so tight I cannot breathe and of dropping me. We struggle to get what we need, both realizing that sometimes all we have in common are our hideous hands and a bone-crushing love.

In the days following our epic fight, I waited for my parents' decision. My emotions ran the gamut. At times, I thought I didn't want to be a Theall anyway, because though I loved these people who were my family, I had to admit that there were times I didn't like them very much. I knew "Michelle" was a name I would keep. After years of thinking I was named after a Beatles song, I learned that Michelle also stood for this: who resembles God. Whether that was a statement or a question didn't matter to me—it had become something sacred to me either way.

I had a good last name too, one I had worked very hard to give some honor to, and I was proud of most of the things I'd done in my life that were associated with it. Changing my name would be erasing myself, my history. For once in my life, I wasn't running. I'd even stopped drinking so much so I could remain present for my son and my partner. I didn't want to start over or forget the past; I had made peace with it.

When my mother finally called me, I knew I could deal with it, whatever she and my father decided. I sat outside on the edge of a lawn chair, gripped the armrest, and steeled myself as she said: "Sweetie, we would never ask you to change your name." I felt the tears wet on my cheeks before I realized I was crying. She said, "If you're going to keep writing about us, change our names to give us some privacy, and give me the chance to read what you're writing. It's only fair that I be given the opportunity to know what's coming." I wept at her words and my broken relief. But I had a choice of my own too.

"I love you, Mom, and I'm grateful, truly relieved to hear you say that," I said. "But I haven't decided yet if I want to be a Theall anymore. If I keep my name and stay in your life, there have to be changes. I can't shift your values or morals, but I don't think I can let Connor be around you if you—either directly or indirectly—refuse the legitimacy of our family. Jill is not my friend or my roommate, she is my partner, my soul mate, and the mother of our child," I told my mom. "Anything else is a lie. One that will wound Connor in so many ways, I can't count them. We wouldn't let Sacred Heart tell him that his family was wrong or allow them to pretend I am a single mother. Why would we let you?"

It's Mother's Day, six months later. My mother sits on our deck, her fingers cradling a cup of coffee, staring at the Flatirons and the foothills. I tilt the umbrella to give her some shade, and we watch the sun make its way across the sky. "Is it too hot out here for you?" my mother asks me. "I'm good," I say. "I like being out here." I feel healthy and strong, and so does Connor. It's hard for me to believe that he will start kindergarten in the fall. He bounds across the yard, stops in front of my mom, and says, "Did you know that squirrels don't get up until eleven A.M.? I saw it in an animal book."

My mother looks at her watch. "But there's one now, and it's only ten A.M."

Connor stares out after a squirrel running along the top of the fence. "Well, the book was written a really long time ago." He seems satisfied and sprints into the house.

My mother's purse, a leopard print with beads and sequins, sits on the table in front of us. She pulls out a tiny box and hands it to me.

"What's this for?" I ask.

She shrugs. "Mother's Day. It's my gift to you."

Behind her, the sun dips below the first Flatiron and splits its rays like fingers reaching out to us from within the gaps of solid rock. I open the lid, and my eyes start to water. Inside, atop a piece of white cotton, rests a sterling silver charm, a circle with a heart carved out of the middle and a tiny diamond at the top of the curve. My mother rises from her chair with effort and places the chain around my neck and latches it in the back. I hold the amulet against my chest. I have to look closely, but when I do, I see that there are words carved into the metal. Etched around the heart, in letters light and thin enough to be a whisper, it says: WE ARE SHAPED BY WHAT WE LOVE.

Ever since that gift from her, I think of my mother and me like a canyon and a river. The canyon defines and contains the river. The river pushes and softens the walls around it. It's the raging love between us that makes us into something more.

ACKNOWLEDGMENTS

Because I know God likes to read, I'll thank Him straightaway for giving me the words and the courage to write this. Writing a memoir is a lot like that dream where you are running down the halls of your high school naked. Several people tactfully told me that if I worked out a little harder, my cellulite would look better beneath the fluorescent lights of publication. For me, those writer friends who strengthened my literary muscles are: Rachel Weaver, Hannah Nordhaus, Buzzy Jackson, Donna Remmert, Sarah Murray, Lisa Jones, Florence Williams, Bonnie-Sue Hitchcock, Deborah Fryer, Rachel Walker, Jean Weiss, Radha Marcum, Nancy Coulter-Parker, and Pam Houston.

This book would not exist, nor would I likely be a writer, without the constant encouragement and gentle critiques of my cousin and notable YA author Gail Giles. Advice to new writers: Find your own Gail who will read the first fledgling manuscript you ever crank out, praise it lavishly, and then, almost as an afterthought, suggest that you highlight all six hundred or so "ly" words and replace them with stronger verbs. Also find yourself a Max Regan. Every time I dug myself into a hole and panicked, Max scooped up all of my dirt and shaped it into something I could stand on.

Tracy Ross showed me that I could survive the fallout of words on paper if I released them like doves seeking peace. And Geoff Van Dyke at *5280 Magazine* saw a story in me and nudged it into the essay that sparked this book. My readers at *Women's Adventure* magazine and attendees at the Creative Conferences in Boulder allowed me a forum to express myself and built my confidence word by word.

Andrea Barzvi let me take a circuitous route to create this book because she is sly and wise and knew I had demons to slay before I could finish the journey. Note to writers ready for publication: Find an agent like Andrea who, while on her way to the hospital to give birth to her first child, will text you, "Don't worry. This won't slow anything down. As soon as I'm finished here, I'm sending out your book proposal."

Tricia Boczkowski, an Irish Catholic, believed in me and my story and its value. Thank you for taking a chance on me and for seeing that this book was about self-acceptance, love, and family, not controversy or condemnation.

My parents gave me the foundation of my faith, and I am forever grateful for that gift and for their steadfast love despite our differences. As a mom, I finally understand the amount of sacrifice it takes to raise another human being and the pain that comes with wanting the best for your child and not always knowing how to give it to them.

To my sister: Thanks for trying to bridge the gap between me and our mom and dad with love and diplomacy. You're a peacemaker with a good heart. Though you never deserved to be put in the middle, you handled it all with infinite grace.

Helen, Susan, Lynn, and Kay widened my idea of family and showed me there's plenty of love to go around.

Petey Pete, for taming me without using a cage and understanding that I needed to write this book, even though my obsession with it would have driven most people away. Only a soul mate could see beyond my excessive movies, naps, and writing vacations to a completed memoir. You never questioned my ability to do this—even though I'm sure you wondered about my sanity.

For my son, for giving me some of the best lines in the manuscript and for making me a better person every day. When God said that "a child shall lead them," I'm pretty sure He meant you.

My pups past and present—Chance, Bear, Daisy, Biscuit, and Winston—for unconditional love and unflagging companionship.

Coffee shops, like Salto and the Laughing Goat, fueled me with creative space and soy mochas. Pam's ranch in Creede with Roany, Deseo, Mary Ellen, Rose, Liam, and Fenton, along with a few feral cats, fed my soul when I needed it most. To Mark, for sharing your home in Steamboat during final edits. Writing conferences like Jackson Hole, Santa Barbara, and Tomales Bay immersed me in the brilliant storytelling of others and filled me with possibility while getting me out of my pajamas and slippers and giving me a reason to shave my legs and bathe. Final note to aspiring writers: You're allowed to overlook personal hygiene when you have writer's block.

For the parents, teachers, parishioners of Sacred Heart, and other members of the Boulder community who stood out in the rain protesting the decision to cast out innocent four-year-olds because of who was raising them, you give me hope and inspire me to be brave and remain faithful in the face of adversity.

And finally, for Mittens, I hope you've forgiven me by now. You were truly an awesome cat.

G

TEACHING
THE CAT
TO SIT

BY

MICHELLE THEALL

ABOUT THIS GUIDE

This reading group guide for Teaching the Cat to Sit *includes an introduction, discussion questions, and ideas for enhancing your book club. The suggested questions are intended to help your reading group find new and interesting angles and topics for discussion. We hope these ideas will enrich your conversation and increase your enjoyment of the book.*

INTRODUCTION

In her poignant memoir, Michelle Theall tells her compelling story of a woman finding that middle place between being a daughter and being a mother as a Catholic gay woman who is raising her son with a loving partner and flying in the face of discrimination.

Author Michelle Theall grew up Catholic in the Texas Bible Belt. She also grew up gay. Throughout her childhood, she found herself at odds with her strict Roman Catholic parents, bullied by her classmates, and kicked out of the very Christian organizations that claimed to embrace her. Shame and longing for her mother's acceptance led her to deny her feelings and eventually run away to a remote stretch of mountains in Colorado. There, she spoke to God every day, but rarely saw another human being.

At forty-three years of age and seemingly settled in her decision to live life openly as a gay woman, Theall and her partner attempt to have their son baptized into the Sacred Heart of Jesus Catholic

Church in the liberal town of Boulder, Colorado. Their quest to have their son accepted into the Church leads Michelle into a battle with both the Church and her mother, an ordeal that leaves her questioning everything she thought she knew about the bonds of family and faith. In order to be a good mother, Michelle begins to realize that she may have to be a bad daughter.

Teaching the Cat to Sit is a moving story that examines the modern roles of motherhood and religion and demonstrates that our ability to love is what ultimately shapes us.

TOPICS AND QUESTIONS
FOR DISCUSSION

1. Explain the significance of the book's title. Why do you think she chose this title for her memoir? Specifically, what does Michelle's childhood relationship with Mittens, her family cat, tell us about her? What does the cat symbolize?

2. Michelle's therapist tells her, "You said your mom's moods dictate how everyone in the family acts and reacts. . . . And yet you say she's fragile, and you have spent your energy trying to protect her from anything upsetting. . . . I guess maybe I'm missing something. She sounds pretty powerful to me" (page 195). Do you agree with Michelle's therapist? Discuss examples of the power that Phyllis, Michelle's mother, has over her family.

3. When Michelle, Jill, and Connor visit Michelle's parents' house for Christmas, she says, "The house smells like pecan pie, but also of Lysol, perfume, and lemon Pledge—sweet and sanitized—welcoming us and asking us not to touch anything at the same time" (page 118). How does Michelle's statement apply to her relationship with her parents during her visit home? In what ways are Michelle and Jill made to feel both welcome and unwelcome?

4. When Michelle and Jill decide to adopt a child, Michelle waits until they are far along in the process before telling her parents and sister about her decision. Why do you think she does so? Do

you agree with her reasoning? Were you surprised by Michelle's family's reaction to her decision to adopt? Why or why not?

5. Michelle writes, "Our first knowledge of right and wrong doesn't come from God—it comes from our mothers" (page 71). Discuss this statement with regard to Michelle's relationship to her mother. What values does Phyllis impart to Michelle that resonate with her? Are the two able to reconcile the differences in their values? In what ways?

6. Of Dale Crandall, Michelle's father says, "He can't be a bad guy if he got full custody. That's something" (page 31). What do you think of Dale Crandall? When Michelle tells her parents of the abuse that she suffered at Dale's hands, how do they react? Were you surprised? Discuss Michelle's attempts to gain closure. Do you think her trip back to Meeker to confront Dale is a good idea? Why or why not?

7. When the time comes to adopt Connor and Jill and Michelle decide that he will take "Theall," Michelle's last name, as his own, she writes, "I made him belong to my family. I created permanent acceptance where I wasn't assured of any" (page 224). What does she mean by this statement, and why is it so important to Michelle that Connor take her last name? Discuss the families portrayed in *Teaching the Cat to Sit*. Compare and contrast the family that Michelle creates for Connor with the one in which she grew up.

8. After Michelle and Jill pull Connor from Sacred Heart, she decides to speak about the school's change in policy, first writing anonymous letters to the editors of the *Boulder Weekly* and *Daily Camera* and ultimately speaking on record. What

accounts for Michelle's activism? Why does she ultimately decide to go on record with her story?

9. Michelle and Jill keep a photograph of Brian and Tara, Connor's biological parents, in his baby book. What are their reasons for doing so? How does Connor respond to seeing their photograph? Discuss the challenges that Michelle and Jill face as they raise Connor in light of his past.

10. When Michelle is diagnosed with multiple sclerosis, she decides to attempt to climb Mount Kilimanjaro. What are her reasons for doing so? Upon asking her guide about alternative routes and procedures, should she need to go back down the mountain instead of climbing with her group, she is told, "There is no way down except to go up" (page 240). How does this statement apply to the rest of Michelle's life?

11. Were you surprised by the revelations about Father Kos? How does Michelle react to them? What effect, if any, do the revelations have on Michelle's relationship both with the Catholic Church and with her mother?

12. After reading Holly's letter, Michelle says, "I'm always telling Connor that our words have power and meaning. Holly's letter is a gut punch and a psalm" (page 245). Why does Holly's letter have such a profound effect on Michelle? Were you surprised to learn what became of Holly after she left Meeker? What are other instances in *Teaching the Cat to Sit* where one's words have power? Discuss them.

13. When Michelle moves to the mountains of Colorado, she finds refuge and, in it, "I allowed myself to realize several different

things" (page 231). What does she learn? Discuss the various revelations that Michelle makes about herself. Why does she ultimately leave her refuge in the mountains?

14. After Michelle and Cassie break up, Coach Scott calls Michelle into her office to find out why her performance as a runner has been so poor lately. Coach Scott tells Michelle, "You haven't learned to use the downhill" (page 175). What does she mean by this statement? How does Coach Scott's training practice apply to Michelle's current situation? What do you think of Coach Scott's advice?

15. At her family reunion, Michelle and Connor are included in the Theall family photo montage, but Jill is not. Why has Jill been slighted? Michelle reacts by telling the reader, "In order to be a good mother, I may have to be a bad daughter" (page 224). Why is this the case? Is she able to reconcile this conflict? If so, how?

16. In the memoir, several of the characters have been abandoned—emotionally or physically—by their mothers, through death, mental illness, or instability. Discuss the role of motherhood and the impact its absence has on the lives of Holly, Father Bill, Father Kos, Brian, Tara, Michelle's mom, and Michelle. What does it mean for Connor to have two moms?

17. Nature versus nurture figures prominently as a theme within the book. Can you come to any conclusions about the dominance of one over the other in the text?

18. Are you disappointed that Michelle offers to change her name? At what point do you feel she finally accepts her identity?

19. Michelle says she sees Wink and Sparrow as a "refuge." Do you agree? Why or why not?

20. How do people stereotype Michelle, and in turn, how does she stereotype others?

21. While the cat is a significant symbol in the book, birds also figure prominently throughout much of the memoir. How many references to them can you find and what are their meanings?

22. Discuss Michelle's faith in God. Does it become stronger because of adversity or in spite of it?

23. Michelle concludes that God made her gay. Do you agree or disagree? Discuss the steps she took to accept her sexuality. What does true acceptance look like and does she attain it?

ENHANCE YOUR BOOK CLUB

1. Read an article from the *Boulder Weekly* (http://www.boulder
   weekly.com/article-1993-parent-sacred-heart-had-other-
   lesbiansrs-children-lscloset-baptismsrs.html) about the Sacred
   Heart policy change and controversy that followed. Discuss it
   in light of what you've learned about the families affected in
   Teaching the Cat to Sit. How does Michelle Theall's memoir
   deepen your understanding of the issues discussed?

2. After being diagnosed with multiple sclerosis, Michelle decides to attempt to climb Mount Kilimanjaro. Learn more
   about Mount Kilimanjaro here: https://en.wikipedia.org/wiki
   /Mount_Kilimanjaro.

3. Read the article Michelle published about being gay in the
   Bible Belt South (http://www.5280.com/magazine/2010/10/all-
   thats-left-god) and discuss her struggles with her sexuality.

4. To learn more about Michelle Theall, read her blog, and
   connect with her online. Visit her official site at http://www
   .michelletheall.com/.

What Happened Next?

*For answers to the following questions,
visit* www.michelletheall.com.

1. What do Michelle and Jill think about the Defense of Marriage Act being overturned? Are they planning to get married?

2. How is Connor doing now?

3. How is Michelle's relationship with her mom and the rest of her family now that the book has been published?

4. Is Father Kos still in jail or did he get paroled?

5. What happened to Mara? With the repeal of Don't Ask, Don't Tell, has she reenlisted?

6. Michelle attended her twenty-five-year reunion for her Texas Tech track team. How was she received by Deanna and her other teammates?

7. Did Michelle ever become friends with Ann again?

8. Is Dale Crandall still alive?

ABOUT THE AUTHOR

MICHELLE THEALL IS THE AUTHOR of two health books, and her syndicated health and fitness column ran with *McClatchy Tribune* for several years. She has appeared on NBC *Today*, MSNBC, the Travel Channel, and the Fox Sports Network, and she garnered two prestigious Folio Awards for her work with *Women's Adventure* magazine. More recently, Theall won two awards of excellence from the North American Travel Journalists' Association for her feature and editorial writing. Michelle currently teaches writing and photography at the Creative Conferences. Her feature essay, *All That's Left Is God*, earned a 2011 GLAAD Media Award nomination and inspired her memoir.

Printed in the United States
By Bookmasters